Africa in The Sixties

Godfrey Mwakikagile

Africa in The Sixties

First Edition

ISBN 978-9987-16-034-1

New Africa Press
Dar es Salaam, Tanzania

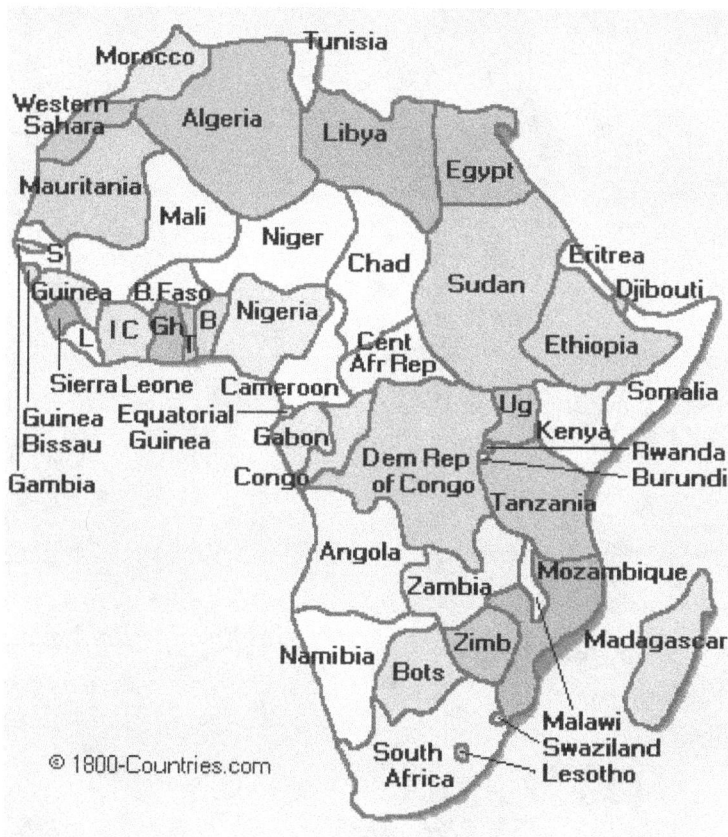

© 1800-Countries.com

Introduction

THIS work is a general survey of Africa in the sixties.

It may not cover everything but it is comprehensive enough in scope and depth as a chronicle of some of the major events which took place during those years.

It focuses on major political developments and other events which have shaped the destiny of the continent through the decades.

The sixties were a turning point in the history of Africa, ushering the dawn of a new era.

To those of us who grew up in Africa during those years, they were the euphoric sixties. The euphoria was a product of a momentous event in the history of the continent: the end of colonial rule.

As we celebrated the end of colonial rule, we felt that we were indeed masters of our own destiny.

But it did not take long for us to realise that we were wrong in many cases. It was a rude awakening even for our leaders as we came face to face with the harsh realities of nationhood.

There were other parts of Africa which had not yet

attained sovereign status. And there was, of course, apartheid South Africa, the citadel of white supremacy on the continent.

But even down there, in that "impregnable" fortress of white power and arrogance, there was a lot of commotion as many people demanded fundamental change. And at no other time in that nation's history was this better demonstrated than during the sixties.

While people across Africa celebrated independence, as one country after another emerged from colonial rule and hoisted its own flag, some parts of the continent were also rocked by violence and other conflicts. The worst, and the most dramatic, were the Congo crisis and the Nigerian civil war.

The Congo crisis was triggered by the secession of Katanga eleven days after the former Belgian Congo won independence on 30 June 1960. Another province, Kasai, also seceded in 1960.

The region that came to be known as Congo – first as Congo Free State, then as Belgian Congo, Republic of the Congo, Democratic Republic of the Congo or Congo-Leopoldville, Congo-Kinshasa, Zaire, and now the Democratic Republic of Congo (DRC) – has suffered so much through the centuries that it has earned the unenviable distinction as the bleeding heart of Africa. As historian Dan Snow stated in his article, "Too Rich for its Own Good: DRC: Cursed by Its Own Wealth," on BBC News Magazine, 8 October 2013:

"The Democratic Republic of Congo is potentially one of the richest countries on earth, but colonialism, slavery and corruption have turned it into one of the poorest.

The world's bloodiest conflict since World War II is still rumbling on today.

It is a war in which more than five million people have died, millions more have been driven to the brink by starvation and disease and several million women and girls have been raped.

The Great War of Africa, a conflagration that has sucked in soldiers and civilians from nine nations and countless armed rebel groups, has been fought almost entirely inside the borders of one unfortunate country – the Democratic Republic of Congo.

It is a place seemingly blessed with every type of mineral, yet consistently rated lowest on the UN Human Development Index, where even the more fortunate live in grinding poverty.

I went to the Congo this summer to find out what it was about the country's past that had delivered it into the hands of unimaginable violence and anarchy.

The journey that I went on, through the Congo's abusive history, while travelling across its war-torn present, was the most disturbing experience of my career.

I met rape victims, rebels, bloated politicians and haunted citizens of a country that has ceased to function – people who struggle to survive in a place cursed by a past that defies description, a history that will not release them from its death-like grip.

The Congo's apocalyptic present is a direct product of decisions and actions taken over the past five centuries.

In the late 15th Century an empire known as the Kingdom of Kongo dominated the western portion of the Congo, and bits of other modern states such as Angola.

It was sophisticated, had its own aristocracy and an impressive civil service.

When Portuguese traders arrived from Europe in the 1480s, they realised they had stumbled upon a land of vast natural wealth, rich in resources – particularly human flesh.

The Congo was home to a seemingly inexhaustible supply of strong, disease-resistant slaves. The Portuguese quickly found this supply would be easier to tap if the interior of the continent was in a state of anarchy.

They did their utmost to destroy any indigenous

political force capable of curtailing their slaving or trading interests.

Money and modern weapons were sent to rebels, Kongolese armies were defeated, kings were murdered, elites slaughtered and secession was encouraged.

By the 1600s, the once-mighty kingdom had disintegrated into a leaderless, anarchy of mini-states locked in endemic civil war. Slaves, victims of this fighting, flowed to the coast and were carried to the Americas.

About four million people were forcibly embarked at the mouth of the Congo River. English ships were at the heart of the trade. British cities and merchants grew rich on the back of Congolese resources they would never see.

This first engagement with Europeans set the tone for the rest of the Congo's history.

Development has been stifled, government has been weak and the rule of law non-existent. This was not through any innate fault of the Congolese, but because it has been in the interests of the powerful to destroy, suppress and prevent any strong, stable, legitimate government. That would interfere – as the Kongolese had threatened to interfere before – with the easy extraction of the nation's resources. The Congo has been utterly cursed by its natural wealth.

The Congo is a massive country, the size of Western Europe.

Limitless water, from the world's second-largest river, the Congo, a benign climate and rich soil make it fertile, beneath the soil abundant deposits of copper, gold, diamonds, cobalt, uranium, coltan and oil are just some of the minerals that should make it one of the world's richest countries.

Instead it is the world's most hopeless.

The interior of the Congo was opened up in the late 19th Century by the British-born explorer Henry Morton Stanley, his dreams of free trading associations with communities he met were shattered by the infamous King of the Belgians, Leopold, who hacked out a vast private empire.

The world's largest supply of rubber was found at a time when bicycle and automobile tyres, and electrical insulation, had made it a vital commodity in the West.

The late Victorian bicycle craze was enabled by Congolese rubber collected by slave labourers.

To tap it, Congolese men were rounded up by a brutal Belgian-officered security force, their wives were interned to ensure compliance and were brutalised during their captivity. The men were then forced to go into the jungle and harvest the rubber.

Disobedience or resistance was met by immediate punishment – flogging, severing of hands, and death. Millions perished.

Tribal leaders capable of resisting were murdered, indigenous society decimated, proper education denied.

A culture of rapacious, barbaric rule by a Belgian elite who had absolutely no interest in developing the country or population was created, and it has endured.

In a move supposed to end the brutality, Belgium eventually annexed the Congo outright, but the problems in its former colony remained.

Mining boomed, workers suffered in appalling conditions, producing the materials that fired industrial production in Europe and America.

In World War I men on the Western Front and elsewhere did the dying, but it was Congo's minerals that did the killing.

The brass casings of allied shells fired at Passchendaele and the Somme were 75% Congolese copper.

In World War II, the uranium for the nuclear bombs dropped on Hiroshima and Nagasaki came from a mine in south-east Congo.

Western freedoms were defended with Congo's resources while black Congolese were denied the right to vote, or form unions and political associations. They were denied anything beyond the most basic of educations.

They were kept at an infantile level of development that suited the rulers and mine owners but made sure that when independence came there was no home-grown elite who could run the country.

Independence in 1960 was, therefore, predictably disastrous.

Bits of the vast country immediately attempted to break away, the army mutinied against its Belgian officers and within weeks the Belgian elite who ran the state evacuated leaving nobody with the skills to run the government or economy.

Of 5,000 government jobs pre-independence, just three were held by Congolese and there was not a single Congolese lawyer, doctor, economist or engineer.

Chaos threatened to engulf the region. The Cold War superpowers moved to prevent the other gaining the upper hand.

Sucked into these rivalries, the struggling Congolese leader, Patrice Lumumba, was horrifically beaten and executed by Western-backed rebels. A military strongman, Joseph-Desire Mobutu, who had a few years before been a sergeant in the colonial police force, took over.

Mobutu became a tyrant. In 1972 he changed his name to Mobutu Sese Seko Nkuku Ngbendu Wa Za Banga, meaning 'the all-powerful warrior who, because of his endurance and inflexible will to win, goes from conquest to conquest, leaving fire in his wake.'

The West tolerated him as long as the minerals flowed and the Congo was kept out of the Soviet orbit.

He, his family and friends bled the country of billions of dollars, a $100m palace was built in the most remote jungle at Gbadolite, an ultra-long airstrip next to it was designed to take Concorde, which was duly chartered for shopping trips to Paris.

Dissidents were tortured or bought off, ministers stole

entire budgets, government atrophied. The West allowed his regime to borrow billions, which was then stolen and today's Congo is still expected to pay the bill.

In 1997 an alliance of neighbouring African states, led by Rwanda – which was furious Mobutu's Congo was sheltering many of those responsible for the 1994 genocide – invaded, after deciding to get rid of Mobutu.

A Congolese exile, Laurent Kabila, was dredged up in East Africa to act as a figurehead. Mobutu's cash-starved army imploded, its leaders, incompetent cronies of the president, abandoning their men in a mad dash to escape.

Mobutu took off one last time from his jungle Versailles, his aircraft packed with valuables, his own unpaid soldiers firing at the plane as it lumbered into the air.

Rwanda had effectively conquered its titanic neighbour with spectacular ease. Once installed however, Kabila, Rwanda's puppet, refused to do as he was told.

Again Rwanda invaded, but this time they were just halted by her erstwhile African allies who now turned on each other and plunged Congo into a terrible war.

Foreign armies clashed deep inside the Congo as the paper-thin state collapsed totally and anarchy spread.

Hundreds of armed groups carried out atrocities, millions died.

Ethnic and linguistic differences fanned the ferocity of the violence, while control of Congo's stunning natural wealth added a terrible urgency to the fighting.

Forcibly conscripted child soldiers corralled armies of slaves to dig for minerals such as coltan, a key component in mobile phones, the latest obsession in the developed world, while annihilating enemy communities, raping women and driving survivors into the jungle to die of starvation and disease.

A deeply flawed, partial peace was patched together a decade ago. In the far east of the Congo, there is once again a shooting war as a complex web of domestic and international rivalries see rebel groups clash with the army and the UN, while tiny community militias add to the general instability.

The country has collapsed, roads no longer link the main cities, healthcare depends on aid and charity. The new regime is as grasping as its predecessors.

I rode on one of the trainloads of copper that go straight from foreign-owned mines to the border, and on to the Far East, rumbling past shanty towns of displaced, poverty-stricken Congolese.

The Portuguese, Belgians, Mobutu and the present government have all deliberately stifled the development of a strong state, army, judiciary and education system, because it interferes with their primary focus, making money from what lies under the Earth.

The billions of pounds those minerals have generated have brought nothing but misery and death to the very people who live on top of them, while enriching a microscopic elite in the Congo and their foreign backers, and underpinning our technological revolution in the developed world.

The Congo is a land far away, yet our histories are so closely linked. We have thrived from a lopsided relationship, yet we are utterly blind to it. The price of that myopia has been human suffering on an unimaginable scale."

The sixties were some of the most turbulent years in the history of post-colonial Africa characterised by military coups and political assassinations.

What came to be known as the Congo crisis best defined that period. It not only put the bleeding of heart of Africa in the international spotlight; it also, in a very tragic way, served as a microcosm of what Africa was all about: a continent in crisis, unstable, and composed of weak countries which were independent in name only.

Africa also lost some of its most illustrious sons during

the turbulent sixties. The most prominent ones were Patrice Lumumba who was assassinated in January 1961, and Dr. Kwame Nkrumah who was overthrown in February 1966 in a military coup engineered and masterminded by the CIA. Nkrumah died six years later, in April 1972, not long after the sixties came to an end.

There were other casualties, not well known like Nkrumah and Lumumba, but no less important. They included President Sylvanus Olympio of Togo who was assassinated in January 1963 in Africa's first military coup.

And there were many other events in the sixties which played a major role in shaping and in determining the course of Africa's destiny in subsequent decades.

Among them were the Sharpeville massacre in South Africa; the Zanzibar revolution; the union of Tanganyika and Zanzibar which was the first union of independent states on the continent; the treason trial of Nelson Mandela; liberation wars in southern Africa; establishment of the Organisation of African Unity (OAU), and many others including border disputes and conflicts in different parts of the continent.

A lot of things happened in the sixties including some of the most dramatic events in the history of post-colonial Africa. And they're all covered in the book, especially the major ones.

The book has its shortcomings as all works do. And this one is no exception. Nobody is perfect.

We are mere mortals, with frailties. The best we can do is strive to be the best we can be in whatever we do.

I only hope that I have done my best in this chronicle and analysis of momentous events which took place on the African continent during the euphoric yet turbulent sixties. I was fortunate to be there during those days.

Its complementary volume, *Remembering The Sixties: A Look at Africa*, addresses similar subjects.

Africa at The Dawn
of The Decade

THE YEAR 1960 stands out in the history of Africa in one fundamental respect. It was the year in which the largest number of African countries won independence, a feat that was not duplicated in any of the following years.

A total of 17 African countries won independence in 1960. Almost all of them were former French colonies with the exception of Nigeria which was once a British colony and won independence on 1 October 1960.

But they were not the first countries on the continent to emerge from colonial rule. They had been preceded by Egypt which won independence from Britain in 1922; Libya from Italy in 1951; Morocco and Tunisia from France in 1956; Sudan from Britain and Egypt also in 1956; and by Ghana and Guinea.

Ghana became the first country in black Africa to emerge from colonial rule. Formerly known as the Gold Coast, Ghana won independence from Britain on 6 March

1957 under the leadership of Kwame Nkrumah. And Guinea under Sekou Toure became the first French colony in sub-Saharan Africa to win independence on 2 October 1958.

Guinea made a dramatic entry into the community of free nations which angered the former colonial power, France, similar to what happened in the former Belgian Congo when Prime Minister Patrice Lumumba gave a fiery speech on independence day denouncing Belgian colonial rule which the Belgian king at the ceremony tried to portray as benevolent to Africans.

Although he was the prime minister and the country's elected leader chosen by parliament of several parties to be the head of government, Lumumba had not even been scheduled to speak on that day – President Joseph Kasavubu was – and many observers say his fiery speech sealed his fate which ended in his brutal assassination only a few month later. As he stated in his speech in Congo's capital, Leopoldville, on June 30, 1960:

"Men and women of the Congo,

Victorious fighters for independence, today victorious, I greet you in the name of the Congolese Government.

All of you, my friends, who have fought tirelessly at our sides, I ask you to make this June 30, 1960, an illustrious date that you will keep indelibly engraved in your hearts, a date of significance of which you will teach to your children, so that they will make known to their sons and to their grandchildren the glorious history of our fight for liberty.

For this independence of the Congo, even as it is celebrated today with Belgium, a friendly country with whom we deal as equal to equal, no Congolese worthy of the name will ever be able to forget that it was by fighting that it has been won [applause], a day-to-day fight, an ardent and idealistic fight, a fight in which we were spared neither deprivation nor suffering, and for which we gave our strength and our blood.

We are proud of this struggle, of tears, of fire, and of blood, to the depths of our being, for it was a noble and just struggle, and indispensable to put an end to the humiliating slavery which was imposed upon us by force.

This was our fate for eighty years of a colonial regime; our wounds are too fresh and too painful still for us to drive them from our memory. We have known harassing work, exacted in exchange for salaries which did not permit us to eat enough to drive away hunger, or to clothe ourselves, or to house ourselves decently, or to raise our children as creatures dear to us.

We have known ironies, insults, blows that we endured morning, noon, and evening, because we are Negroes. Who will forget that to a black one said *tu*, certainly not as to a friend, but because the more honourable *vous* was reserved for whites alone?

We have seen our lands seized in the name of allegedly legal laws which in fact recognized only that might is right.

We have seen that the law was not the same for a white and for a black, accommodating for the first, cruel and inhuman for the other.

We have witnessed atrocious sufferings of those condemned for their political opinions or religious beliefs; exiled in their own country, their fate truly worse than death itself.

We have seen that in the towns there were magnificent houses for the whites and crumbling shanties for the blacks, that a black was not admitted in the motion-picture houses, in the restaurants, in the stores of the Europeans; that a black travelled in the holds, at the feet of the whites in their luxury cabins.

Who will ever forget the massacres where so many of our brothers perished, the cells into which those who refused to submit to a regime of oppression and

17

exploitation were thrown? [applause]

All that, my brothers, we have endured.

But we, whom the vote of your elected representatives have given the right to direct our dear country, we who have suffered in our body and in our heart from colonial oppression, we tell you very loud, all that is henceforth ended.

The Republic of the Congo has been proclaimed, and our country is now in the hands of its own children.

Together, my brothers, my sisters, we are going to begin a new struggle, a sublime struggle, which will lead our country to peace, prosperity, and greatness.

Together, we are going to establish social justice and make sure everyone has just remuneration for his labour [applause].

We are going to show the world what the black man can do when he works in freedom, and we are going to make of the Congo the centre of the sun's radiance for all of Africa.

We are going to keep watch over the lands of our country so that they truly profit her children. We are going to restore ancient laws and make new ones which will be just and noble.

We are going to put an end to suppression of free thought and see to it that all our citizens enjoy to the full the fundamental liberties foreseen in the Declaration of the Rights of Man [applause].

We are going to do away with all discrimination of every variety and assure for each and all the position to which human dignity, work, and dedication entitles him.

We are going to rule not by the peace of guns and bayonets but by a peace of the heart and the will [applause].

And for all that, dear fellow countrymen, be sure that we will count not only on our enormous strength and immense riches but on the assistance of numerous foreign countries whose collaboration we will accept if it is offered freely and with no attempt to impose on us an alien culture of no matter what nature [applause].

In this domain, Belgium, at last accepting the flow of history, has not tried to oppose our independence and is ready to give us their aid and their friendship, and a treaty has just been signed between our two countries, equal and independent. On our side, while we stay vigilant, we shall respect our obligations, given freely.

Thus, in the interior and the exterior, the new Congo, our dear Republic that my government will create, will be a rich, free, and prosperous country. But so that we will reach this aim without delay, I ask all of you, legislators and citizens, to help me with all your strength.

I ask all of you to forget your tribal quarrels. They exhaust us. They risk making us despised abroad.

I ask the parliamentary minority to help my Government through a constructive opposition and to limit themselves strictly to legal and democratic channels.

I ask all of you not to shrink before any sacrifice in order to achieve the success of our huge undertaking.

In conclusion, I ask you unconditionally to respect the life and the property of your fellow citizens and of foreigners living in our country. If the conduct of these foreigners leaves something to be desired, our justice will be prompt in expelling them from the territory of the Republic; if, on the contrary, their conduct is good, they must be left in peace, for they also are working for our country's prosperity.

The Congo's independence marks a decisive step towards the liberation of the entire African continent [applause].

Sire, Excellencies, Mesdames, Messieurs, my dear fellow countrymen, my brothers of race, my brothers of struggle-- this is what I wanted to tell you in the name of the Government on this magnificent day of our complete independence.

Our government, strong, national, popular, will be the

health of our country.

I call on all Congolese citizens, men, women and children, to set themselves resolutely to the task of creating a prosperous national economy which will assure our economic independence.

Glory to the fighters for national liberation!

Long live independence and African unity!

Long live the independent and sovereign Congo!"

Lumumba's militancy had been preceded elsewhere, in Guinea, under another fiery and uncompromising African nationalist: Ahmed Sekou Toure.

Both were dynamic leaders. But it was Ahmed Sekou Toure's militancy which became one of the most prominent features in the early years of the African independence struggle when he defied French wishes and refused to keep his country in the French community in 1958, about two years before Lumumba led Congo to independence on 30 June 1960.

Sekou Toure's militancy started early in his life. He did not go far in school in terms of formal education but was well-read and very knowledgeable like a number of other African leaders who also never got the chance to go to college.

Zambian president, Kenneth Kaunda, was one of them. He completed standard six, what Americans call sixth grade, and worked as a school teacher before entering politics.

Yet he successfully led his country to independence and was one of the most prominent and most knowledgeable leaders in post-colonial Africa. Sekou Toure was another one among several.

Born in 1922 of peasant origin like most of his contemporaries including the majority of African leaders, Sekou Toure received primary school education but was expelled from a trade school for leading a food strike when he was only 15 years old.

A firebrand, he became actively involved in trade union activities and rose to prominence as a national leader of the African trade-union federation he formed after breaking away from the Communist French trade-union confederation.

Sekou Toure also formed the Democratic Party of Guinea. His party lost the 1954 elections which were rigged against him by the French colonial authorities. But in 1957, he won complete control of the Guinea National Assembly, clearing the way for him to lead his country to independence.

In the referendum of September 1958, he won endorsement – by an overwhelming majority – of his position for immediate independence and led Guinea to become the first African French colony to emerge from colonial rule; and by doing so, helped blaze the trail for African emancipation together with Kwame Nkrumah who, only the year before in 1957, became the first black African leader to lead his country to independence.

The independence struggle which had already been going for many years in different parts of Africa was finally beginning to bear fruit, with the sixties being the most important years in the history of African decolonisation.

But with decolonisation came problems as was tragically demonstrated by the events in Congo when the country descended into chaos only eleven days after country won independence from Belgium, triggered by the secession of Katanga Province under the leadership of Moise Tshombe backed by Western interests.

Therefore, while 1960 was hailed as the dawn of a new era for Africa when 17 countries on the continent won independence in that year, it was also a sign and a warning of things yet to come and about which African countries could do very little to avert the catastrophes that befell the continent in subsequent years.

Some of those events were linked to or were influenced

by what was going on in the United States during that period. The Congo crisis was one of those events in which the United States was actively involved in pursuit of its national and geopolitical interests as the main rival of the Soviet Union in Africa and in other parts of the Third World.

Another major event was the civil rights movement in the United States which had a lot in common with the African independence struggle.

As we look at the chronology of the main events on the African continent through the years, we see that Africa has come a long way since the sixties. And she still has a long way to go in terms of achieving the goals she set out to achieve at the dawn of independence in the 1960s.

1960:
Dawn of A New Era

THE YEAR 1960 was one of the most important in the history of Africa. It was the year when the largest number of African countries won independence.

A total of 17 countries won independence that year, mostly from France. It was a feat that was not duplicated in any of the following years and 1960 was declared Africa's Year by the United Nations because of the unprecedented number of countries which won independence in that year.

The countries which won independence in 1960 were:

Dahomey (renamed Benin), 1 August 1960; Upper Volta (now Burkina Faso), 5 August 1960; Cameroon, 1 January 1960; Central African Republic, 13 August 1960; Chad, 11 August 1960; Congo-Brazzaville, 15 August 1960; Congo-Leopoldville (renamed Congo-Kinshasa, Zaire, and now the Democratic Republic of Congo), 30 June 1960.

Gabon, 17 August 1960; Ivory Coast (renamed Cote D'Ivoire), 7 August 1960; Madagascar, 26 June 1960; Mali, 20 June 1960; Mauritania, 28 November 1960; Niger, 3 August 1960; Nigeria, 1 October 1960; Senegal, 20 August 1960; Somalia, 1 July 1960; and Togo 27 April 1960.

They were all former French colonies except Nigeria and Somalia. Nigeria won independence from Britain. Somalia was an amalgamation of British Somaliland in the north and Italian Somaliland in the south. The two colonies agreed to unite and emerged from colonial rule as one country, Somalia.

But while 1960 was hailed as Africa's Year, and Africans across the continent celebrated the dawn of a new era heralded by the achievement of independence by a large number of countries, marking the beginning of the end of colonial rule on the continent, the year was also marred by some of the bloodiest events in the history of the continent.

The initial euphoria of independence was dampened when the former Belgian Congo descended into chaos just a few days after the country won independence, turning this giant African nation into the bleeding heart of Africa. "It was the best of times, it was the worst of times," to quote Charles Dickens. And Africa has never fully recovered from the convulsions caused by the Congo crisis in the turbulent sixties. Half a century later, Congo is still bleeding.

In a very tragic way, the Congo crisis demonstrated how vulnerable Africa was to foreign intrigue, with foreign powers turning the continent's potentially richest country into a playground and combat theatre in their contest for control of the continent.

Africans couldn't do anything about it.

While ethnic and regional rivalries fuelled and may even have helped to ignite the conflict in Congo, there is no question that the crisis was largely engineered by

Western financial, economic and political interests led by the former colonial power, Belgium, and by the United States, the leader of the Western world.

And while Lumumba was a staunch nationalist and Pan-Africanist and wanted Congo to be genuinely independent without being dominated by either the East or West, he was not anti-Western as he was portrayed in the western media.

He even sought assistance from the West to help contain the situation and restore stability to Congo but was rebuffed by the United States and other Western powers; and for good reason, of course, since they were the ones who had engineered the whole thing.

Lumumba's predicament reminds one of what happened to Sekou Toure when he also sought assistance from the West. After the French cut off economic aid to Guinea, Sekou Toure asked for assistance from the United States but was rebuffed. President Dwight Eisenhower dismissed him as a dangerous leftist and a Soviet ally who did not deserve help from any Western country. But unlike Lumumba, he survived assassination and coup attempts through the years.

When Lumumba was assassinated, Africa entered a new era. It was a turning point in the history of the continent.

The assassination of Lumumba, and subsequent chaos that ensued following his assassination and Western intervention in Congo, was one of the biggest tragedies in the history of Africa since the advent of colonial rule. And it still haunts the continent today more than 50 years after Congo won independence from Belgium in June 1960.

Once Africa's great hope as its richest country, richer than South Africa in terms of minerals and agricultural potential right in the heart of the continent, Congo became the bleeding heart of Africa because of foreign intervention. And it is still battered and traumatised.

At the centre of this maelstrom was the United States

and Belgium, the most active and most prominent players on the Congo scene in the sixties and thereafter. In fact, for decades until the fall of Mobutu in May 1997, the largest CIA station in Africa was in Congo's capital, Kinshasa. The country was then known as Zaire, renamed by Mobutu in 1971.

Lumumba's fate and that of Congo would not have turned out the way it did had Western countries not intervened, wreaking havoc on an unprecedented scale since Congo's independence in 1960 well into the 1990s and beyond at a cost of more than 6 million lives.

The civil wars which broke out in the nineties, tearing the country apart, were largely a result of that, with the West having propped up a rotten regime under Mobutu for more than 30 years, triggering an uprising against his kleptocratic and blood-soaked reign of terror during which he and his Western masters bled the country to death, leaving it an empty shell.

One of Africa's richest countries became one of the poorest. And it all started because Western countries, led by the United States, did not want Lumumba to remain in power and lead this huge, rich country in the heart of Africa.

Lumumba was a strong nationalist and Pan-Africanist leader who was determined to lead Congo as a truly independent country. And that was anathema to the West. Western countries were equally determined to secure, maintain, and perpetuate their hegemonic control over Congo and the rest of the continent in order to preserve, protect and promote their own interests to the detriment of Africans, and largely succeeded in doing so.

In many fundamental respects, Congo became a test case of what the West intended to do to African countries after they won independence. And that was to neutralise them and render their independence meaningless by turning them into client states of the West or by simply destroying them if they resisted Western intervention.

Lumumba and his country became the first casualties.

The downward spiral started with the secession of Katanga Province led by Moise Tshombe.

Tshombe used the chaos that ensued soon after the country won independence as an excuse to seek assistance from Belgium to restore law and order in his province. Belgian paratroopers flew into Katanga but with a larger mission in mind: to support the secession of the mineral-rich province.

As the chaos spread across the country, Lumumba sought UN assistance and the United Nations created a peacekeeping force for the country. But just before the arrival of UN peacekeeping forces which had the mandate to make arrangements for the withdrawal of Belgian troops as requested by Lumumba, Tshombe declared independence for his province. The UN forces arrived on July 15th.

Katanga seceded on 11 July 1960, only a few days after the country won independence on June 30th under the leadership of Patrice Lumumba as the first democratically elected leader of this vast country of more than 200 ethnic groups.

Just a few days after Katanga seceded, Tshombe ordered mobilisation of his forces on July 20th to resist UN intervention and went on to recruit mercenaries to bolster his defence, making the situation worse for Lumumba as the legitimate leader of the Congolese government which wanted to keep the country united.

Lumumba assumed power as prime minister after winning a plurality of votes and was endorsed by the national parliament composed of representatives of different political parties all of which were regionally entrenched except Lumumba's Congolese National Movement – *Mouvement National Congolaise* (MNC) – which transcended ethno-regional loyalties and had support in all parts of the country. The MNC was founded on 5 October 1958. Lumumba was one of its founding members and later its president. The other founders of the party were Cyrille Adoula and Joseph Ileo.

His political base was in Stanleyville, in his home region of eastern Congo. But as a leader of a supra-tribal party, he did not see that as his only strength. He had followers across the country.

Formed less than two years before the Belgians formally relinquished power, the MNC was the driving force behind the independence movement. In mid-1959, the party split into two groups.

One was more militant and was led by Lumumba, a situation similar to what happened in Ghana during the independence struggle when Kwame Nkrumah left the conservative United Gold Coast Convention (UGCC), of which he had served as secretary-general, and went on to form the more radical Convention People's Party (CPP) in 1949 which led the country to independence by campaigning on the slogan, "Independence Now."

Lumumba pursued the same goal, invoking virtually the same slogan. And his party won support across the country in a relatively short time.

The other faction of the Congolese National Movement was led by Joseph Ileo, Cyrille Adoula and Albert Kalonji. It was a moderate group and all three leaders went on to play important roles in the country soon after independence and after Lumumba was assassinated.

Ileo and Adoula each served as prime minister at different times; and Albert Kalonji – a conservative who once served as Lumumba's minister of agriculture – is remembered probably more than anything else as the leader who led another secessionist province, South Kasai, thus threatening the territorial integrity of the new republic. Among all these leaders, Lumumba emerged as the only true nationalist leader transcending tribal and regional loyalties.

And the fact that he came from a small tribe or ethnic group, the Batatele, native to Orientale, a province in eastern Congo – which includes Stanleyville, now called Kisangani – and to North Kasai where he was born, was a factor that made him more acceptable to many smaller ethnic groups across the country who feared domination by larger groups.

The large ethnic groups included the Bakongo whose most prominent son was President Joseph Kasavubu; and the Lunda, of whom Moise Tshombe was its most well-known leader who was also related to the royal family of this large ethnic group. The son of a successful business man in Katanga, Tshombe was the son-in-law of the emperor of the Lunda people.

And there was the Luba, another large ethnic group dominant in Kasai Province whose most prominent member was Albert Kalonji. There were other groups which were bigger than Lumumba's, the Batatele.

President Kasavubu was the leader of *Alliance des Bakongo* (ABAKO) – the Alliance of the Bakongo – a party with an ethnic base solidly anchored among his people who constituted the largest ethnic group in the country and after whom the country itself and the Congo River were named.

But Lumumba's status as a member of a small ethnic group was also a liability since it did not provide him with a strong ethnic base from which he could derive and mobilize support the way Kasavubu did from the Bakongo; and even the way Etienne Tshisekedi did from the Luba, his people, years later when he sought the presidency in the 1990s and beyond long after Lumumba was dead.

Although Lumumba did not come from a large ethnic group, the MNC faction he led emerged victorious in the first legislative elections of May 1960 and won the largest number of votes among all the parties in the country.

His minority status as a member of the small Batatele tribe was also a powerful incentive among many members of parliament who supported him for his prime ministerial position after his party won the largest number of votes in the May 1960 elections.

But it was his appeal to nationalist sentiments transcending ethnic and regional interests more than anything else which made him the most popular leader in Congo. Many people saw him as a unifying factor and the leader of all Congolese, not just those of his small tribe or ethnic groups in the eastern part of the country where he came from.

He was the exact opposite of Moise Tshombe, his arch-enemy and the leader of secessionist Katanga Province.

The events leading to Katanga's secession occurred in rapid succession soon after the country won independence.

The army mutinied against its Belgian officers. The Belgian government deployed troops ostensibly to protect and rescue its citizens and other Europeans who were supposedly under siege and in danger of being killed by Africans. Katanga declared independence, and the country dissolved in anarchy, prompting Lumumba to seek assistance from other African countries and the United Nations to restore law and order and save the country from breaking up along ethno-regional lines. As Brian Urquhart, who was in Congo during that time, stated years later in his article "The Tragedy of Lumumba" in *The New York Review of Books*, 4 October 2001:

"Belgium's exploitation of the Congo was the darkest episode in all the murky history of European colonialism.

To feed King Leopold II's manic appetite for ivory and rubber, mutilations, mass executions, and the use of the *chicotte* - a hippopotamus hide whip that cut through skin and muscle - administered by the indigenous *Force Publique* commanded by Belgian officers had halved the population within a few years and left a legacy of oppression and cruelty that poisoned forever the relations of Congolese and Belgians.

At Congo's independence on June 30, 1960, the young

King Baudoin, in a paternalistic speech, praised his ghastly ancestor's achievements. Lumumba's fiery response brought into the open the latent rage and resentment of his people (before he spoke, Lumumba was seen scribbling notes when the king was giving his speech).

Perhaps for the first time, Belgian officials realized that after independence, with Patrice Lumumba as prime minister, things would not, as they had hoped, go on much as before.

The Congo, unlike most African colonies, had no longstanding liberation movement either at home or abroad, or any internationally recognized independence leaders like Mandela, Kenyatta, Nkrumah, Nkomo, Nujoma, and others. Such liberationist activity as there was had been sanctioned only in 1957 and was led by Joseph Kasavubu, who was to become the Congo's first president.

Lumumba, a former postal clerk and beer salesman, became the leader of the nationalist, supratribal party, the *Mouvement National Congolaise* (Congolese Nationalist Movement), in Stanleyville, his political base. He was arrested for the first time in November 1959 and then released to take part in the Brussels Roundtable that set the scene for the Congo's suddenly accelerated independence, precipitated in part by Charles De Gaulle's abrupt granting of independence to France's African colonies. Congolese independence was in every way a last-minute arrangement.

Whether because they believed that independence would be little more than a formality or because of the superiority and contempt they felt for their unfortunate African subjects, the Belgians, unlike other colonial powers, made no practical arrangements for an independent Congo.

No Congolese had ever taken part in the business of government or public administration at any important level. Only 17 (other reports say only 16) out of a population of 13.5 million had university degrees. There was not one Congolese officer in the *Force Publique*, which was to become the *Armee Nationale Congolaise* (ANC). No colony had ever faced independence so ill-prepared.

Events in the first days of independence went at a dizzying pace. The army mutinied and threw out its Belgian officers. Europeans were roughed up, and there were reports of white women being raped. The Belgian population panicked and left. Belgian paratroopers were deployed to protect the remaining Europeans.

These troops, believed by the Congolese to have been sent to reverse independence, clashed with the soldiers of the ANC – which had no officers – in the major cities. With the connivance of Belgium, the richest province, Katanga, whose president was Moise Tshombe, seceded from the new republic. Public administration, law, and order evaporated and were replaced by chaos and anarchy."

Brian Urquhart was in a unique position to make those observations not only because he was in Congo during that time but also because he worked with Dr. Ralph Bunche, a black American senior diplomat who was also the UN undersecretary-general. Dr. Bunche was also in Congo during that time. As Urquhart explained:

"I should explain here my own connection with the Congo. I was Ralph Bunche's chief assistant and in that capacity was in the Congo throughout the summer and early fall of 1960.

We were in touch with Lumumba more or less on a daily basis during this time, until he broke off relations with Bunche.

In the fall of 1961, after Hammarskjold's death on a mission to the Congo, I became the UN representative in

Katanga, was kidnapped and severely beaten up by Moise Tshombe's troops, and was in charge of the UN side during two weeks of fierce fighting after which Tshombe agreed to end secession and reunite Katanga with the Congo.

Bunche, who had drafted the chapters of the UN Charter on decolonization and trusteeship and was awarded the 1950 Nobel Peace Prize for negotiating the armistice agreements between Israel and its Arab neighbors, had a unique record as a promoter and expediter of decolonization and was the friend and mentor of many of the African independence leaders.

Lumumba once asked me angrily why Hammarskjold had sent '*ce negre Americain*' to the Congo. I replied with some heat that Hammarskjold had only sent the best man in the world to deal with such a situation. Lumumba did not revert to this subject."

Although the anarchic situation in Congo had been precipitated by a series of dramatic events soon after independence, the most tragic before Lumumba's assassination was the secession of Katanga Province.

Katanga's secession was followed by secessionist threats from other provinces. One such threat was carried out when Albert Kalonji of Kasai Province, which was the homeland of the Luba people in south-central Congo, declared himself king of South Kasai. Kasai's secession only made things worse.

Bordered by Katanga on the southeast, southern Kasai declared independence on 14 June 1960, 16 days before Congo's independence, and declared itself the Federal State of South Kasai. The northern part of Kasai province did not secede.

On 8 August 1960, the state of South Kasai officially became a "sovereign" entity, with Bakwanga, now Mbuji-Mayi, as its capital. Albert Kalonji became president of South Kasai and Joseph Ngalula was appointed head of government or prime minister.

On 12 April 1961, an assembly of South Kasai leaders and elders declared Alber Kalonji's father an emperor, invested with the title Mulopwe which means emperor or king in the Luba language.

But the new emperor immediately abdicated his throne in favour of his son Albert Kalonji, the président of South Kasai. From then on, Albert Kalonji ruled South Kasai as Mulopwe - Emperor/King - Albert I Kalonji.

The head of the Congolese government during that chaotic period was still Patrice Lumumba. To end the secession, he sent troops to South Kasai. The soldiers, who came from the national army, were led by Joseph Mobutu. After four months of fighting, the province was retaken and brought under control. Albert Kalonji was arrested on 31 December 1961, ending the secession.

On 7 September 1962, Kalonji escaped from prison and attempted to regain the province. He set up a new government but it was dissolved less than a month later.

The secession of South Kasai was one of the major problems the country faced in the early sixties. But it was Katanga's secession which posed the greatest threat to the territorial integrity of Congo. Its leader, Moise Tshombe, was resolutely opposed to any reconciliation and the establishment of a central government as the supreme authority over the whole country.

Even before Congo won independence, Tshombe made it clear that he preferred a loose federation in which the provinces would be able to exercise considerable power over their own affairs. It was a kind of autonomy which amounted to virtual independence with a very weak central government.

Before he declared Katanga a republic soon after the province seceded from the rest of the country, Tshombe already had formidable influence in his home region because of his family ties to the royal family of the Lunda, the largest ethnic group in Katanga; also because of his dominant position as president of *Confédération des associations tribales du Katanga* (CONAKAT) – the Confederation of Associations of Katanga – the biggest and strongest political party in Katanga Province. He was co-founder of the party, together with Godefroid Munongo who became his close confidant. Munongo also played a major role in Lumumba's assassination.

The party was also supported by the Belgian colonial authorities and their government in Brussels.

Founded in the 1950s, CONAKAT was regionalist and wanted the mineral wealth of the province to benefit only the indigenous people of Katanga.

In January – February 1960, Tshombe attended the Brussels Roundtable, a conference on Congo's independence. The meeting was also attended by other Congolese leaders including Lumumba and Kasavubu under the auspices of the Belgian government.

At that meeting, Tshombe demanded that once the country won independence on June 30th it should form a loose federation of independent states based on the existing regional structure whose provinces were defined by their ethnic identities more than anything else.

He did not prevail but left no doubt in any one's mind that a unitary state for Congo was the farthest thing from his mind. He wanted no part of it; nor did his sponsors, the Belgians, who wanted to control the mineral wealth of Katanga once the province seceded.

In the general elections of 1960, CONAKAT won and secured control of the provincial legislature in Elisabethville, capital of Katanga Province, giving Tshombe considerable power not only in his home province but in the country as a whole as the leader of the richest province and of one of the most powerful and best organized political parties in Congo, even though it was regionally entrenched like the rest except Lumumba's which transcended ethno-regional loyalties.

Emboldened by this victory and support from the Belgian authorities, and his pre-eminent position on the country's political scene as the leader of the richest province, he pulled Katanga out of Congo and declared the province a republic only 11 days after the country won independence. It was a bold and dangerous move, and it had dire consequences for the entire country for decades to come. Even today, Congo has not yet recovered from what ensued in the country during those turbulent years as a result of Katanga's secession and intervention by external forces.

After Katanga's secession, Tshombe worked closely with Belgian advisers and business leaders as he had in the past and even appointed a Belgian officer as the commander of his army, in spite of the fact that the Belgians saw him as a racist who worked with whites only to secure his own interests. They denounced Lumumba the same way, although those who knew Lumumba, including his political opponents, say he was not a racist but an uncompromising nationalist and Pan-Africanist.

But there is no question that Tshombe was a tribal chauvinist and champion of the Lunda people and other Katangese but especially the Lunda, his fellow tribesmen. And he refused to cooperate with the UN and the central government under Lumumba to restore the integrity of Congo, maintaining that Katanga was an independent state and had the right to be one.

In August 1960, he was elected president of Katanga and maintained a large army of mercenaries. Many of them came from apartheid South Africa and other countries including France and Belgium. When the United Nations asked Tshombe to end Katanga's secession, he refused and opposed UN troops which had been sent to Congo to restore law and order. UN forces were later given the mandate to end Katanga's secession by force and fighting began.

As chaos continued, Congolese leaders tried to restore stability in the country. In February 1961, they formed a provisional government. Joseph Ileo was chosen to be the prime minister.

Conferences to negotiate reunification of the country were held in the first half of 1961 and were attended by representatives from all of the country's six provinces.

In July 1961, the secession of South Kasai under Albert Kalonji formally ended, and in August, Cyrille Adoula was named Congo's prime minister.

Adoula emerged on the national scene as a moderate trade union leader before independence. Antoine Gizenga was named deputy prime minister. Earlier, Gizenga had served in the same position under Lumumba.

Lumumba served as prime minister from 24 June – 5 September 1960; Joseph Ileo from 12 September 1960 – 27 July 1961; and Adoula from 2 August 1961 – 20 June 1964.

Antoine Gizenga served as prime minister of a rival nationalist government of Lumumba's followers based in Stanleyville from 13 December 1960 – 5 August 1961.

Formation of the government of national unity in July 1961 took place after politicians from all parts of the country, including Katanga, were invited to Leopoldville in July to discuss new political arrangements under a federal constitution. They agreed to keep Kasavubu as president.

But to appease Lumumba's followers, Lumumba's deputy prime minister, Antoine Gizenga, was brought into the government. Before then, he was head of a rival government in Stanleyville, one of the three centres of power in the country during that period. The other two were Leopoldville, the nation's capital, and Elisabethville, the capital of the secessionist Katanga Province.

Among all three, the government in Stanleyville, Lumumba's political stronghold, claimed to be and was seen by its supporters as the only nationalist government in Congo in the tradition of Lumumba.

Although Tshombe and other politicians in Katanga were also invited to the conference, they refused to attend.

It was a conference of rival groups and politicians, with different ideologies, but succeeded in reaching compromises in order to form a national government and keep the country united under a federal constitution.

While all these compromises were being made, the situation in Katanga Province not only remained highly volatile but deteriorated. Tshombe refused to negotiate with the United Nations to end Katanga's secession and his refusal to do so was the last straw.

UN forces began rounding up mercenaries in Katanga Province on 28 August 1960. It was the beginning of a long struggle against the secessionist province and its mercenary fighters which went on until January 1963 when Katanga's secession was finally brought to an end.

About 100,000 Congolese are estimated to have died during the Congo crisis, the bloodiest on the continent in the first years of African independence.

While Katanga's secession formally ended on 15 January 1963, and the central government took over Katanga Province with UN military assistance, another rebellion broke out in Kwilu Province in the west in January 1964 under the leadership of Pierre Mulele.

The rebellion spread to other parts of the country, followed by an uprising led by Gaston Soumialot in Kivu Province in the east. It lasted until December 1964.

In June the same year, Tshombe was recalled from exile by President Kasavubu and was appointed prime minister, replacing Cyrille Adoula, in an attempt to achieve national reconciliation. But the honeymoon between Tshombe and Kasavubu did not last long.

Disagreements between President Kasavubu and Prime Minister Tshombe led to a government paralysis. In October 1965, Kasavubu dismissed Tshombe and appointed Evariste Kimba as prime minister.

In November the same year, Mobutu overthrew the government and proclaimed himself president. Evariste Kimba served as prime minister of Congo for less than one month from 18 October to 14 November 1965. Earlier, from 1960 – 1963, he was the foreign affairs minister of the separatist Katanga Province.

Kimba and other opponents of Mobutu's regime – ex-ministers Jérôme Anany, Emmanuel Bamba and André Mahamba – were publicly hanged in the nation's capital Kinshasa in June 1966 in an attempt by Mobutu to intimidate his other opponents into submission. It was in the same year that Leopoldville was renamed Kinshasa in compliance with Mobutu's policy of Africanisation. But along with Africanisation was bloodshed because of the turmoil the country had been plunged into after Katanga's secession and because of Mobutu himself as a ruthless dictator.

All this downward spiral took place within five years after the country won independence when Lumumba became prime minister, only to be neutralized after three months in office. His biggest challenge, right away, was the secession of Katanga Province.

The central government under Lumumba was powerless and couldn't do anything to end the secession of Katanga Province on its own and even with the help of troops from other African countries. As Ahmed Ben-Bella, former president of Algeria who was overthrown in June 1965, said about the African countries which tried to help Lumumba and his followers and about the situation in Congo in the sixties when he was interviewed in Geneva, Switzerland on 4 November 1995: "We arrived in the Congo too late."

Ben-Bella was interviewed by Jorge Castaneda, the author of *Companero*: *The Life and Death of Che Guevara* in which he quotes the former Algerian leader.

A number of African countries – Ghana, Tanzania, Guinea, Mali, Algeria and Egypt – tried to help the nationalist forces in Congo. But, by then, Lumumba was gone. He was assassinated on 17 January 1961.

When Ben-Bella said "We arrived in the Congo too

late, he was referring to the attempts made by the six African countries which intervened later in Congo to help the nationalist forces when they were fighting the Western-backed government in Leopoldville whose leaders played a major in the elimination of Lumumba.

But Lumumba's supporters did not give up the fight. His closest advisers and many of his followers including Laurent Kabila (who was in his twenties then) quickly left the capital Leopoldville soon after his assassination and went to the rural areas of eastern Congo, mainly Kivu, and Tanzania to mobilise forces and continue fighting.

Therefore, although Lumumba was gone, his nationalist followers who had regrouped and settled in the northeast continued to fight for his cause well into 1967.

He also had supporters in other parts of the country including Katanga, and in Kwilu Province in the west where resistance led by Lumumba's minister of education and heir apparent, Pierre Mulele, continued until Mulele's assassination by Mobutu on 9 October 1968, although the guerilla campaign by Mulele and his followers virtually ended in 1966.

Mulele, who was living in exile in Brazzaville, was tricked by Mobutu into returning to Leopoldville after Mobutu said he had given amnesty to those who had waged war against the central government and that they could return home to join their fellow countrymen in building the nation.

He didn't mean it. He sent his foreign minister Justin Bomboko to Brazzaville to lure Mulele back to Leopoldville. Bomboko had earlier also served as foreign affairs minister under Lumumba and knew Mulele well as a colleague in the first independence cabinet.

Six African leaders, more than any others on the African continent, made the most determined attempt to help the Congolese nationalist forces in their war against the puppet government in Leopoldville and its Western sponsors during the turbulent the sixties.

They were Julius Nyerere of Tanzania, Kwame Nkrumah of Ghana, Gamal Abdel Nasser of Egypt, Ben-Bella of Algeria, Sekou Toure of Guinea, and Modibo Keita of Mali.

They even had a group of their own within the Organization of African Unity (OAU) known as "the Group of Six," and secretly worked together as Ben-Bella said in the same interview with Jorge Castaneda who was then a professor at New York University. Castaneda later became Mexico's minister of foreign affairs under President Vincente Fox.

The interview with Ben-Bella is one of the most sad reminders of what unfolded in Congo in the turbulent sixties.

Tragically, Lumumba's fate was sealed from the beginning when he emerged on the political scene as the country's most influential leader. Western governments, led by the United States, saw him as a threat to their geopolitical interests in Congo and in Africa as a whole because of his strong nationalist views and beliefs as a Pan-Africanist.

On 18 August 1960, a CIA dispatch from Congo to Washington described Lumumba as "a commie playing the commie game." The American ambassador to Congo during that time was Clare Hayes Timerlake.

Americans and other Westerners saw Patrice Lumumba as another Castro and a friend of the Russians who would give the Soviets the upper hand in the heart of Africa at the expense of the West, in spite of the fact that he was not a communist or an ideological ally of the Soviets in the rivalry between the East and the West.

The Americans, including President Dwight Eisenhower and his successor John F. Kennedy and their advisors as well as congressional leaders, saw Congo as the most prized possession in Africa in pursuit of their geopolitical interests and competition with the Soviet Union because of the country's vast mineral wealth and

41

strategic location including its proximity to the white-ruled countries in southern Africa which were ideological allies of the West against Eastern-bloc countries during the Cold War.

Therefore they did everything they could to gain control of the country and prevent the Soviets from getting it, even if it meant going to war, especially by using surrogate forces to secure Western interests. To them, Lumumba symbolized the worst they could think of. All attempts to portray Lumumba in his true colours and try to explain to the rest of the world what type of leader he really was were ignored or dismissed as lies by Western leaders, especially the Americans.

One young American reporter who was on the scene when the tragic events were unfolding in Congo during that period provided a detailed account of Western machinations against Lumumba masterminded by the United States. She produced what were probably some of the most balanced reports coming out of Congo during those tragic years.

Her name was D'Lynn Waldron. She was 23 years old in 1960 when she was in Congo. She worked for *The Cleveland Press and News* in Cleveland, Ohio, and her despatches from Congo before independence were published in that newspaper, although she complained that her editors in the United States censored and slanted her reports to portray Lumumba and the Congolese people in a negative light and added to the published reports some things she never wrote or said.

These are some of the things she said about what happened and what was going on when she was in Congo with Lumumba:

"In the spring of 1960, I was the only foreign correspondent covering Patrice Lumumba in Stanleyville just before Independence, and as such and an American, I became Lumumba's confidant and the one he entrusted to

42

mediate between himself and the Belgian administration and to get the word to Eisenhower and the American people that he was absolutely not a Communist....

It was well known in the Congo before Independence that Belgium and the banking and mining interests were arranging for the coming Independence to disintegrate into chaos so they could take back Katanga with its gold, uranium and copper, and Kasai with its industrial diamonds, while dumping the unprofitable remainder of the Congo.

The 'White Congolese' of Belgian descent were even more aware of this and more angered by the betrayal of a trust, than almost any 'Black African,' except Patrice Lumumba.

It was these disaffected White Congolese, and especially the colonial governor of Kasai, who told me exactly what the plans of the banking and mining interests were. I even have their hand-drawn maps showing the parts of the country that would be reclaimed from the chaos. The governor of Kasai was so disgusted with the Belgian government that he took down from his wall his prized historical maps of the Congo and handed them to me (I still have them).

Before I went up the Congo River to Stanleyville, which was Lumumba's political headquarters, I had read newspaper stories and been told by some people in the Belgian Colonial Administration that Lumumba was a madman and a Communist puppet of Russia.

What I found was a thoughtful, dignified, dedicated man who naively believed that if... Eisenhower were told the truth, Eisenhower would no longer listen to the Belgian lie that he, Lumumba, was a Communist.

My cabled newspaper stories had things added and removed by Scripps-Howard, and all references to Lumumba's admiration for America and his requests to President Eisenhower for training for his people were cut out.

Lumumba rightly believed that the Russians didn't like him any more than the Belgians did, because he was not a Communist and because he would never do the bidding of any foreign power. Lumumba only wanted what was best for the Congo and that was his death warrant. The Russians would have killed Lumumba, if the Western powers hadn't done it first.

I was with Lumumba in his living room in Stanleyville when Lumumba got the telegram which said that instead of Gizenga's staying in Accra for training with Nkrumah's people, Gizenga had been taken straight from the airport in an Aeroflot plane to Moscow. Lumumba was terrified by this and said to me, 'The Russians will use Gizenga as my Judas.'

However, Gizenga's subsequent life indicates that the Russians would have found him as dedicated to the Congo and as difficult to dictate to as Lumumba. (See the e-mail about their family's travails written to me by Dorothee Gizenga in July 30, 2003.)

The Russians had thought they would be able to wrap Gizenga in Lumumba's mantel and take control of the Congo. Gizenga did establish himself as Lumumba's heir in the Eastern Congo, but, like the rest of the Congo, the area descended into tribal war, plus Maoist inspired massacres aimed at the 'elite', which included anyone who could read, or even wore eyeglasses....

Before Independence, I know from personal knowledge, that Lumumba asked Eisenhower to provide training in government administration for Congolese, who the Belgians had deliberately kept from learning the most basic skills necessary to run a country. Eisenhower replied that would be interfering in Belgium's internal affairs, a position which was later repeated to me by the State Department.

After Independence, when the Congo needed international assistance to restore order, Prime Minister Lumumba asked Eisenhower to send American troops.

44

However, Eisenhower continued to falsely label Lumumba a Communist and handed Lumumba's unwanted request over to Dag Hammarskjold. Hammarskjold, along with Conor Cruise-O'Brien, was part of the cabal that used the UN to destroy the Congo's Independence, in order to take back Katanga on behalf of Western mining interests.

To try to force Eisenhower to send American troops to restore order in the Congo, Lumumba threatened to bring in Russians troops. This was highly publicized by the American government, and no mention was made of the fact that this was only a threat and Lumumba was appealing to Eisenhower to send American troops. (see the book *Congo Cables* with the actual cables to and from Washington regarding the Congo and Lumumba, as assembled by Madeline Kalb).

Right up to his being turned over to Katanga to be assassinated, Lumumba pinned his hopes on America and his travelling companion and confidant was Frank Carlucci, who it has since been revealed in Congressional investigations was an American intelligence officer and presumably part of Operation Zaire Rifle, the American plot to assassinate Lumumba.

I left the Congo overland just before Independence through Ruanda and Urundi and the Mountains of the Moon to bring Lumumba's requests for help addressed to President Eisenhower to the American Consulate in Uganda, because mail and cables were being stopped by the Belgian postal authorities. The American consulate refused to accept anything from Lumumba. They said he would have to use the Belgian Post and Telegraph in the Congo for any messages he wanted to send to President Eisenhower.

One this site, and indexed below, are newspaper stories I wrote from the Congo which were highly edited back in the States, and documents including Lumumba's own written responses to my questions on his future plans for the Congo, and in Lumumba's own handwriting with my notes using the same pen, the statement I carried to the Belgians in charge of Stanleyville at the height of the crisis."

The preceding comments are on her web site which features scanned copies of some of the original pages from the *The Cleveland Press and News* containing some of her dispatches from Congo. Her web site, "Patrice Lumumba, Stanleyville, Belgian Congo D'Lynn Waldron," is:
http://www.dlynnwaldron.com/Lumumba.html
She witnessed some of the most tragic events which unfolded in Congo in the sixties.

Although she provided first-hand accounts of what was going on, and dealt with Lumumba on personal basis, she was ignored by Western leaders including her editors at her newspaper in Cleveland, Ohio, because what she wrote and said did not conform to the ideological dictates and interests of Western nations which wrongly, and deliberately, portrayed Lumumba as a communist, hence their enemy.

Patrice Lumumba was prime minister of Congo for only three months. Yet his influence went far beyond his brief term in office, and beyond Congo. He was the dominant figure on the country's political scene even after he was removed from office and even after he was arrested and put in jail towards the end of 1960.

Although the year 1960 was dominated by the Congo crisis, there were other events which took place in different parts of Africa. And they deserve attention for a comprehensive picture of what happened on the continent during that period.

But probably the most significant event was the secession of Katanga Province on 11 July 1960, eleven days after the country won independence. It was in the news everyday.

I remember when I was growing up in Rungwe District in the Southern Highlands in southwestern Tanzania in a region bordering what was then Nyasaland (now Malawi) and Northern Rhodesia (renamed Zambia) that the conflict in Congo was the dominant story broadcast by the Tanganyika Broadcasting Corporation (TBC) based in the capital Dar es Salaam, about 540 miles away on the east coast.

We also listened almost everyday to broadcasts from Elisabethville, the capital of Katanga Province which is also about 800 miles from my home district. We also listened to broadcasts from Leopoldville, the capital of the former Belgian Congo.

The broadcasts we listened to were in Kiswahili – a language also spoken in Congo – on shortwave radio. And they are still vivid in my memory 50 years later because of the tragic events and countless lives lost in that country in 1960 and in the following years.

Although the people of Congo celebrated independence in 1960, they also became the victims of one of the worst tragedies that befell Africa during the post-colonial era. And what happened in Congo in 1960 is indelibly etched in the minds of many people not only in that country but in other parts of Africa as well. And that was only the beginning of the tragedies that the continent suffered in the sixties.

Another tragic event was the Sharpeville massacre in South Africa on 21 March 1960 when 69 unarmed, peaceful black protesters were killed. Among those killed were 8 women and 10 children.

Most of them were shot in the back as they fled from the police. At least 180 black Africans were injured and there are reports that as many as 300 suffered injuries at the hands of the police.

The protests were organised by the Pan Africanist Congress (PAC), a party led by Robert Mangaliso Sobukwe who was a professor of African studies at Witwatersrand University, South Africa's leading academic institution especially for English speakers.

The demonstrators lived in the black township of Sharpeville on the outskirts of the white town of Vereeniging in the Transvaal, about 30 miles south of Johannesburg.

The township was created in compliance with the country's apartheid laws to keep the races apart. The people who were shot were protesting against the notorious pass laws which dehumanised them and forced them to carry pass books all the time and restricted them to certain areas while whites enjoyed unlimited access to all parts of the country and enjoyed a lifestyle and privileges blacks could only dream of. As David Sibeko stated in explaining why the Pan-Africanist Congress directed its wrath against and focused its campaign on the pass laws in his article, "The Sharpeville Massacre: Its Historic Significance in the Struggle Against Apartheid":

"The pass system was deliberately chosen because: (i) it is the linchpin of apartheid; and (ii) of all the apartheid laws none is so pervasive, and few are as perverted, as the pass laws.

They show no respect for the sanctity of marriage – men are forcibly separated from their wives or vice versa because one of them cannot obtain the permit to reside in the same area. They tear away children from their parents: a child above the age of 16 needs a special permit to live with its parents outside the bantustan reservation, otherwise it must find accommodation in one of the location barracks they call hostels in South Africa.

They deny men and women the universal right to sell their labour to whom they choose; every African man or woman seeking employment has to obtain a special permit to look for work – within a limited period, usually 14 days; otherwise they face deportation to the `homeland' bantustan reservation they most likely have never known.

The indignities are legion and falling foul with any of the pass law regulations leaves an African open to arrest and imprisonment. Sentences are most frequently served out on prison farms, under the most primitive conditions.

The best known African campaign before Sharpeville was the potato boycott. It came as a result of exposures in newspapers like the *Post* about conditions for African prisoners in the potato prison farms of Bethal, in the Eastern Transvaal.

Investigative reporters found that prisoners are dressed in nothing but sacks, they sleep on damp cement floors and are out working the potato fields with bare hands from the crack of dawn until dusk. They are continuously whipped by jailers on horse back, and the one meal a day they eat is always half-cooked dried maize without any protein. Many die from disease and torture before they complete the relatively short terms of imprisonment, between two and six months.

The pass laws, therefore, affect every living black person."

Sibeko went on to explain how the campaign in Sharpeville against pass laws was organized and conducted and what the leaders, including Mangaliso Robert Sobukwe, expected and wanted to be done:

"In this non-violent campaign there is none that could have been more concerned to avoid the shedding of even an ounce of blood than the leadership of the PAC. Mr. Stanley Motjuwadi, a long-time journalist with *Drum* and its current editor, recalls in the issue of his magazine of November 22, 1972:

'A day after the Sharpeville shootings I had an interview in Johannesburg's Fort prison with Mangaliso Robert Sobukwe ... He was awaiting trial on a charge of incitement and seemed to have aged overnight. He was depressed and almost at the point of tears – the Sharpeville tragedy had really hit him hard.'

Any who have followed Sobukwe's role at the head of

PAC know full well the man's courage: he went through nine years of imprisonment without flinching and all those who have seen him, during his imprisonment and now under house arrest, including Members of Parliament from the ruling National Party and the white opposition parties, testify that his convictions remain as strong and his determination as unwavering.

Mindful of the panic a threat to their power creates in despots, Mr. Sobukwe wrote to the Commissioner of Police of South Africa, on the eve of the campaign, emphasising that the PAC campaign against passes would be non-violent and imploring the Commissioner to instruct his men to refrain from the use of violence in an attempt to put down demonstrations. As a further precaution Mr. Sobukwe sternly told PAC leaders and cadres all over the country:

'My instructions, therefore, are that our people must be taught now and continuously that in this campaign we are going to observe absolute non-violence.'"

The authorities did exactly the opposite. Their racist attitude towards blacks, and their total disregard for the lives of black people whom they did not even consider to be equal human beings, largely explains why they opened fire on the peaceful demonstrators. As Lieutenant-Colonel D.H. Pienaar bluntly put it, the mere gathering of blacks was seen as provocation by the white authorities and, by implication, justified the shooting. And typical of the stereotypes about blacks among many white racists, he went on to say:

"The Native mentality does not allow them to gather for a peaceful demonstration. For them to gather means violence."

That alone was enough justification for the white police to shoot the demonstrators. In justifying the shooting, Pienaar was also quoted by BBC saying: "It started when hordes of natives surrounded the police station. If they do these things, they must learn their lessons the hard way."

In fact, the authorities stated that the police opened fire because they panicked and feared for their lives; a ridiculous assertion as if heavily armed security forces were indeed under siege and were threatened by unarmed, peaceful demonstrators many of whom were women and children. And as David Sibeko explained what happened on that fateful day, Monday, 21 March 1960:

"It is appropriate to focus on Sharpeville itself at this stage. Under the chairmanship of Nyakale Tsolo, the PAC branch at Sharpeville approached almost every house and the men's hostel in the township, mobilising support for the strike against passes planned for Monday, March 21, 1960.

The full story of Sharpeville is still to be told, hopefully by those who helped to make this history. I was fortunate as head of the regional executive committee of the Vaal from 1963 to work in the underground amongst many of the organisers and participants in the historic event. Like most veterans of war the people of Sharpeville hate to relive their wartime experience but I was able to learn from direct participants a great deal of what took place.

Not a single bus moved out of Sharpeville to take passengers to work on that Monday. PAC task force members started out before the break of dawn lining up marchers in street after street. By daybreak the marchers, under the leadership of the task force, were moving to a preappointed open ground, where they merged with other demonstrators.

In line with the instruction of the Party leadership, when all the groups had been assembled, the 10,000 and more men, women and children proceeded to the local police station - chanting freedom songs and calling out campaign slogans 'Izwe lethu' (Our land); 'I Africa'; 'Awaphele ampasti' (Down with passes); 'Sobukwe Sikhokhle' (Lead us Sobukwe); 'Forward to Independence, Tomorrow the United States of Africa'; and so on and so forth.

When the marchers reached Sharpeville's police station a heavy contingent of police was lined up outside, many on top of British-made Saracen armoured cars. Mr. Tsolo and other members of the Branch Executive moved forward – in conformity with the novel PAC motto of 'Leaders in Front' – and asked the white policeman in command to let them through so that they could surrender themselves for refusing to carry passes. Initially the police commander refused but much later, towards 11 a.m, they were let through.

The chanting of freedom songs was picking up and the slogans were being repeated with greater volume. Journalists who rushed there from other areas, after receiving word that the campaign was a runaway success in this mostly ignored African township, more than 30 miles south of Johannesburg, confirm that for all their singing and shouting the crowd's mood was more festive than belligerent.

But shortly after the PAC branch leaders had been let through into the police station, without warning, the police facing the crowd opened fire and in two minutes hundreds of bodies lay sprawling on the ground like debris.

The joyful singing had given way to murderous gunfire, and the gunfire was followed by an authentic deadly silence, and then screams, wild screams and cries of the wounded.

Littering the ground in front of that police station in nearby dusty streets were 69 dead and nearly 200 injured men, women and children; a revolting sight which appalled decent human beings the world over as pictures of the massacre got around.

The same pattern of events had taken place in nearby Vanderbijl Park, where two Africans were gunned down by white police a few minutes later, and at Langa and Nyanga, a thousand miles away in Cape Town, where five people were shot dead by white police.

With that savagery the apartheid regime sealed the path of non-violence and PAC resolved to continue the struggle through arms in future."

Other reports including witness accounts tell basically the same story that the shooting was unprovoked, the protesters were unarmed and did not in way threaten the police.

What is clear is that the police response and shooting was a reflex action triggered by the "natural" bias and hostility prevalent among many whites who saw black people as worthless human beings, if not just some creatures who were less than human; a sentiment forcefully expressed by one leader of the ruling National Party which instituted apartheid. As Sibeko wrote about the reaction among many whites, including leaders, after the shooting:

"It was a revealing comment, the one made by Carel de Wet, the Member of Parliament for Vanderbijl Park, a former cabinet minister in Mr. Vorster's Government, who is currently serving a second term as ambassador to the Court of St. James. He complained: 'Why did the police kill only two kaffirs in my constituency?' Clearly the mass killings were by design and they were intended to 'teach the kaffirs a lesson.'"

And the lesson assumed another dimension because of the highly symbolic value and significance of the place where it was taught and, not only for blacks in Sharpeville, but for black people all over the country.

The town of Vereeniging, of which Sharpeville was an

53

integral part as a segregated township for blacks, occupies a special place in the history of South Africa, especially in the history of white nationalism in that country.

It was in that town on 13 March 1902, that the treaty which ended the Anglo-Boer War was signed and the whites of South Africa – the British and the Afrikaners – patched up their differences in pursuit of a common objective to consolidate their position as the dominant racial group in the country at the expense of blacks and other non-whites.

Almost 60 years later, the same place became the scene of bloodshed and one of the worst racial incidents in South African history when powerless blacks protested against the inhuman treatment they endured everyday at the hands of their white oppressors. And the words "Sharpeville massacre" were indelibly etched in the consciences of many people around the world as a constant reminder of the brutal treatment black Africans suffered under the apartheid regime.

The government viewed the protest against the pass laws as a challenge to its authority and the legitimacy of the abominable institution of apartheid whose walls finally came tumbling down more than 40 years later in 1994 when the country held its first multi-racial democratic elections and Nelson Mandela, the leader of the African National Congress (ANC), was elected president of a country that had been dominated by whites for more than 300 years.

The consistency of the reports from different sources and by different people of different backgrounds and political persuasions including news reporters lends credibility to the conclusion that the shooting of the protesters was unprovoked and the Sharpeville massacre could have been easily avoided had the police reacted with restraint and concern for the well-being of the demonstrators. But because the protesters were black, it was a different story, and their fate was sealed simply because of who and what they were. As the assistant editor of *Drum* magazine, Humphrey Tyler, who was at the scene, described what happened:

"Protestors were chanting 'Izwe Lethu' which means 'Our land' or gave the thumbs up 'freedom' salute, and shouted 'Afrika.,' nobody were afraid, in actual fact they were in a cheerful mood. There were plenty of police and more ammunition than uniforms.

A Pan Africanist leader approached us and said his organization and the marches were against violence and were demonstrating peacefully. Suddenly I heard chilling cries of 'Izwe Lethu' it sounded mainly like the voices of women. Hands went up in the famous black power salute. That is when the shooting started.

We heard the clatter of machine guns one after the other. The protestors thought they were firing blanks or warning shots. One woman was hit about 10 yards away from our car, as she fell to the ground her companion went back to assist, he thought she had stumbled.

Then he tried to pick her up, as he turned her around he saw her chest had been blown away from the hail of bullets. He looked at the blood on his hand and screamed 'God she had been shot.'

Hundreds of kids were running like wild rabbits, some of them were gunned down. Shooting only stooped when no living protestor was in sight."

The protesters were told by the leaders of the Pan-Africanist Congress to leave their passes at home and to offer no bail, seek no defence, and pay no fine, if arrested. About 5,000 people – some reports say 7,000 or more – are said to have participated in the protest that morning, marching through Sharpeville to the municipal offices at the entrance of the township.

Before the protests, Sobukwe wrote the police

commissioner on 16 March 1960, stating that the Pan-Africanist Congress would hold a five-day, disciplined, peaceful protest against the pass laws starting on March 21st. And he further stated at a press conference on March 18th that he was sure the protesters would conduct themselves in a peaceful manner. As he put it:

"I have appealed to the African people to make sure that this campaign is conducted in a spirit of absolute non-violence, and I am quite certain they will heed my call. If the other side so desires, we will provide them with an opportunity to demonstrate to the world how brutal they can be."

And they did.

Sobukwe was sentenced to three years in prison for leading the demonstrations against the pass law. He was released on 3 May 1963, but was immediately rearrested and sent to Robben Island where he spent six years in detention and solitary confinement without trial. The provision of the law which empowered the government to continue detaining anyone found guilty of "incitement" came to be known as the "Sobukwe clause."

He was released from Robben Island on 8 May 1969 but was not really free. He was placed under house arrest in Kimberley until his death on 27 February 1978. He was 54.

Born to poor Xhosa parents on 5 December 1924, he was an excellent student and a gifted orator. He also earned more degrees, in economics and law, from the University of London after he was released from Robben Island and will always be remembered for the Shapervelle massacre and as the most prominent black leader in South Africa besides Mandela.

He was also a man of peace.

Had the apartheid regime agreed to talk to him, and with Mandela and other anti-apartheid leaders, there would have been no Shaperville and other bloody incidents including the Soweto uprising in 1976.

The Sharpeville massacre was one of the most significant events in the struggle against apartheid and was not even eclipsed years later by the events in Soweto when hundreds of school children were massacred by the South African police and security forces in June 1976, an event that is widely acknowledged as having signalled the beginning of the end of apartheid. As Ambrose Reeves, a minister in South Africa, stated in "The Sharpeville Massace: A Watershed in South Africa":

"History records that on May 13, 1902, the treaty which ended the Anglo-Boer war was signed at Vereeniging, then a small town some thirty miles from Johannesburg. Nobody could then have realised that some fifty-eight years later the whole world would learn of another event occurring in that part of the Transvaal; this time in the African township of Sharpeville.

As with most towns on the Reef, as the white population of Vereeniging grew so did the township for Africans on the outskirts of the town....

The events at Sharpeville on March 21, 1960,... shocked the world and...are still remembered with shame by civilised men everywhere.

Early that morning a crowd of Africans estimated at between 5,000 and 7,000 marched through Sharpeville to the municipal offices at the entrance to the township.

It appears that much earlier that day members of the Pan Africanist Congress had gone around Sharpeville waking up people and urging them to take part in this demonstration. Other members of the PAC prevented the bus drivers going on duty with the result that there were no buses to take the people to work in Vereeniging.

Many of them set out on bicycles or on foot to their

places of work, but some were met by Pan Africanists who threatened to burn their passes or "lay hands on them" if they did not turn back. However, many Africans joined the procession to the municipal offices quite willingly.

Eventually this demonstration was dispersed by the police, using tear gas bombs and then a baton charge, some sixty police following them into the side streets. Stones were flung and one policeman was slightly injured. It was alleged that several shots were fired by Africans and that only then some policemen opened fire without an order from their officer to do so. Fortunately nobody was hurt.

I was not at Sharpeville when the shooting occurred but it was familiar territory to me. Time and again I officiated at the large African Anglican church there and knew intimately many of the congregation, some of whom were to be involved in the events of that tragic day. I could so well visualise the scene.

Near my home in the northern suburbs of Johannesburg was a large zoo situated in acres of parkland. By a curious anomaly the lake near the zoo was the meeting place for Africans working in the northern suburbs on a Sunday afternoon.

Work finished for the day they would leisurely make their way there in small groups - a gay, colourful, jostling crowd - families and individuals - some political, some not, chatting, laughing, singing, gesticulating and occasionally fighting. The thud of home-made drums could be heard shattering the Sunday calm, and over all the plaintive notes of the penny whistle - shrill and penetrating. It could so easily have been like that on that crisp autumn morning in Sharpeville. Like that, but so very different.

During the morning news spread through the township that a statement concerning passes would be made by an important person at the police station later that day. The result was that many who had been concerned in the earlier demonstration drifted to the police station where they waited patiently for the expected announcement. And all the time the crowd grew.

Reading from the police report on what subsequently happened the Prime Minister told the House of Assembly that evening that the police estimated that 20,000 people were in that crowd. This seems to have been a serious exaggeration.

From photographs taken at the time it is doubtful if there were ever more than 5,000 present at any particular moment, though it may well be that more than this number were involved at one time or another as people were coming and going throughout the morning.

They were drawn to the crowd by a variety of reasons. Some wanted to protest against the pass laws; some were present because they had been coerced; some were there out of idle curiosity; some had heard that a statement would be made about passes.

But whatever may have brought them to the police station, I was unable to discover that any policeman ever tried either to find out why they were there or make any request for them to disperse. And this in spite of the fact that the presence of this crowd seems to have caused a good deal of alarm to the police. So much so that at ten o'clock that morning a squadron of aircraft dived low over the crowd, presumably to intimidate them and encourage them to disperse. This was surely a most expensive way of trying to disperse a crowd.

The police claimed that the people in the crowd were shouting and brandishing weapons and the Prime Minister told the Assembly that the crowd was in a riotous and aggressive mood and stoned the police. There is no evidence to support this.

On the contrary, while the crowd was noisy and excitable, singing and occasionally shouting slogans it was not a hostile crowd. Their purpose was not to fight the police but to show by their presence their hostility to the pass system, expecting that someone would make a statement about passes.

Photographs taken that morning show clearly that this was no crowd spoiling for a fight with the police. Not only was the crowd unarmed, but a large proportion of those present were women and children. All through the morning no attack on the police was attempted.

Even as late as one p.m. the Superintendent in charge of the township was able to walk through the crowd, being greeted by them in a friendly manner and chatting with some of them. Similarly, the drivers of two of the Saracen tanks stated subsequently that they had no difficulty in driving their vehicles into the grounds surrounding the police station. And their testimony was borne out by photographs taken of their progress.

As the hours passed the increasing number of people in the crowd was matched by police reinforcements. Earlier there had only been twelve policemen in the police station: six white and six non-white. But during the morning a series of reinforcements arrived until by lunch time there was a force of nearly 300 armed and uniformed men in addition to five Saracens.

Yet in spite of the increased force that was then available, no one asked the crowd to disperse and no action was taken to arrange for the defence of the police station. The police just strolled around the compound with rifles slung over their shoulders, smoking and chatting with one another.

Scene was set for explosive situation

So the scene was set. Anyone who has lived in the Republic of South Africa knows how explosive that situation had already become. On the one side the ever-growing crowd of noisy Africans - the despised Natives - the Kaffirs who, at all costs, must be kept down lest they step outside the place allotted to them. On the other side the South African police.

Every African fears them, whether they be traffic police, ordinary constables or members of the dreaded Special Branch. Most policemen expect unquestioning deference from Africans. If this is not forthcoming they immediately interpret it as riot and rebellion. In part this is due to the widespread prejudice of white people the world over to those who happen to have a different coloured skin than their own. But in South Africa it is underpinned by the hatred, fear and contempt that so many white police have for all non-white people.

The only action taken during that morning appears to have come not from the police but from two Pan Africanist leaders who urged the crowd to stay away from the fence around the perimeter of the compound so that they did not damage it. Then Lieutenant Colonel Pienaar arrived in the compound. He appears to have accepted that he had come into a dangerous situation and therefore made no attempt either to use methods of persuasion on the crowd or to attempt to discover what the crowd was waiting for.

Instead, about a quarter of an hour after his arrival he gave the order for his men to fall in. A little later he said, "Load five rounds". But he said no more to any of his officers, or to the men. Later, Colonel Pienaar stated that he thought his order would frighten the crowd and that his men would understand that if they had to fire they would not fire more than five rounds. Unfortunately, this was not understood by the policemen under his command.

During this time Colonel Spengler, then head of the Special Branch, was arresting two of the leaders of the Pan Africanist Congress. Afterwards he arrested a third man. Colonel Spengler said subsequently that he was able to carry out his arrests because while the crowd was noisy it was not in a violent mood.

It is extremely difficult to know what happened next. Some of the crowd near the gate of the police station compound said later that they heard a shot. Some said that they heard a policeman say, 'Fire.' Others suddenly became aware that the police were firing in their midst. But all agreed that practically all of them turned and ran away once they realised what was happening.

A few, it is true, stood their ground for some seconds, unable to understand that the police were not firing blanks. Lieutenant Colonel Pienaar was quite clear that he did not give the order to fire. Moreover, he declared that he would not have fired in that situation. It was stated later that two white policemen opened fire and that about fifty others followed suit, using service revolvers, rifles and sten guns.

Police action caused devastating consequences

But whatever doubts there may be of the sequence of events in those fateful minutes, there can be no argument over the devastating consequences of the action of the police on March 21, 1960, in Sharpeville. Sixty-nine people were killed, including eight women and ten children, and of the 180 people who were wounded, thirty-one were women and nineteen were children.

According to the evidence of medical practitioners it is clear that the police continued firing after the people began to flee: for, while thirty shots had entered the wounded or killed from the front of their bodies no less than 155 bullets had entered the bodies of the injured and killed from their backs. All this happened in forty seconds, during which time 705 rounds were fired from revolvers and sten guns.

But whatever weapons were used the massacre was horrible. Visiting the wounded the next day in Baragwanath Hospital near Johannesburg, I discovered youngsters, women and elderly men among the injured. These could not be described as agitators by any stretch of the imagination. For the most part they were ordinary citizens who had merely gone to the Sharpeville police station to see what was going on. Talking with the wounded I found that everyone was stunned and mystified by what had taken place. They had certainly not expected that anything like this would happen.

All agreed that there was no provocation for such savage action by the police. Indeed, they insisted that the political organisers who had called for the demonstration had constantly insisted that there should be no violence or fighting.

Arrests follow massacre

To make matters worse, some of the wounded with whom I spoke in hospital stated that they were taunted by the police as they lay on the ground, being told to get up and be off. Others who tried to help were told to mind their own business.

At first there was only one African minister of the Presbyterian Church of South Africa who tried to help the wounded and the dying. It is true that later the police assisted in tending the wounded and summoned ambulances which conveyed the injured to Vereeniging and Baragwanath Hospitals. Later still, 77 Africans were arrested in connection with the Sharpeville demonstration, in some cases while they were still in hospital.

In fact, it was clear on my visits to the wards of Baragwanath Hospital that many of the injured feared what would happen to them when they left hospital. This wasn't surprising, for Baragwanath Hospital was an extraordinary sight. Outside each of the wards to which the wounded were taken were a number of African police, some white policemen, and members of the Special Branch in civilian clothes.

The attitude of the South African Government to the event at Sharpeville can be seen from its reaction to the civil claims lodged the following September by 224 persons for damages amounting to around 400,000 arising from the Sharpeville killings.

The following month the Minister of Justice announced that during the next parliamentary session the Government would introduce legislation to indemnify itself and its officials retrospectively against claims resulting from action taken during the disturbances earlier that year. This was done in the Indemnity Act, No. 61 of 1961. Not that money could ever compensate adequately for the loss of a breadwinner to a family or make up for lost limbs or permanent incapacity. But it would have been some assistance.

It is true that in February 1961 the Government set up a committee to examine the claims for compensation and to recommend ex gratia payments in deserving cases. But this is not the same thing, and in fact by October 1962 no payments had been made.

Failure of police to communicate with the people

Few commentators since Sharpeville have attempted to justify the action of the police that day. In fact, many of them have drawn special attention to the complete failure of the police to attempt to communicate with the crowd at the police station. If it had been a white crowd the police would have tried to find out why they were there and what they wanted.

Surely their failure to do so was due to the fact that it never occurred to them, as the custodians of public order, either to negotiate with the African leaders or to try to persuade the crowd to disperse. Their attitude was summed up by the statement of Lieutenant Colonel Pienaar that "the Native mentality does not allow them to gather for a peaceful demonstration. For them to gather means violence."

The same point was demonstrated even more graphically by one of his answers at the Court of Enquiry under Mr. Justice Vessels. When he was asked if he had learnt any useful lesson from the events in Sharpeville, he replied, 'Well, we may get better equipment.'

Not that all members of the South African Police Force are cruel or callous. No doubt many of them were shocked by what happened. At the same time what happened at Sharpeville emphasises how far the police in South Africa are cut off from sympathy with or even understanding of Africans. And this is underlined by the fact that at no time did the police express regret for this tragic happening.

Yet it would be folly to attempt to fasten the whole blame for the events at Sharpeville on the police. By the mass of repressive legislation which has been enacted every year since 1948, the South African Government has given the police a task which ever becomes more difficult to fulfill.

The pass laws

It was this legislation which was indirectly responsible for the tragedy of Sharpeville, and in particular the "pass laws". Indeed, the immediate cause of many in the crowd assembling at the police station was the growing resentment of Africans to the system of passes.

This system originated in 1760 in the Cape Colony to regulate the movement of slaves between the urban and the rural areas. The slaves had to carry passes from their masters. Subsequently, the system was extended in various forms to the whole country and was eventually collated in the Native (Urban Areas) Consolidation Act of 1945.

This Act made provision for a variety of passes including registered service contracts and for passes permitting men to seek work in particular areas. But through the years an increasing number of Africans had been given exemption from these laws.

This was the situation which obtained until 1952 when a new act ironically called 'The Abolition of Passes Act' made it compulsory for every African male, whether he had previously had to carry passes or no, to carry a reference book. If the holder had previously been exempted from the pass laws he was now privileged to carry a reference book with a green instead of a brown cover! But the contents were identical.

The advent of the reference books meant that technically there were no longer any such things as passes. But, as will be understood, to the Africans reference books are passes for they contain all the details which were previously entered on the various pass documents. They contain the holder's name, his tax receipt, his permit to be in an urban area and to seek work there, permits from the Labour Bureau, the signature each month of his employer to show that he is still in the employment he was given permission to take, as well as other particulars.

Even more objectionable than having to possess a reference book is the fact that this book must be produced on demand to any policeman or any of the fifteen different classes of officials who may require to see it. Failure to produce it on demand constitutes an offence for which an African may be detained up to thirty days while inquiries are being made about him.

What this means in practice can be seen from the fact that in the twelve months ending June 30, 1966 no less than 479,114 Africans were prosecuted for offences against the "pass laws". At the time of Sharpeville there were 1,000 prosecutions a day for these offences. By 1966, this had risen to over 1,300 a day. These figures speak for themselves.

In 1960 a new development occurred when the Government of South Africa decided for the first time in South African history to extend the pass laws to African women. In their case another fear was added that they might be subjected to manhandling by the police with a further loss of human dignity. In fact, by the time of Sharpeville it was estimated that three-quarters of African women were in possession of reference books.

But many of the women who had not obtained

reference books were strenuously opposed both to the pass system and to its extension to themselves. To them reference books stood for racial identification, and therefore for racial discrimination.

Intolerable economic situation

But this was by no means the only reason for unrest in Sharpeville. Anyone who knew the township at that time was aware that there had been increasing tension among the inhabitants because in that area wages were too low and rents were too high. Prior to March of that year rent had been increased in Sharpeville and this had added to the burdens of Africans living there.

The previous year (1959) a study of the economic position of Africans in Johannesburg had shown that 80 per cent of Africans were living at or below the poverty datum line. The probability is that the lot of Africans in Sharpeville was worse than in Johannesburg.

A survey carried out by the Johannesburg Non-European Affairs Department in 1962 in Soweto showed that 68 per cent of families there had an income below the estimated living costs. A subsequent study in 1966 showed that this figure remained the same. So in spite of the increased prosperity of South Africa the economic position of a high percentage of Africans does not seem to have improved much since Sharpeville.

African wages in Sharpeville in 1960 were low, partly because African trade unions were not (and still are not) recognised for the purpose of bargaining with employers. But also, the continuing colour bar in commerce and industry meant, and still means, high minimum wages for white workers and low maximum wages for the black workers who make up the great majority of the labour force. All this means two wage structures in South Africa which have no relation to one another: in the fixing of the black wage structure the workers frequently have no say at all.

Several months before the tragic events at Sharpeville it was becoming obvious that those living in the township were facing an intolerable economic situation. It is too easy to dismiss the Sharpeville demonstration at the police station as the work of agitators and the result of intimidation. All that those who led the demonstration did was to use a situation which, for political and economic reasons, was already highly explosive.

Growing resistance

Not that Sharpeville was an isolated incident. The ten years before Sharpeville had seen feverish activity by the opponents of apartheid. By means of boycotts, mass demonstrations, strikes and protests, the non-white majority had attempted by non-violent means to compel those in power to modify their racist policies. For example, on June 26, 1952, the Campaign of Defiance against Unjust Laws had been launched.

The same day three years later (June 26, 1955) 3,000 delegates had adopted the Freedom Charter which had been drafted by the Congress Alliance. This took place at a massive gathering at Kliptown, Johannesburg.

The following year the Federation of South African Women held a series of spectacular demonstrations against the extension of the pass system to African women. These culminated in a mass demonstration at the Union Buildings, Pretoria, on August 9, 1956. Some 10,000 women gathered there in an orderly fashion to present 7,000 individually signed protest forms.

Again, from January 7, 1957, many thousand African men and women for months walked eighteen to twenty miles a day to and from work in Johannesburg in a boycott of the buses. Although in this particular case they gained their objective, all the various endeavours by Africans to secure change by peaceful means brought little tangible result.

The surprising thing was that in all this activity there was very little violence on the part of boycotters, demonstrators and strikers. In spite of great and frequent provocation by the police, Africans remained orderly and disciplined. They were in truth non-violent. As could be expected there were, however, occasions when the resentment and frustration of Africans spilled over into violence.

One such occasion was at Cato Manor near Durban on June 17, 1959. On that day a demonstration of African women at the beer hall destroyed beer and drinking utensils and was dispersed by the police. Several days later the Director of the Bantu Administration Department met 2,000 women at the beer hall.

Once they had stated their grievances they were ordered to disperse. When they failed to do so the police made a baton charge. General disorder and rioting followed, with the result that damage estimated at 100,000 (Rands) was done to vehicles and buildings. Later that day Africans attacked a police picket and were driven off with sten guns.

After this, things remained comparatively quiet in Cato Manor until a Sunday afternoon in February, 1960, when the smouldering resentment of Africans there again burst into flame. An ugly situation developed in which nine policemen lost their lives. This was a deplorable business. Whatever may be said of the actions of the South African police these men died while carrying out their duties. The blame for their deaths must in the first instance lie on those who murdered them.

The fact that these deaths occurred in Cato Manor only a few weeks before the demonstration at Sharpeville must have been well known to the police gathered at the police station in Sharpeville that morning. Certainly more than one spokesman of the South African Government linked these two affairs together. There is not the slightest evidence, however, that there was in this sense any connection between the tragedies of Cato Manor and Sharpeville.

But in another sense they were both intimately connected because more indirectly they both arose out of the action of those in power during the previous decade, who had taken every possible step to ensure that the whole life of the millions of Africans was encased within the strait-jacket of compulsory segregation.

Civilisation without mercy

Yet there the similarity ended. The crowd at Sharpeville was not attacking anything or anyone. Further, there is abundant evidence to show that they were unarmed. While nothing can justify the killing of police at Cato Manor, that incident cannot in any way exonerate the vicious action of the police at Sharpeville. As the late Sir Winston Churchill pointed out in a debate in the British House of Commons on July 8, 1920:

"There is surely one general prohibition which we can make. I mean the prohibition against what is called 'frightfulness'. What I mean by frightfulness is the inflicting of great slaughter or massacre upon a particular crowd of people with the intention of terrorising not merely the rest of the crowd, but the whole district or the whole country." (This is precisely what the police did at Sharpeville).

On that occasion Sir Winston concluded his speech with some words of Macaulay – '... and then was seen what we believe to be the most frightful of spectacles, the strength of civilisation without mercy.' These are words which aptly summarise all that happened at Sharpeville that March morning.

Many people inside South Africa, though shocked for a time by the events at Sharpeville, ended by dismissing them as just one incident in the long and growing

70

succession of disturbances that down the years have marked the implementation of apartheid. Certainly the Government of South Africa, though badly shaken in the days immediately following Sharpeville, soon regained control of the situation.

On March 24, the Government banned all public meetings in twenty-four magisterial districts. On April 8, the Governor-General signed a proclamation banning the African National Congress and the Pan Africanist Congress as unlawful organisations, the result being that they were both driven underground. But neither of them became dormant.

At the same time the Government mobilised the entire Citizen Force, the Permanent Force Reserve, the Citizen Force Reserve and the Reserve of Officers, and the whole of the Commando Force was placed on stand-by. Already on March 30, in Proclamation No. 90, the Governor-General had declared a state of emergency which lasted until August 31, 1960.

During that time a large number of prominent opponents of government policy of all races were arrested and detained without being brought to trial. In addition some 20,000 Africans were rounded up, many of whom were released after screening.

So after some months eventually, at least superficially, life in South Africa became at least relatively normal. But underneath the external calm dangerous fires continue to smoulder: fires that can never be extinguished by repressive measures coupled with a constant and growing show of force.

Outside South Africa there were widespread reactions to Sharpeville in many countries which in many cases led to positive action against South Africa: action which still continues. But here, too, most people, even if they have heard of Sharpeville, have relegated what happened there to the archives of history, just one of the too many dark pages in the human story.

Sharpeville marked a watershed in South Africa

Yet it is my personal belief that history will recognise that Sharpeville marked a watershed in South African affairs. Until Sharpeville, violence for the most part had been used in South Africa by those who were committed to the maintenance of the economic and political domination of the white minority in the Republic.

Down the years they had always been ready to use force to maintain the status quo whenever they judged it necessary to do so. When the occasion arose they did not hesitate to use it. Over and over again, non-white civilians were injured by police action or by assaults on them when in prison.

Until Sharpeville the movements opposed to apartheid were pledged to a policy of non-violence. But on March 21, 1960, when an unarmed African crowd was confronted by 300 heavily armed police supported by five Saracen armoured vehicles, an agonising reappraisal of the situation was inevitable. Small wonder is it that, having tried every peaceful method open to them to secure change without avail, the African leadership decided that violence was the only alternative left to them.

Never again would they expose their people to another Sharpeville. As Nelson Mandela said in court at his trial in October 1962:

'Government violence can do only one thing and that is to breed counter-violence. We have warned repeatedly that the Government, by resorting continually to violence, will breed in this country counter-violence among the people till ultimately if there is no dawning of sanity on the part of the Government, the dispute between the Government and my people will finish up by being settled in violence and by force.'

Outwardly things may go on in South Africa much as before. Visitors may find a booming economy, the white minority may seem secure in their privileged position for any foreseeable future, some urban Africans may have higher living standard than formerly. But all this ought not to deceive anybody.

The fact is that for the first time both sides in the racial struggle in South Africa are now committed to violence; the white minority to preserve the status quo; the non-white majority to change: change from society dominated by apartheid to one that is non-racial in character. Already there are clear indications that the opponents of apartheid are turning deliberately to violence.

The fact that at the moment this is being expressed through small bands of guerillas who may be neither very well trained nor well-equipped does not mean that they ought therefore to be dismissed as having little significance.

After all, we have the examples of Algeria, Cuba and Viet Nam before us as powerful reminders of what may result from very small and weak beginnings.

In spite of the present calm in South Africa and a prosperity unparallelled in its history, within the Republic the seeds of violence have already been sown. Unless there is a radical change in the present political and economic structures of South Africa, that which has already been sown will be harvested in a terrible and brutal civil war which might easily involve the whole African continent in conflict before it ends.

Indeed it may be that in the present situation in the Republic of South Africa are hidden forces which will involve humanity in a global racial conflict unless the present racist policies there are changed radically.

The choice before the international community has been a clear one ever since Sharpeville. Either it takes every possible step to secure the abandonment of the present policies in South Africa or the coming years will bring increasing sorrow and strife both for South Africa and for the world.

Sharpeville was a tragedy showing most plainly that the ideology of apartheid is a way of death and not of life. Can the nations recognise this before it is too late?"

The apartheid regime obviously did not recognise that and was reinforced in its belief that it would survive because some of the most powerful countries in the world, especially the industrialized nations in the West, continued to support it.

It did not take the massacre seriously. It believed that the white power structure was invincible, virtually an impregnable fortress that could withstand the most sustained assault even by its fiercest opponents. And it invoked the inspired canon of the Scripture to justify its diabolical policies as if they had been sanctioned by God and white people had divine mandate to rule members of "the lesser breed": black people and other non-whites.

Shortly after the massacre, the apartheid regime declared a state emergency which lasted from 30 March to 31 August 1960.

The emergency declaration was prompted by widespread demonstrations, protests and strikes across the country in condemnation of the massacre and what the apartheid regime perceived to be a threat to the nation's security and white domination of the country.

More than 18,000 people including most of the country's leading anti-apartheid politicians of all races were arrested when the emergency was declared. And on April 8th, both the African National Congress (ANC) and the Pan Africanist Congress (PAC) were declared illegal, forcing them to go underground and resort to other means to bring about change in the country.

The establishment of Umkhonto we Sizwe (The Spear of the Nation), the military wing of the African National Congress; and of Poqo, PAC's armed wing, was largely inspired by the Sharpeville massacre and by the government's refusal to negotiate with the opponents of apartheid and find ways to achieve racial equality in the country without resorting to violence.

Although both the ANC and the PAC were banned in South Africa, they remained active in the country and from their operational bases in other countries such as Tanzania and Zambia. It was not until 30 years later, in 1990, that they were unbanned.

Thus, instead of bringing about fundamental change, the government became even more repressive following the Sharpeville massacre. In October 1960, the white electorate voted for a republican form of government under the leadership of the National Party dominated by Afrikaners and which instituted apartheid in 1948. South Africa withdrew from the Commonwealth in March 1961. On May 31st the same year, it became republic.

The withdrawal of South Africa from the Commonwealth was a result of a concerted effort by African leaders to keep the apartheid regime out of this community of nations of former British colonies. The campaign was led by Julius Nyerere who made it clear that if South Africa remained a member, his country Tanganyika would not join the Commonwealth once it became independent. As he bluntly stated: "To vote South Africa in, is to vote us out."

There is no question that the Shaperville massacre galvanized the anti-apartheid movement worldwide. It drew worldwide condemnation and played a critical role in changing the attitude of many African leaders who had earlier embraced non-violence as a means to achieving racial justice in the land of apartheid. After the massacre, armed struggle was seen a viable alternative that could be used to compel the apartheid regime to accept fundamental change. And it was effectively used through the years as a complementary strategy, along with diplomacy, to achieve this goal.

Coincidentally, the year 1960 was also a year of hope and optimism for Africa. Millions of Africans across the continent celebrated the dawn of a new era marking the end of colonial rule when 17 countries won independence, the largest number in a single year.

Many events had taken place across the continent through the years but independence was different. It was a phenomenal event and probably the most significant since the advent of colonial rule. As British Prime Minister Harold Macmillan said in his speech to the South African parliament in Cape Town on 3 February 1960, "the wind of change is blowing through this continent," as more and more Africans in the colonies demanded the right to rule themselves. And "whether we like it or not, this growth of national consciousness is a political fact."

The rulers of apartheid South Africa did not like what he said and expressed their displeasure. But, as the saying goes, the rest is history.

1961

PROBABLY the most significant event that occurred in Africa in 1961 was the assassination of Patrice Lumumba. And it had a profound impact on Congo and beyond for years.

The chaos that Congo endured for decades was partly attributable to the elimination of Lumumba from the country's political scene and as the most important leader and unifying force in Congo's post-colonial history.

He was assassinated on 17 January 1961. His brutal murder and the ensuing chaos in Congo dominated the news in Africa for the rest of the year and became one of the dominant subjects of discussion in the following years not only in Africa but in other parts of the world.

Right from the beginning, Lumumba's enemies within Congo, especially Moise Tshombe and Joseph Mobutu, were blamed for his assassination. And there is no question that they played a major role.

It was Mobutu who, as the head of the army and the most powerful Congolese leader, seized power on 14

September 1960. Also, it was he who supported Joseph Kasavubu as the country's president after Kasavubu dismissed Lumumba as prime minister on September 5th and replaced him with Joseph Ileo. And it was he who arrested Lumumba and later transferred him to his arch-enemy, Moise Tshombe in Katanga Province, to be killed.

Quite often, Lumumba's assassination is largely blamed on internal actors, the Congolese themselves, as a conspiracy between Mobutu, Kasavubu, Tshombe, Joseph Ileo, Albert Kalonji and Lumumba's other enemies in the country. The impression some people might get is that all these people were independent actors and made their own decisions, without external involvement, on what to do with Lumumba. And they did play a big role in his elimination.

But Lumumba's assassination involved even much bigger people and actors than Lumumba's Congolese enemies. It was a conspiracy which went far beyond the circle of his enemies within Congo. Although his fellow Congolese played an important role in his elimination, they were no more than puppets manipulated at will by outside powers, in spite of the fact that even they themselves would have killed him, on their own, if they had the opportunity to do so and even if there was no foreign intervention.

One of the biggest players on the scene and in Lumumba's assassination was Belgium, the former colonial power, which sent troops to Congo after independence ostensibly to rescue its citizens and other whites after the country descended into chaos precipitated by the secession of Katanga Province under the leadership of Moise Tshombe on 11 July 1960.

Katanga's secession was instigated and encouraged by Belgium and other western financial and political interests. And the real motive for Belgium's intervention was to provide military, economic and political support to Tshombe to ensure that the secession of Katanga was successful.

The Belgians had powerful financial interests in this mineral-rich province. They did not want it to remain an integral part of Congo under the control of the country's central authority, especially under the leadership of Lumumba whom they saw as a threat to their economic and political interests in the country because of his strong nationalist credentials as a leader who wanted to keep the country independent and united and free from external interference.

Although the Belgians were the most decisive force in Lumumba's assassination, they earned this status and unenviable distinction mainly because they were highly visible on the political scene in Congo as the former colonial rulers. Far more sinister was the involvement of the United States in Lumumba's arrest and subsequent assassination.

As the most powerful country in the West where the plot for Lumumba's elimination was conceived and hatched, it would not be an overstatement to say that it was the United States which was the dominant force in Congo. It was also the United States which could have prevented this tragic event from happening had the leaders in Washington chosen to do so. They orchestrated the whole thing, despite denials through the years and attempts to blame only the Belgians as the main architects of the conspiratorial and assassination plot against Lumumba.

As late as the 1990s, reports continued to circulate, as they had through the years since the sixties, that the Belgians were the main players on Congo's political scene and in the assassination of Lumumba. Even in the mid-seventies, a committee of the United States Senate which, under the chairmanship of Senator Frank Church of Idaho, investigated the role of the CIA in the assassination of foreign leaders concluded that there was no evidence to show that the United States was involved or played a role in Lumumba's assassination.

Yet, it was President Dwight Eisenhower who ordered Lumumba's assassination and authorized the CIA to carry out the plot. And Belgium could not have done anything without the approval of the United States as the leader of the Western world.

But it is also true that CIA agents were involved right from the beginning in the plot to assassinate Lumumba, despite denials of the involvement of some of them such as Laurence Devlin who was the CIA station chief in Congo during that time. Devlin also befriended Lumumba using his diplomatic cover as just another official at the American embassy in Leopoldville to conceal his true identity as a CIA agent.

In an interview from his home in Princeton, New Jersey, in 1996, Devlin denied any personal involvement and claimed he was against Lumumba's assassination and that of other foreign leaders as a political weapon to secure and promote American interests.

Some people have tried to minimize the role played by the United States in the assassination of Lumumba. There are even those, including former UN undersecretary-general Brian Urquhart, who have tried to exonerate the United States from this crime. Yet there is plenty of evidence to refute that. The United States played a major role in the commission of this crime.

Also, America's direct involvement in the assassination of Lumumba did little to help the United States win friends in Africa – besides Tshombe and Mobutu – and keep other countries out of the Congo imbroglio; it accomplished exactly the opposite.

The CIA plot to assassinate Lumumba started with the Eisenhower Administration and remains, to this day, one of the saddest chapters in the history of relations between the United States and Africa. That the United States was largely responsible for his assassination is an open secret, as much as it has been for decades.

It is as much a sad story about the weakness of African countries as it is one of total disregard for the interests, rights and wellbeing of Africans – for racist reasons as well, not just economic and geopolitical – by the world's most powerful country whose white majority, according to national surveys, still refuse to accept African Americans as full human beings; hence the belief among millions of whites – if not the vast majority – that black people are genetically inferior to them and members of others races, a racist doctrine given pseudoscientific validity by *The Bell Curve* and other works.

Therefore by killing Lumumba, American leaders were just getting rid of "another nigger," although the main reasons were geopolitical, ideological, and economic: control of Congo, the heart of Africa, by the United States and her Western allies.

Evidence against the United States is overwhelming, although some people, while conceding American complicity in Lumumba's assassination, tend to minimise her role. One of them is Jon Lee Anderson who wrote an excellent biography of Che Guevara, entitled *Che Guevara: A Revolutionary Life*, which also deals with the Congo crisis.

Yet he downplays America's role in the assassination of Lumumba. He also fails or deliberately refuses to see the United States – not necessarily as a global tyrant although it is hard to refute that after America's invasion of Iraq and threats to invade other countries – as an imperial power capable of manipulating and controlling world events to the detriment of weak countries.

The United States controls their economies; intimidates, manipulates, and even overthrows their governments, and has even ordered and sponsored the assassination of leaders the American government doesn't like.

Yet some people fail to see or are unwilling to accept that, sometimes out of blind patriotism in the case of

Americans, although Anderson is not cast in that mould as a blind patriot. His book is massive and rich in detail. But that does not compensate for lack of objective analysis. As Jane Franklin stated in "Che Guevara: Guerilla Heroica," her review of Anderson's book, in *The Nation:*, 19 May 1997:

"Anderson seems not to share Guevara's view of US imperialism, and downplays the US role in global events.

Speaking at a 1961 rally to mobilize Cubans for the imminent US invasion, Guevara cited the recent murder of Patrice Lumumba as 'an example of what the empire is capable of '....In the many pages devoted to events in the Congo, Anderson contests this claim.

Though he reports a plan by Dr. Sidney Gottlieb of the CIA's 'medical division' to poison Lumumba, he states that 'before the CIA could get close to Lumumba, however, his own Congolese rivals did.'

But the CIA and the US Embassy had already connived with these Congolese rivals – Moise Tshombe and Joseph Mobutu – to murder Lumumba. Mobutu, who turned Lumumba over to Tshombe to kill, was actually on the CIA payroll.

Four years later, when Guevara left Cuba to fight against Tshombe and Mobutu on the side of Lumumba's followers, the CIA had already dispatched a band of Cuban exiles, trained for the Bay of Pigs, to fly bombing raids for Tshombe. This CIA operation, ignored by Anderson, suggests that Washington shared Guevara's view of the dimensions of the struggle." – (Jane Franklin, "Che Guevara: Guerilla Heroica," *The Nation*, New York, May 19, 1997, p.28. See also Jon Lee Anderson, *Che Guevara: A Revolutionary Life*, Nnew York: Grove Press, 1997).

Some supporters of President Dwight Eisenhower refused – and even today probably still refuse – to accept the fact that the president could have authorised such a plot to assassinate Lumumba.

Yet he is the same leader who didn't care how many people were killed in order to "fight communism" in Latin America; nor did he have any qualms about overthrowing the populist government of Guzman Arbenz in Guatemala in 1954 or the government of Dr. Mohammad Mossadeq in Iran a year earlier in 1953 because it nationalised the oil industry which belonged to the Iranians – not to the British or the Americans.

Then there was the plot to assassinate Castro, also conceived and hatched by the Eisenhower Administration; and next, the one against Lumumba.

Just as in the case of Castro when Eisenhower felt that the CIA was not doing enough, and fast enough, to eliminate him, the president also felt that the intelligence agency was not working fast enough to get rid of Lumumba. As Christopher Andrew states in his book, *For the President's Eyes Only: Secret Intelligence and the American Presidency from Washington to Bush*:

"Just as Eisenhower had regarded the 5412 Committee's February (1960) proposals for dealing with Castro as too feeble, so he was equally critical of its initial plans for covert actions against Patrice Lumumba.

When the committee met to discuss action against Lumumba on August 25, Gordon Gray reported that the president 'had expressed extremely strong feelings on the necessity for very straightforward action in this situation, and he wondered whether the plans as outlined were sufficient to accomplish this.'

Thus admonished, the committee 'finally agreed that planning for the Congo would not necessarily rule out consideration" of any particular kind of activity that might contribute to getting rid of Lumumba." – (Christopher Andrew, *For the President's Eyes Only: Secret Intelligence and the American Presidency from*

Washington to Bush, New York: Harper Perennial, 1997, pp. 293 – 301).

As part of the plot to eliminate Lumumba, the CIA also launched a smear campaign against the Congolese prime minister and prepared different kinds of poisons to accomplish their mission.

All that was revealed in 1975 during US Senate investigations – conducted by the Select Committee on Intelligence Activities chaired by Democratic Senator Frank Church of Idaho – into assassinations of foreign leaders by the CIA.

The hearings also covered CIA plots – some of them successful – to overthrow foreign governments including a number of them in Africa: for example, Nkrumah's in Ghana which the CIA succeeded in overthrowing in February 1966; Nyerere's in Tanzania which the CIA tried more than once in the mid-sixties to overthrow; and Lumumba's, of course, with Lumumba himself being targeted for assassination not just for removal from office. And the smear campaign against him by the CIA knew no bounds. As Christopher Andrew further states in his book:

"Allen Dulles (the CIA director, also known as the DCI – Director of Central Intelligence) told Eisenhower that Lumumba was insane; later reports alleged that he was also 'a dope fiend.'

On September 21 the DCI reported to an NSC (National Security Council) meeting, chaired by the president, that 'Lumumba was not yet disposed of.' Still fascinated by the use of poisons in covert action, Richard Bissell (head of CIA's covert operations) instructed a CIA scientist to prepare biological toxins designated to assassinate or incapacitate an unnamed 'African leader' (Patrice Lumumba)." – (Ibid., p. 253).

More than a decade later, the CIA was still denying its

involvement in the assassination of Lumumba in spite of overwhelming evidence implicating the American intelligence agency in the diabolical plot.

In a television interview on 27 February 1975, conducted by Daniel Schorr of CBS News, CIA Director William Colby was asked about the agency's role in assassinations: "Has the CIA ever killed anyone in this country?" Schorr asked. "Not in this country," replied Colby. The CIA chief was then asked about assassinations abroad. He refused to give any names.

Schorr suggested Dag Hammarskjold, the UN secretary-general killed in a mysterious plane crash in Ndola, Northern Rhodesia (now Zambia) in 1961. "No, of course not!" said Colby. But when Schorr mentioned Patrice Lumumba, also killed in 1961, Colby refused to comment.

The plot included infecting Lumumba's tooth paste with deadly bacteria. The CIA doctor who was responsible for these poisons, Sidney Gottlieb, flew to Congo with his poison kit. But things didn't work out well for him and the other CIA agents trying to kill Lumumba. They couldn't get the poisoned tooth paste to Lumumba.

As for Sidney Gottlieb, that was not even his real name. It was the name he used when he worked for the CIA. Born in 1918, his real name was Joseph Scheider. He joined the CIA after getting a Ph.D. in chemistry from the California Institute of Technology (CalTech).

He joined the CIA soon after he got his Ph.D. and worked as a member of the Technical Services Staff (TSS). He eventually became head of the Chemical Division at the CIA. His failure to kill Lumumba was one of his biggest disappointments. He died on 10 March 1999.

Finally, the CIA concluded that getting rid of Lumumba right away was the best solution. And that is exactly what it did, in collusion with Tshombe and Mobutu.

American involvement in Lumumba's elimination has been amply documented. There is no doubt that Washington played a critical role in his removal from power and subsequent assassination. As Dr. Stephen Weissman who was staff director of the US House of Representatives Subcommittee on Africa from 1986 to 1991 stated in his article, "Opening the Secret Files on Lumumba's Murder," in *The Washington Post*, July 21, 2002:

"In his latest film, 'Minority Report,' director Steven Spielberg portrays a policy of 'preemptive action' gone wild in the year 2054. But we don't have to peer into the future to see what harm faulty intelligence and the loss of our moral compass can do. U.S. policies during the Cold War furnish many tragic examples. One was U.S. complicity in the overthrow and murder of Congolese Prime Minister Patrice Lumumba.

Forty-one years ago, Lumumba, the only leader ever democratically elected in Congo, was delivered to his enemies, tortured and summarily executed. Since then, his country has been looted by the U.S.-supported regime of Mobutu Sese Seko and wracked by regional and civil war.

The conventional explanation of Lumumba's death has been that he was murdered by Congolese rivals after earlier U.S. attempts to kill him, including a plot to inject toxins into his food or toothpaste, failed. In 1975, the U.S. Senate's 'Church Committee' probed CIA assassination plots and concluded there was 'no evidence of CIA involvement in bringing about the death of Lumumba.'

Not so. I have obtained classified U.S. government documents, including a chronology of covert actions approved by a National Security Council (NSC) subgroup, that reveal U.S. involvement in -- and significant responsibility for -- the death of Lumumba, who was mistakenly seen by the Eisenhower administration as an African Fidel Castro.

The documents show that the key Congolese leaders who brought about Lumumba's downfall were players in 'Project Wizard,' a CIA covert action program. Hundreds of thousands of dollars and military equipment were channeled to these officials, who informed their CIA paymasters three days in advance of their plan to send Lumumba into the clutches of his worst enemies.

Other new details: The U.S. authorized payments to then-President Joseph Kasavubu four days before he ousted Lumumba, furnished Army strongman Mobutu with money and arms to fight pro-Lumumba forces, helped select and finance an anti-Lumumba government, and barely three weeks after his death authorized new funds for the people who arranged Lumumba's murder.

Moreover, these documents show that the plans and payments were approved by the highest levels of the Eisenhower administration, either the NSC or its 'Special Group,' consisting of the national security adviser, CIA director, undersecretary of state for political affairs, and deputy defense secretary.

These facts are four decades old, but are worth unearthing for two reasons. First, Congo (known for years as Zaire) is still struggling to establish democracy and stability. By facing up to its past role in undermining Congo's fledgling democracy, the United States might yet contribute to Congo's future. Second, the U.S. performance in Congo is relevant to our struggle against terrorism. It shows what can happen when, in the quest for national security, we abandon the democratic principles and rule of law we are fighting to defend.

In February (2002), Belgium, the former colonial power in Congo, issued a thousand-page report that acknowledged 'an irrefutable portion of responsibility in the events that led to the death of Lumumba.' Unlike Belgium, the United States has admitted no such moral responsibility.

Over the years, scholars (including myself) and

journalists have written that American policy played a major role in the ouster and assassination of Lumumba. But the full story remained hidden in U.S. documents, which, like those I have examined, are still classified despite the end of the Cold War, the end of the Mobutu regime and Belgium's confession.

Here's what they tell us that, until now, we didn't know, or didn't know for certain:

* In August 1960, the CIA established Project Wizard. Congo had been independent only a month, and Lumumba, a passionate nationalist, had become prime minister, with a plurality of seats in the parliament. But U.S. presidential candidate John F. Kennedy was vowing to meet 'the communist challenge' and Eisenhower's NSC was worried that Lumumba would tilt toward the Soviets.

The U.S. documents show that over the next few months, the CIA worked with and made payments to eight top Congolese -- including President Kasavubu, Mobutu (then army chief of staff), Foreign Minister Justin Bomboko, top finance aide Albert Ndele, Senate President Joseph Ileo and labor leader Cyrille Adoula -- who all played roles in Lumumba's downfall.

The CIA joined Belgium in a plan, detailed in the Belgian report, for Ileo and Adoula to engineer a no-confidence vote in Lumumba's government, which would be followed by union-led demonstrations, the resignations of cabinet ministers (organized by Ndele) and Kasavubu's dismissal of Lumumba.

* On Sept. 1, the NSC's Special Group authorized CIA payments to Kasavubu, the U.S. documents say. On Sept. 5, Kasavubu fired Lumumba in a decree of dubious legality. However, Kasavubu and his new prime minister, Ileo, proved lethargic over the following week as Lumumba rallied supporters. So Mobutu seized power on Sept. 14. He kept Kasavubu as president and established a

temporary 'College of Commissioners' to replace the disbanded government.

* The CIA financed the College and influenced the selection of commissioners. The College was dominated by two Project Wizard participants: Bomboko, its president, and Ndele, its vice-president. Another CIA ally, Lumumba party dissident Victor Nendaka, was appointed chief of the security police.

* On Oct. 27, the NSC Special Group approved $250,000 for the CIA to win parliamentary support for a Mobutu government. However, when legislators balked at approving any prime minister other than Lumumba, the parliament remained closed. The CIA money went to Mobutu personally and the commissioners.

* On Nov. 20, the Special Group authorized the CIA to provide arms, ammunition, sabotage materials and training to Mobutu's military in the event it had to resist pro-Lumumba forces.

The full extent of what one U.S. document calls the 'intimate' relationship between the CIA and Congolese leaders was absent from the Church Committee report. The only covert action (apart from the assassination plots) the committee discussed was the August 1960 effort to promote labor opposition and a no-confidence vote in the Senate.

How did Lumumba die?

After being ousted Sept. 5, Lumumba rallied support in parliament and the international community. When Mobutu took over, U.N. troops protected Lumumba, but soon confined him to his residence. Lumumba escaped on Nov. 27. Days later he was captured by Mobutu's troops, beaten and arrested.

What happened next is clearer thanks to the Belgian report and the classified U.S. documents. As early as Christmas Eve 1960, College of Commissioners' president Bomboko offered to hand Lumumba over to two secessionist leaders who had vowed to kill him.

One declined and nothing happened until mid-January 1961, when the central government's political and military position deteriorated and troops guarding Lumumba (then jailed on a military base near the capital) mutinied. CIA and other Western officials feared a Lumumba comeback.

On Jan. 14, the commissioners asked Kasavubu to move Lumumba to a 'surer place.' There was 'no doubt,' the Belgian inquiry concluded, that Mobutu agreed. Kasavubu told security chief Nendaka to transfer Lumumba to one of the secessionist strongholds. On Jan. 17, Nendaka sent Lumumba to the Katanga region. That night, Lumumba and two colleagues were tortured and executed in the presence of members of the Katangan government. No official announcement was made for four weeks.

What did the U.S. government tell its Congolese clients during the last three days of Lumumba's life? The Church Committee reported that a Congolese 'government leader' advised the CIA's Congo station chief, Larry Devlin, on Jan. 14 that Lumumba was to be sent to 'the home territory' of his 'sworn enemy.' Yet, according to the Church Committee and declassified documents, neither the CIA nor the U.S. embassy tried to save the former prime minister.

The CIA may not have exercised robotic control over its covert political action agents, but the failure of Devlin or the U.S. embassy to question the plans for Lumumba could only be seen by the Congolese as consent. After all, secret CIA programs had enabled this group to achieve political power, and the CIA had worked from August through November 1960 to assassinate or abduct

Lumumba.

Here, the classified U.S. chronology provides an important postscript. On Feb. 11, 1961, with U.S. reports from Congo strongly indicating Lumumba was dead, the Special Group authorized $500,000 for political action, troop payments and military equipment, largely to the people who had arranged Lumumba's murder.

Devlin has sought to distance himself from Lumumba's death. While the CIA was in close contact with the Congolese officials involved, Devlin told the Church Committee that those officials 'were not acting under CIA instructions if and when they did this.'

In a recent phone conversation with Devlin, I posed the issue of U.S. responsibility for Lumumba's death. He acknowledged that, 'It was important to [these] cooperating leaders what the U.S. government thought.' But he said he did 'not recall' receiving advance word of Lumumba's transfer. Devlin added that even if he had objected, 'That would not have stopped them from doing it.'

By evading its share of moral responsibility for Lumumba's fate, the United States blurs African and American history and sidesteps the need to make reparation for yesterday's misdeeds through today's policy.

In 1997, after the Mobutu regime fell, the Congolese democratic opposition pleaded in vain for American and international support.

Since then, as many as 3 million lives have been lost as a result of civil and regional war. The United States has not supported a strong U.N. peacekeeping force or fostered a democratic transition. The collapse in late April 2002 of negotiations between Congolese factions threatens to reignite the smoldering conflict or ratify the partition of the country.

Our government's actions four decades ago in Congo also have special meaning after the tragedy of Sept. 11. They warn that even as we justly defend our land and our people against terrorists, we must avoid the excessive fear and zeal that lead to destructive intervention betraying our most fundamental principles."

Such intervention by the United Stated led to one of the worst crises in the history of post-colonial Africa. And the Congo crisis continued to be a dominant news item throughout the sixties.

The year 1961 was one of the worst right from the beginning. Lumumba had just been assassinated early that year, and Katanga's secession continued to threaten the territorial integrity of one of Africa's biggest countries right in the heart of the continent.

But it was Lumumba's assassination that dominated the news. Almost everything that unfolded in Congo during those tragic years was directly or indirectly related to his ouster from power and subsequent assassination.

Probably the only way Lumumba could have been saved would have been to prevent him from leaving his official residence in Leopoldville. Instead, he left the nation's capital,. determined to go to Stanleyville, his political stronghold in eastern Congo.

The situation in the Congo was out of control because of a combination of factors: Katanga's secession, internal disputes including secessionist threats from other provinces; and power rivalry between Lumumba and Kasavubu instigated and fueled by the United States and Belgium whose officials and intelligence agents backed Kasavubu and did everything they could to sow seeds of confusion and discord with Lumumba's camp.

When in July 1960 Lumumba appealed to the United Nations for help to send troops to end Katanga's secession and restore law and order, and ask Belgian troops to withdraw from Congo, NATO allies, especially the United States, Belgium and France expressed strong reservations on such involvement by the UN.

However, the UN Security Council finally authorised

the provision of military assistance to the beleaguered nation until Congo's own security forces would be ready to take over. In spite of such an offer of assistance, UN forces couldn't do much. They were sent to Congo but only with limited mandate. They were not authorised to intervene in internal conflicts and could use force only in self-defence.

The first UN troops to go to Congo were from African countries: Ghana, Guinea, Ethiopia, Liberia, Morocco and Tunisia, They arrived two days after the UN Security Council authorised the mission. More than troops, initially all from African countries, were deployed throughout the country towards the end of July 1960 except in the secessionist province of Katanga whose army included mercenaries from South Africa, Belgium, France and other countries.

By the end of July, the total UN military contingent was 8,396, of whom 2,340 were Ghanaians, 2,087 Tunisians, 1,220 Moroccans, 1,160 Ethiopians, 741 Guineans, 225 Liberians and 623 Swedes. A little later, an Irish battalion was added. Eventually 28 countries contributed troops, making a total of 19,828 UN soldiers in Congo.

The UN force in Congo – known as UNOC, a French acronym for "UN Congo" – remained predominantly African. White troops, Swedish and Irish, came from countries which were considered to be neutral.

But it was clear that, because of their limited mandate, and given the size of the country roughly equal to the size of Western Europe, they were not enough for the task. Compounding the problem was the fact that Belgian troops did not want to leave Congo for obvious reasons and because of the kind of support they had including encouragement from the United States whose leaders did not like Lumumba anymore than the Belgians and the leaders of the other Western countries did. They wanted him out of power, and dead.

Finally, after the Belgian troops left Congo,

Lumumba's primary concern was to find ways to end Katanga's secession. But because of their limited mandate, UN troops could not intervene and use force to try to end the secession of Katanga even though most of them came from African countries and may have wanted to reunite the country.

African leaders were sympathetic towards Lumumba and wanted to end Katanga's secession. They included Ghanaian President Kwame Nkrumah whose troops were the first to arrive in Congo. But he was also fully aware of the inability of the independent African countries alone to end the secession of Katanga even if Lumumba had invited them to do so without external help.

The problem was compounded by the unwillingness of Western powers to authorise the UN to send a much larger force to Congo to end Katanga's secession. Their refusal to do so amounted to *de facto* recognition of Katanga as a legal sovereign entity, to the consternation of Lumumba and other African leaders.

In August 1960, the first UN troops arrived in Katanga in a gradual attempt to replace Belgian troops which, in spite of denials by the Belgian authorities, provided the backbone of the secessionist province together with the mercenaries who also helped sustain Moise Tshombe in power. But UN forces did not go into Katanga on a combat mission. And Katanga continued to defy the central authority under Lumumba, insisting that it was an independent state and no longer an integral part of the former Belgian Congo.

In response to such defiance, and because of the inability of UN troops to end the secession by force, Lumumba sent troops from his national army – *Armee Nationale Congolaise* (ANC) – to the secessionist province in August 1960 to try to end the rebellion.

He also sent troops to Kasai Province where secessionists in the southern part of the province under the leadership of Albert Kalonji also declared independence.

Unfortunately, the soldiers from the Congolese national army were not well-trained and therefore not prepared to engage the secessionist forces in both provinces. With the UN equivocating, Lumumba was compelled under very difficult circumstances to seek assistance from the Soviet Union to try to defeat the secessionists. The Soviets responded by sending military advisers, trucks and ten transport planes.

But even they were not enough. The situation in the secessionist provinces was too dangerous and the Soviet advisers and their planes were forced to withdraw. Although troops from the national army was no match for the secessionist forces in Katanga, they were able to engage the secessionists in Kasai Province whose dominant ethnic group was and still is the Luba, but with tragic consequences.

More than 1,000 Lubas – or Baluba – were killed in August 1960 in the unsuccessful operation. About 250,000 ended up as refugees, further alienating and infuriating many people in the province who were already against Lumumba.

Lumumba's enemies used this tragedy in Kasai Province as an excuse to undermine his authority; and President Joseph Kasavubu, with the encouragement of American and Belgian officials including CIA agents, dismissed Lumumba from the government on September 5th accusing him of using arbitrary powers as prime minister and plunging the country into civil war.

About 30 minutes later, Lumumba retaliated and announced on the radio that he had dismissed President Kasavubu from office and appealed to the Congolese people to rally around him. Lumumba's enemies were aware of what they were facing: With his popularity and oratorical skills, Lumumba had the ability to rally support across the country no other Congolese could match.

He was such a powerful orator that his enemies thought he had something else working in his favour. As Keith

Kyle, a BBC reporter who was in Congo during the crisis and the ensuing civil war ignited by Katanga's secession, stated in his 1995 paper, "The UN in Congo: Initiative on Conflict Resolution and Ethnicity":

"Lumumba was a charismatic speaker whose power over other people was so compelling that many of his enemies felt that there was witchcraft in it. It was probably one of the reasons he had to die that, like the Roman consul Marius, when under arrest he could bewitch his jailers."

His enemies had already decided what they were going to do. And Western countries sided with Kasavubu whom they had supported all along in his rivalry with Lumumba.

And in spite of his dismissal by Kasavubu, Lumumba still commanded support.

He maintained that he was the legitimate head of the Congolese government and his claim was confirmed by the vote of confidence he got in parliament.

But nine days later on the evening of September 14th after Lumumba and Kasavubu dismissed each other from office, Joseph Mobutu – ostensibly to fill the vacuum left by the two leaders who had dismissed each other – seized power, urged by American and Belgian officials to do so. He said Kasavubu, Lumumba and the parliament were suspended until the end of the year.

He went on to explain that this was only a temporary measure, for three months, during which the country would be governed by a "College of Commissioners" comprising technocrats – Congolese university graduates and others; a ridiculous proposition in a country which had only 16 university graduates when it won independence a few months earlier. He said the "College of Commissioners" would be headed by one of the Congolese university graduates.

It was an act of betrayal.

Mobutu once served as Lumumba's personal secretary and at the time of the coup was the head of the national army, appointed by Lumumba. And all that time, he was on the CIA payroll, without Lumumba's knowledge. Lumumba was also betrayed by another close political associate, Victor Nendaka, who was secretly working with the American and Belgian officials against him in Leopoldville.

But Mobutu was Lumumba's most conspicuous former ally who betrayed him. It is true that he broke with Lumumba. But it later became obvious that he had been against him all the time when he was working under him.

And when he executed the CIA-inspired coup with just as much Belgian support, he established his own power base but also in alliance with the Kasavubu camp.

He announced on the radio that he had temporarily seized power to neutralise two rival governments, Lumumba's and Kasavubu's, and the national parliament until the end of the year. Other western countries, besides Belgium and the United States, also supported Mobutu. But Kasavubu remained head of state. And under pressure from the United States, the UN General Assembly recognized the Kasavubu/Mobutu regime as the country's legitimate authority.

As the country further degenerated into chaos, Lumumba was being guarded by UN troops in his official residence in Leopoldville. His enemies wanted him arrested but the UN secretary-general, Dag Hammarskjold, refused to authorise UN troops to do so.

Throughout the crisis, the American ambassador in Leopoldville asked Kasavubu and Mobutu to arrest Lumumba.

But they did not and could not do so for a number of reasons including opposition by the UN to such a move whose repercussions no one could fully anticipate and which could have gone beyond anyone's imagination.

The recognition of the Kasavubu/Mobutu alliance by

the UN General Assembly as the new legitimate authority in Congo further weakened Lumumba who was already isolated in his official residence in Leopoldville, guarded by UN troops.

The UN troops surrounded his house to prevent his enemies from entering the premises to capture or kill him. Forming the outer ring, surrounding UN troops, were Mobutu's soldiers waiting for an opportunity to grab Lumumba should he venture out and beyond the premises of his official residence.

All that was too much for Lumumba. The last straw for him was when, in a move orchestrated by the United States, the UN General Assembly recognised the government of Kasavubu allied with Mobutu, thus virtually withdrawing formal recognition from Lumumba as the legitimate leader of Congo.

In an attempt to mobilise support, Lumumba decided to leave Leopoldville and go to Stanleyville, his home and political base. He hid in the back of a car and left his official residence in an attempt to get to Stanleyville on the same day Kasavubu was celebrating his victory at the United Nations where his government had won formal recognition from the General Assembly as the legitimate authority in Congo in place of Lumumba.

Lumumba's departure from Leopoldville was undoubtedly motivated by good intentions and nationalist commitment. But it was a tragic mistake. He had been under protection for two months.

He had been repeatedly warned by UN officials that if he left his residence, it would no longer be their responsibility to protect him, and he would be doing so at his own risk. Yet, as the country's elected leader, he was powerless and became virtually a prisoner under the UN's protective custody.

The head of the UN mission in Congo gave orders to UN troops across the country not to take sides between Lumumba and his enemies.

This was in compliance with UN's policy of neutrality and non-interference in the internal affairs of Congo. UN soldiers were given orders not to stop Lumumba from going to Stanleyville or anywhere in the country. They were also ordered not to stop Lumumba's enemies from pursuing or hunting him down.

His enemies finally caught up with him at Mweka in Kasai Province. Born in the small village of Onalua in Katako Kombe district, northern Kasai Province, on 2 July 1925, it was ironic and tragic that the beginning of his end took place in the same province in which he was born.

After his arrest at Mweka, he was flown back to Leopoldville. All these events – Lumumba's secret departure from his official residence and subsequent arrest – took place in December 1960.

This was the last chance the UN troops had to protect Lumumba. They could have saved him. Had the UN intervened before he was captured at Mweka, his enemies would not have had the chance to lay their hands on him. After all, the UN had protected him at his residence for two months and could have extended the same protection to him outside his residence and anywhere else in the country, since he was entitled to such protection as Congo's elected national leader.

After his capture, a photograph was taken showing him dishevelled and with his hands tied behind his back. He was then imprisoned together with his compatriots, Joseph Okito and Maurice Mpolo at Thysville, a military camp outside the capital.

The photograph also shows Mobutu with his hands across his chest and his soldiers laughing at Lumumba and his colleagues who were also brutally manhandled. Even more than 50 years later, it remains one of the most tragic images of Congo, and Africa, from those turbulent years.

Yet, even in custody under strict guard by his enemies, Lumumba still inspired awe and fear among them. To avoid any mistakes and his escape with the help of his loyal supporters, they first decided to transfer him secretly to Kasai Province where one of his arch-enemies, Albert Kalonji, swore to get rid of him and use his skull as a flower vase.

But before they flew him to Kasai, they found out at the last minute that there were UN troops stationed at Bakwanga airfield in Kasai Province. So Kasavubu and Mobutu together with Belgian and American officials and Lumumba's other enemies in leadership positions in Congo decided to send him to another place, Katanga, where another big enemy of Lumumba, Moise Tshombe, was in charge.

He was flown from Leopoldville to Elisabethville, the capital of Katanga, on 17 January 1961 and was brutally beaten by Luba guards throughout his six-hour flight to the province. When the plane landed in Elisabethville, Lumumba was pushed out and shoved down the steps together with Maurice Mpolo and Joseph Okito.

Lumumba and his colleagues were so badly beaten by the Luba soldiers on the plane that when they arrived in Elisabethville, Katengese officials and soldiers said the three captives were almost dead on arrival. And the Luba soldiers on plane felt justified in what they did to Lumumba and his compatriots because of what they said Lumumba did to their people in Kasai Province when he sent troops to fight the secessionists; a mission which ended in the tragic death of many innocent people massacred by undisciplined Congolese soldiers from the national army (ANC). And as John Reader stated in his book, *Africa: A Biography of the Continent*, about the last days of Lumumba and his compatriots:

"Lumumba's supporters regrouped in Stanleyville. At the end of November Lumumba decided to join them – a fatal move. He was arrested en route and handed over to Mobutu's army.

Lumumba was consigned to a military prison, but his

supporters continued to have an unsettling effect on the country at large....Kasavubu and his (American and Belgian) advisers decided that he should be sent to Elisabethville, the Katangan capital, where the errant Tshombe was in charge.

On 17 January 1961, Lumumba and two colleagues (Maurice Mpolo and Joseph Okito) were flown to Katanga, where a Swedish warrant officer with the United Nations forces witnessed their arrival:

'The first to leave the aeroplane was a smartly dressed African. He was followed by three other Africans, blind-folded and with their hands tied behind their backs. The first of the prisoners to alight had a small beard [Lumumba].

As they came down the stairs, some of the *gendarmes* ran to them, pushed them, kicked them and brutally struck them with rifle butts; one of the prisoners fell to the ground. After about one minute the three prisoners were placed in a jeep which drove off....'

Neither Lumumba nor his colleagues were ever seen again. It is believed they were taken to a farmhouse on the outskirts of Elisabethville, where they died at the hands of Katangese officials and Belgian mercenaries." – (John Reader, *Africa: A Biography of the Continent*, New York: Vintage, 1999, pp. 659, 660, and 662).

A UN investigation years later concluded that Lumumba was shot by a Belgian officer in the presence of Moise Tshombe and other Katangese officials including the highly notorious Godefroid Munongo, a cabinet member in Tshombe's government who was interior minister and in charge of security in Katanga.

Munongo was also, together with Tshombe, a founding member of the Confederation of Associations of Katanga (CONAKAT), the largest political party in Katanga Province and one of the largest in the country.

He was of Tanzanian origin, a descendant of King

Msiri. Born in 1830 near Tabora in western Tanganyika, Msiri was a trader – in slaves, copper, ivory and guns – and a member of the Nyamwezi ethnic group in western Tanzania (then Tanganyika) who settled in Congo and established a kingdom in Katanga in the 19th century.

He and some of his fellow Nyamwezi tribesmen from what is now Tanzania settled in southern Katanga around 1856. By 1868, he had taken control of much of Katanga and was crowned king of Garaganja, what came to be known as Katanga Province, after he succeeded in taking over most of the mineral-rich region from its previous rulers of the dominant Lunda ethnic group.

Godefroid Munongo, Tshombe's hatchet man, was not only Msiri's direct descendant; he was also the most prominent "immigrant" in the government of the secessionist region. So, when he served in the Katangese government dominated by Tshombe's dominant ethnic group, the Lunda, he was not a member of a large ethnic group.

Ironically, in spite of his minority status as a member of the small Bayeke ethnic group, he was notorious for having been responsible for the persecution of the members of the Luba ethnic group living in Katanga Province. While the Lunda dominated Katanga, the Luba were the dominant ethnic group in neighbouring Kasai Province, although their historic – hence ancestral – home is northern Katanga where many of them have always lived.

Yet, in carrying out this persecution, Munongo felt that he was more of an authentic Katangan than the Luba from Kasai were, despite his Tanzanian origin as a Nyamwezi.

So, he had a reputation as a tribalist like his boss, Moise Tshombe. And both were delighted to see that Lumumba had been arrested and sent to Katanga for them to preside over his fate.

Also present during Lumumba's execution were American CIA agents and Belgian officials as well as intelligence officers. And as Professor Adam Hochschild of the University of California-Berkeley stated in his book, *King Leopold's Ghost: A Story of Greed, Terror, and Heroism in Colonial Africa*:

"An inspired orator whose voice was rapidly carrying beyond his country's borders, Lumumba was a mercurial and charismatic figure. His message, Western governments feared, was contagious. Moreover, he could not be bought. Anathema to American and European capital, he became a leader whose days were numbered.

Less than two months after being named the Congo's first democratically chosen prime minister, a U.S. National Security Council subcommittee on covert operations, which included CIA chief Allen Dulles, authorized his assassination. Richard Bissell, CIA operations chief at the time, later said, 'The President [Dwight D. Eisenhower]...regarded Lumumba as I did and a lot of other people did: a mad dog...and he wanted the problem dealt with.'

Alternatives for dealing with 'the problem' were considered, among them poison – a supply of which was sent to the CIA station chief (Laurence Devlin) in Leopoldville – a high-powered rifle, free-lance hit men. But it proved hard to get close enough to Lumumba to use these, so, instead, the CIA supported anti-Lumumba elements within the factionalized Congo government, confident that before long they would do the job. They did.

After being arrested and suffering a series of beatings, the prime minister was secretly shot in Elizabethville in January 1961. A CIA agent ended up driving around the city with Lumumba's body in his car's trunk, trying to find a place to dispose of it...

The key figure in the Congolese forces that arranged Lumumba's murder was a young man named Joseph Desire Mobutu, then chief of staff of the army and a

103

former NCO in the old colonial *Force Publique.* Early on, the Western powers had spotted Mobutu as someone who would look out for their interests. He had received cash payments from the local CIA man and Western military attaches while Lumumba's murder was being planned....

I had been writing about human rights for years, and once, in the course of half a dozen trips to Africa, I had been to the Congo.

That visit was in 1961. In a Leopoldville apartment, I heard the CIA man, who had too much to drink, describe with satisfaction exactly how and where the newly independent country's first prime minister, Patrice Lumumba, had been killed a few months earlier.

He assumed that any American, even a visiting student like me, would share his relief at the assassination of a man the United States government considered a dangerous leftist troublemaker." – (Adam Hochschild, *King Leopold's Ghost: A Story of Greed, Terror, and Heroism in Colonial Africa,* New York: Houghton Mifflin, 1998, pp. 301 – 302).

Lumumba and his compatriots Maurice Mpolo and Joseph Okito were physically and verbally abused, brutally tortured and humiliated in every conceivable way until the very last minute of their lives.

Even after they were pushed out of the plane and hit with rifle butts and dumped at the airport in Elisabethville by the Luba guards, they continued to suffer. They were given a thorough beating by Tshombe's henchmen at the airport. And the Luba guards who had tortured them all the way from Leopoldville participated in this orgy of violence. As Brian Urquhart who once served in Congo during the crisis and later as UN undersecretary-general stated in his article, "The Tragedy of Lumumba," in *The New York Review of Books*, October 4, 2001:

"After Lumumba and his two companions (Maurice

Mpolo and Joseph Okito) were dumped, bloody and disheveled, in a remote corner of the Elisabethville airfield, they were beaten again with rifle butts, and thrown onto a jeep and driven two miles from the airport to an empty house in the bush, where a veteran Belgian officer, Captain Julien Gat, took charge.

A series of visitors – the notorious Katangese interior minister Godefroid Munongo and other ministers, Tshombe himself, and various high-ranking Belgians – came to the house to gloat over the prisoners, who were again beaten.

Some of the Belgian visitors later spoke of Lumumba's courage and dignity under this treatment, but none saw fit to stop it.

The soldiers were ordered to kill Lumumba if UN troops located the house.

During the evening, drinking heavily, Tshombe and his ministers decided that the three should be executed at once.

Around 9:30 PM the inebriated Katangese ministers returned to the house in the bush. After once again being beaten up, the prisoners were stuffed into a car with Captain Gat and police commissioner Frans Verscheure, and, in a convoy that also carried Tshombe, Munongo, and four other 'ministers,' were driven at high speed to a remote clearing fifty kilometers out in the wooded savanna.

Joseph Okito, the former vice-president of the Senate, was the first to face the firing squad; next came Maurice Mpolo, the first commander of the Congolese National Army; and finally Patrice Lumumba. Their corpses were thrown into hastily dug graves.

This was not the end of the atrocious affair. During the night, the Belgians, increasingly apprehensive, began to concoct an elaborate cover plan under which Lumumba and his companions had been well treated, but had later managed to escape and had been killed by the inhabitants of an unnamed 'patriotic' village.

The Belgians also decided that the corpses must disappear once and for all. Two Belgians and their African assistants, in a truck carrying demijohns of sulphuric acid, an empty two-hundred-liter barrel, and a hacksaw, dug up the corpses, cut them into pieces, and threw them into the barrel of sulphuric acid.

When the supply of acid ran out, they tried burning the remains. The skulls were ground up and the bones and teeth scattered during the return journey.

The task proved so disgusting and so arduous that both Belgians had to get drunk in order to complete it, but in the end no trace was left of Patrice Lumumba and his companions. Lumumba was 36 years old." – (Brian Urquhart, "The Tragedy of Lumumba," *The New York Review of Books*, October 4, 2001).

Lumumba's dignified composure was evident throughout his ordeal since his capture. It was also reflected even in his last message to his wife written before he was flown to Elisabethville and handed over to Katangan authorities for execution. The letter was also a farewell message to the Congo and to Africa as a whole:

"My dear wife,

I am writing these words not knowing whether they will reach you, when they will reach you, and whether I shall still be alive when you read them.

All through my struggle for the independence of my country, I have never doubted for a single instant the final triumph of the sacred cause to which my companions and I have devoted all our lives.

But what we wished for our country, its right to an honourable life, to unstained dignity, to independence without restrictions, was never desired by the Belgian imperialists and the Western allies, who found direct and indirect support, both deliberate and unintentional, amongst certain high officials of the United Nations, that organization in which we placed all our trust when we called on its assistance.

They have corrupted some of our compatriots and bribed others. They have helped to distort the truth and bring our independence into dishonour.

How could I speak otherwise?

Dead or alive, free or in prison by order of the imperialists, it is not myself who counts.

It is the Congo, it is our poor people for whom independence has been transformed into a cage from whose confines the outside world looks on us, sometimes with kindly sympathy, but at other times with joy and pleasure.

But my faith will remain unshakeable.

I know and I feel in my heart that sooner or later my people will rid themselves of all their enemies, both internal and external, and that they will rise as one man to say No to the degradation and shame of colonialism, and regain their dignity in the clear light of the sun.

We are not alone. Africa, Asia and the free liberated people from all corners of the world will always be found at the side of the millions of Congolese who will not abandon the struggle until the day when there are no longer any colonialists and their mercenaries in our country.

As to my children whom I leave and whom I may never see again, I should like them to be told that it is for them, as it is for every Congolese, to accomplish the sacred task of reconstructing our independence and our sovereignty: for without dignity there is no liberty, without justice there is no dignity, and without independence there are no free men.

Neither brutality, nor cruelty nor torture will ever bring me to ask for mercy, for I prefer to die with my head unbowed, my faith unshakable and with profound trust in the destiny of my country, rather than live under subjection and disregarding sacred principles.

History will one day have its say, but it will not be the history that is taught in Brussels, Paris, Washington or in the United Nations, but the history which will be taught in the countries freed from imperialism and its puppets.

Africa will write its own history, and to the north and south of the Sahara, it will be a glorious and dignified history.

Do not weep for me, my dear wife. I know that my country, which is suffering so much, will know how to defend its independence and its liberty.

Long live the Congo! Long live Africa!

Patrice"

His death was not announced until almost a month later on 13 February 1961.

The tragic news of Lumumba's death sent shock waves throughout Africa and many parts of the world. His death only plunged the country deeper into chaos.

The country was already in deep crisis. When Lumumba was killed, Katanga Province, which he tried to subdue although at a great risk since his national army was not strong enough to end the secession, was still defiant and refused to reunite with the rest of the country. And his death only encouraged the secessionists even further to assert their independence.

Many other parts of the country were also in a rebellious mood since there was no strong central authority to exercise control over this vast expanse of territory. Besides the secession of Katanga Province, secessionists in South Kasai, whom Lumumba tried to neutralise when he sent troops there in August 1960, continued to pose a big threat to the territorial integrity of Congo and were emboldened to pursue their goal after their nemesis had been eliminated.

Also, different groups in other provinces contemplated similar moves, only in varying degrees.

Then there were the supporters of Lumumba. Saddened and angered by his assassination, many of his supporters in different parts of the country vowed to carry on the struggle for Congo's liberation from the clutches of Western imperialists who played a major role in the ouster and elimination of their leader, the only true nationalist politician of national stature Congo had produced just before independence.

Lumumba's loyalists constituted the core of the nationalist forces which went on to launch guerilla warfare in an attempt to topple the Western-backed government in Leopoldville. The strongest insurgencies were in the eastern part of the country, Lumumba's political stronghold, and in Kwilu Province in the west, the home of Lumumba's education minister and heir-apparent, Pierre Mulele.

But it was not until three years after Lumumba was assassinated that these insurgencies got underway, first in Kwilu Province in January 1964. However, some of the civil unrest in the country was fuelled by Lumumba's supporters who refused to recognise the regime in Leopoldville.

Elsewhere in Africa, the year 1961 was not marked by any significant events of continental scope like the Congo crisis. It was mainly a year of celebration and of anticipation as more and more countries moved towards independence.

In the 17 countries which won independence in the previous year, many people were highly optimistic of the future under the new leadership of fellow Africans, hoping and expecting that their lives would improve dramatically now that they were no longer under colonial rule.

It was a period of rising expectations – as they were described back then – among millions of people in the initial euphoria of independence, although events in

Congo were an ominous warning of what could happen in any of the countries on the continent if foreign intrigue and ethno-regional rivalries were encouraged to flourish on their soil after the end of colonial rule.

Hardly a year passed without at least one or two African countries winning independence in that decade.

In 1961, two African countries, Tanganyika and Sierra Leone, won independence. Both won independence from the same colonial power: Britain. Sierra Leone won independence on April 21st and Tanganyika on December 9th.

Tanganyika's independence would later prove to be critical in the history of the continent in one fundamental respect: liberation. And it helped to change the destiny of a significant part of the African continent, mainly southern Africa.

It was the first country in the region to win independence and became a haven and training ground for freedom fighters from the countries of southern Africa still under white minority rule.

Soon after Tanganyika won independence, Julius Nyerere offered sanctuary to the people of southern Africa fleeing persecution and oppression in their countries and invited the freedom fighters to establish their operational bases in the country.

It was also in the same month and in the same year, December 1961, that the military wing of the African National Congress (ANC), Umkhonto we Sizwe (the Spear of the Nation), launched a campaign of sabotage in South Africa as an integral part of a concerted effort to bring down the apartheid regime.

Less than two years later after the Organization of African Unity (OAU) was founded in Addis Ababa, Ethiopia, in May 1963, Tanganyika (later renamed Tanzania in 1964 after uniting with Zanzibar) was chosen

110

by the African leaders to be the headquarters of the OAU Liberation Committee and all the African liberation movements. And they all went on to open their offices in Tanzania's capital, Dar es Salaam. They also established guerrilla training camps in the country.

The decision by African leaders to choose Tanzania as the headquarters of the OAU Liberation Committee angered Nkrumah who wanted his country, Ghana, to be the headquarters. His rivalry with Nyerere came out into the open at the OAU summit the following year in Cairo, Egypt, in July 1964 when he denounced Nyerere as "an imperialist agent" who could not be trusted to handle such responsibility.

During the army mutiny in Tanganyika in January 1964, Nyerere sought British assistance – from the former colonial power – to subdue the mutineers, a decision that earned him the uncomplimentary title, "imperialist agent," from Nkrumah.

The mutiny in Tanganyika inspired soldiers in neighbouring Kenya and Uganda to follow suit. They mutinied in the next few days.

The leaders of the two countries, Jomo Kenyatta of Kneya, and Milton Obote of Uganda who coincidentally was a close friend of Nkrumah, also sought military assistance from their former colonial rulers, the British, like Nyerere did, to quell the mutineers.

In the eyes of Nkrumah, seeking military assistance from a former colonial power was tantamount to betrayal of the African cause, and surrender of sovereignty. But he did not apply the same judgement to Kenyatta and Obote, calling them imperialist agents, the way he did Nyerere, although they also sought the same assistance from the same former colonial power, Britain.

And unlike Kenyatta and Obote, Nyerere did not even let British troops stay long in his country but called an emergency session of the OAU to seek military assistance from fellow Africans to replace British soldiers. Nigeria agreed to do so and sent troops to Tanganyika to assist in providing security and defence while the country was rebuilding its army.

The OAU meeting was held in Dar es Salaam, Tanzania, from 12 February 1964 and lasted for about one week. It was attended by the African ministers of foreign affairs. It was chaired by Tanzania's minister of external affairs and defence, Oscar Kambona.

What was behind all that name-calling by Nkrumah was not because he really believed Nyerere was an imperialist agent; it was because he saw Nyerere as a rival and as his biggest threat to his stature as a continental leader.

Although 13 years younger than Nkrumah, Nyerere was rising fast as a leader of continental stature who was highly respected by his colleagues across the continent. He had a lot of influence in African affairs especially concerning liberation of southern Africa from white minority rule – in a way Nkrumah did not expect him or want him to be. As Professor Ali Mazrui stated in his lecture at the University of Ghana Legon, Accra, in 2002:

"Julius K. Nyerere of Tanzania was regarded as revolutionary partly because he became the most radical voice of Pan-Africanism after the overthrow of Nkrumah. Nyerere was also regarded as a revolutionary innovator in socialism and a left-wing experimentalist....

In the debates between incremental Pan-Africanism and rapid unification Nkrumah found a rival in Julius K. Nyerere of Tanzania....

Nyerere's reputation came much later as a symbol of post-independence African radicalism rather than of pre-independence African militancy....the torch of African radicalism, after the coup which overthrew Nkrumah in 1966, was in fact passed to Nyerere.

The great voice of African self-reliance, and the most active African head of government in relation to liberation in Southern Africa from 1967 until the 1980s was in fact Julius Nyerere....

In reality Nkrumah and Nyerere had already begun to be rivals as symbols of African radicalism before the coup which overthrew Nkrumah. Nkrumah was beginning to be suspicious of Nyerere in this regard.

The two most important issues over which Nyerere and Nkrumah before 1966 might have been regarded as rivals for continental pre-eminence were the issues of African liberation and African unity.

It was soon clear that the most difficult problems of decolonization were likely to be the Portuguese dependencies and Rhodesia.

The Organization of African Unity, when it came into being in May 1963, designated Dar es Salaam as the headquarters of liberation movements.

The choice was partly determined by the proximity of Dar es Salaam to southern Africa as the last bastion of colonialism and white minority rule. But the choice was also determined by the emergence of Nyerere as an important and innovative figure in African politics.

Nkrumah's Ghana did make a bid to be the headquarters of liberation movements but Nkrumah lost the battle. If the reason had simply been that Dar es Salaam was closer to the arenas of colonial conflict, Nkrumah might have accepted this more readily.

But at least as important a reason for the success of Dar es Salaam in being designated the Mecca of liberation movements was the fact that Nkrumah, by mid-1963, had already accumulated several enemies, especially in French-speaking Africa. Nkrumah's encouragement of dissidents from neighboring countries, although it had yet to reach the proportions it reached in 1965, had begun to rear its head as a grievance among neighbours....

As the years went by Nkrumah felt that freedom fighters were not simply those who were fighting against colonial rule but also those who were fighting against their own African neo-colonial regimes. This was domestic revolution versus anti-colonialism first phase.

The hospitality he extended to rebels from his French-speaking neighbours, and even to dissidents from Nigeria, made him less and less acceptable as a patron of major Pan-African ventures, especially if these depended on the blessing of the Organization of African Unity. In 1963 suspicion of Nkrumah was already strong enough to make it unlikely that Accra, Ghana, would be acceptable as the official liberation capital of the African continent. Nkrumah strongly resented this reaction.

The other major arena in which Julius Nyerere was a rival to Nkrumah was the arena of regional integration. For years Nkrumah had been the eloquent voice of Pan-Africanism and the symbol of the continent's quest for greater integration. On a more modest scale Nkrumah had even attempted to lead a union first between Guinea and Ghana, and later between Guinea, Ghana and Mali....But these...attempts at unification which Nkrumah had led proved abortive.

Then in 1961 and 1962 it appeared as if Nyerere was going to succeed in leading the East African countries to a regional federation of Tanzania, Kenya and Uganda. By June 1963 the three heads of government in East Africa – Kenyatta, Obote, and Nyerere – felt confident enough to announce plans to form an East African federation before the end of the year.

In 1960 Nyerere had already stolen the limelight on federalism in Africa by announcing his readiness to delay Tanganyika's independence until Kenya and Uganda became independent if this would facilitate the formation of an East African federation. In June 1963 Kenya was still not independent, but the other two had attained theirs.

This time the clarion call was not for Tanzania to delay its independence but for Kenya to speed up its own timetable of decolonization. The British were called upon to grant Kenya independence by December 1963 so as to enable it to join in a federation with the other two.

It was in this sense that Nyerere had by that time become a symbol of African unification, apparently standing a greater chance of success in effective inter-territorial integration than Nkrumah had stood in his own ventures with Guinea and Mali.

Nkrumah's reaction was not overly subtle. He propounded a new thesis that sub-regional unification of the kind envisaged in East Africa was in fact simply 'Balkanization writ large.'

Further, the enterprise was likely to compromise the bigger ambition of a continental union in Africa. It was a case of the good being the enemy of the best – and East Africans who accepted the minimally good achievement of sub-regional federation would no longer have the incentive to embark on continental union as a more effective bulwark against neo-colonialism and poverty. Nkrumah pointed out that his own country could not very easily join an East African federation. This proved how discriminatory and divisive the whole of Nyerere's strategy was for the African continent.

Nyerere treated Nkrumah's counter-thesis with contempt. He asserted that to argue that Africa had better remain in small bits than form bigger entities was nothing more than 'an attempt to rationalize absurdity.'

He denounced Nkrumah's attempt to deflate the East African federation movement as petty mischief-making arising from Nkrumah's own sense of frustration in his own Pan-African ventures.

Nyerere was indignant. He went public with his attack on Nkrumah. He referred to people who pretended that they were in favour of African continental union when all they cared about was to ensure that 'some stupid historian in the future' praised them for being in favour of the big continental ambition before anyone else was willing to undertake it.

Nyerere added snide remarks about 'the

Redeemer' (Nkrumah's self-embraced title of the Osagyefo).

On balance, history has proved Nkrumah wrong on the question of Nyerere's commitment to liberation. Nyerere was second to none in that commitment.

At that Cairo conference of 1964 Nkrumah had asked 'What could be the result of entrusting the training of Freedom Fighters against imperialism into the hands of an imperialist agent?'

Nyerere had indeed answered 'the good Osagyefo' with sarcasm and counter-argument. But Nyerere was also already trying to sharpen his country's militancy in anti-colonial policy. At Cairo he took the posture of a leader disillusioned with the arts of persuasion in matters of liberation. He now demanded rigorous action to expel Portugal from Africa. As he put it:

'I am convinced that the finer the words the greater the harm they do to the prestige of Africa if they are not followed by action ...Africa is strong enough to drive Portugal from our Continent. Let us resolve at this conference to take the necessary action.'

Nyerere did indeed attempt to take the lead in this new militancy. He became the toughest spokesman against the British on the Rhodesian question. His country played a crucial role at the OAU Ministerial meeting at which it was decided to issue that fatal ultimatum to Britain's Prime Minister, Harold Wilson – 'Break Ian Smith or Africa will break with you.'"

Therefore, Nkrumah and Nyerere had an adversarial relationship. But they still worked together. Even in his book *Dark Days* in Ghana, Nkrumah was critical of the United States because of her role in undermining African leaders, including himself and Nyerere.

Nyerere also was highly critical of the people who

overthrew Nkrumah. Yet Nkrumah himself tried to undermine Nyerere because he saw him as his biggest rival on the continent and in the international arena. And he worked closely with Tanzania's minister of foreign affairs, Oscar Kambona, to undermine Nyerere.

Kambona was very close to Nkrumah and had his own ambitions to replace Nyerere. Nkrumah also worked with another Tanzanian cabinet member, probably Abdullah Kassim Hanga (simply known as Kassim Hanga), to undermine Nyerere.

Hanga was also close to Sekou Toure, Nkrumah's ideological compatriot, and even sought exile in Guinea after he fled Zanzibar when he was accused of plotting to overthrow Zanzibari President Abeid Karume who was also the first vice-president of Tanzania (the second vice-president was Rashidi Kawawa). Hanga lived in Guinea until 1967 before returning to Tanzania mainland after Nyerere guaranteed him security.

Another Tanzanian cabinet member, Abdulrahman Mohamed Babu, was also close to Nkrumah, ideologically. They shared Marxist views and and both espoused scientific socialism, unlike Nyerere who was the most prominent proponent of African socialism, called *ujamaa* (Swahili for familyhood), which he contended was rooted in the African traditional way of life of sharing and communal living.

Hanga was a very close friend of Kambona. They were close since their student days in Britain where they were also roommates. And both were involved in a plot to overthrow the government. Kambona was the mastermind of a coup to overthrow Nyerere in October 1969 and supported his friend, Hanga, in an attempt to overthrow the government of Zanzibar where he once served as prime minister and as vice president under Karume.

Before and after Kambona left Tanzania in July 1967 and went into self-imposed exile in Britain, he wrote Nkrumah and informed him about his plan to overthrow

Nyerere. Nkrumah supported Kambona and agreed with him that Nyerere should be overthrown.

The letters exchanged between the two leaders are in the archives of the Tanzanian government. Some Tanzanian officials, who wanted to remain anonymous, said they saw and read the letter Nkrumah wrote Kambona supporting him in his attempt to overthrow Nyerere.

Kambona also wrote Nkrumah to tell him that formation of the East African Community – comprising Kenya, Uganda and Tanzania – was "an imperialist plot." Yet Kambona himself had publicly supported it and travelled to Kenya and Uganda to facilitate its formation, while at the same time working behind-the-scenes to undermine it.

Kambona's position on the establishment of the East African Community – which he described as an imperialist plot – was in accord with Nkrumah's (opposed to regional federations) and was clearly an attempt to undermine Nyerere who supported it.

Nyerere was also – among all the East African leaders – the strongest proponent of an East African federation. Nkrumah was resolutely opposed to that and did everything he could to undermine Nyerere in his attempt to form such a union.

Therefore what Kambona did and continued to do, with Nkrumah's encouragement and support, was an integral part of a grand design to frustrate Nyerere in his quest for regional integration and political unification of the three East African countries.

On 5 June 1963, the three East African leaders – Jomo Kenyatta of Kenya, Milton Obote of Uganda, and Julius Nyerere of Tanganyika – signed an agreement to form an East African federation before the end of the year. Aware of Nkrumah's opposition to such a union and other regional federations which he described as "balkanisation on a grand scale," Nyerere responded to Nkrumah by stating at a press conference in Nairobi, Kenya:

"We must reject some of the pretensions that have been made from outside East Africa. We have already heard the curious argument that the continued 'balkanisation' of East Africa will somehow help African unity.... These are attempts to rationalize absurdity." – (Julius Nyerere, quoted by Richard Cox, *Pan-Africanism in Practice: An East African Study*, Oxford University Press, 1964, p. 77; Ali A. Mazrui, *Towards A Pax Africana: A Study of Ideology and Ambition*, Oxford University Press, 1967, p. 71).

Nkrumah's interference infuriated Nyerere so much that he wrote Nkrumah about it:

"His meddling became so apparent that on 6th August, 1963, President Nyerere of Tanzania wrote him a very angry letter on this subject." – Donald S. Rothchild, *Politics of Integration: An East African Documentary*, Institute of Development Studies, University College of Nairobi; East African Publishing House, Nairobi, Kenya, 1968, p. 112).

Yet Nkrumah himself was not really opposed to regional federations. He turned against them, and tried to frustrate Nyerere, only after he failed in his attempts to form such unions before May 1963 when the Organisation of African Unity (OAU) was founded in Addis Ababa, Ethiopia. As long as he could be the leader of such federations, he had no problem with them. If he could not, he opposed them and did everything he could to block or undermine them.

He himself had tried to form such federations in West Africa when he first proposed formation of a union with Guinea. His friend, President Ahmed Sekou Toure of Guinea, agreed and the Ghana-Guinea Union was formed in November 1963. In fact, the union's flag looked like

Ghana's flag which has a black star; the union's flag had two black stars. The Ghana-Guinea Union was renamed the Union of African States in May 1959.

Mali, under the leadership of President Modibo Keita, who was Nkrumah's and Sekou Toure's ideological compatriot, joined the union in April 1961. Another black star was added to the union's flag to represent Mali. The flag now had three stars representing the three member states.

But the union did not last long. It collapsed in 1962. In fact, right from the beginning, the union was more symbolic than functional.

Nkrumah's failure to unite the countries he wanted to unite in West Africa led to further frustration. He used another argument to sabotage Nyerere's quest for federation in East Africa. He tried to discredit the proposed federation, contending that countries which were far from East Africa would not be able to join it, thus making it discriminatory.

Yet when he formed the Ghana-Guniea-Mali Union with his friends, Ahmed Sekou Toure and Modibo Keita, he did not say the union was discriminatory since it would be impossible for countries such as Tanganyika (there was no Tanzania then) and Kenya to join the union because they were so far way in East Africa.

Ghana itself does not even share borders with Guinea and Mali the way the latter two share theirs. Yet Nkrumah saw no problem in uniting his country with Guinea and Mali; nor did he say Ghana's union with Congo which he and Lumumba agreed to form in August 1960, with Leopoldville as the capital and with Nkrumah himself being the driving force behind it, would be impractical or discriminatory. Yet when Nyerere wanted to form an East African federation, it was a different story, with Nkrumah insisting the union of the three East African countries would be discriminatory and divisive:

"Nkrumah pointed out that his own country could not very easily join an East African federation. This proved how discriminatory and divisive the whole of Nyerere's strategy was for the African continent.

Nyerere treated Nkrumah's counter-thesis with contempt. He asserted that to argue that Africa had better remain in small bits than form bigger entities was nothing more than 'an attempt to rationalize absurdity.'

He denounced Nkrumah's attempt to deflate the East African federation movement as petty mischief-making arising from Nkrumah's own sense of frustration in his own Pan-African ventures.

Nyerere was indignant. He went public with his attack on Nkrumah. He referred to people who pretended that they were in favour of African continental union when all they cared about was to ensure that 'some stupid historian in the future' praised them for being in favour of the big continental ambition before anyone else was willing to undertake it." – (Ali A. Mazrui in his lecture "Nkrumahism and The Triple Heritage: Out of the Shadows" at the University of Ghana-Legon in 2002; Ali A. Mazrui in Opoku Agyeman, *Nkrumah's Ghana and East Africa: Pan-Africanism and African Interstate Relations*, Fairleigh Dickinson University Press, 1992, p. 16; Ali Al'Amin Mazrui, *Nkrumah's Legacy and Africa's Triple Heritage between Globalization and Counter-Terrorism*, Ghana Universities Press, 2004, p. 35).

Nkrumah was opposed to formation of an East African federation for another reason besides his concern that regional federations would be an obstacle to immediate continental unification. He saw Nyerere not only as a rival; he did not want to see him or anybody else succeed when he himself had failed to achieve such a goal. Not only did he fail to form a functional union in West Africa; his attempt to unite Ghana with Congo also failed.

In August 1960, he signed a secret agreement with

Congo's prime minister, Patrice Lumumba, who was also his friend, to unite their countries. Congo's capital Leopoldville was chosen to be the capital of the new federation. The union was only on paper. Nothing was done to make it functional.

But even any attempt to make the Ghana-Congo union functional would not have have succeeded, considering the tragic events which unfolded in Congo during that period, especially the conflict in Katanga following the secession of the province, and the arrest and assassination of Lumumba.

If Nkrumah was really opposed to regional federations and believed only in immediate continental unification, he would not have tried to form any. Instead, he tried to form three: the Ghana-Guinea Union in November 1958, the Ghana-Congo Union in August 1960, and the Ghana-Guinea-Mali Union in July 1961.

He was the driving force behind all those regional efforts to form political unions under one government. He and his colleagues – Sekou Toure and Modibo Keita – also said other African countries were free to join the unions in order to achieve continental unification. It was only after those unions failed that he started to denounce formation of regional federations, contending that they would be an obstacle to continental unification.

The Ghana-Guinea-Mali Union collapsed in 1962, only a short time before the Organisation of African Unity)OAU) was formed in Addis Ababa, Ethiopia, the following year, when Nkrumah made an impassioned call for immediate continental unification:

"Nkrumah spoke and wrote of a United States of Africa as if it were not only a practical possibility but an urgent necessity:

'The emergence of such a mighty stabilising force in this strifeworn world should be regarded...not as the shadowy dream of a visionary, but as a practical proposition which the peoples of Africa can and should translate into reality. There is a tide in the affairs of every people when the moment strikes for political action. We must act now. Tomorrow may be too late.'

Nyerere shared Nkrumah's goals, but as a gradualist believed that they could only be achieved painfully by a long-step-by-step process. Thus Nyerere could support regional associations such an East African Federation as initial steps, whereas Nkrumah saw such intermediate associations of states as standing in the way of greater unity.

It is true that Ghana, with Nkrumah's blessing, participated in the Ghana-Guinea-Mali Union, but this union was seen as an open association with invitations for all African states to join: it could be enlarged easily and could be the nucleus of African unity, especially since it bridged Anglophone Africa and Francophone Africa.

Despite Nkrumah's enormous investment in his diplomacy, by 1962 he had become 'virtually the only prominent exponent in Africa' of continental union government.

Nkrumah's utopianism was sharply revealed at the May 1963 conference of African statesmen which established the OAU: he proposed 'a formal declaration that all the independent African states here and now agree to the establishment of a Union of African States' and 'machinery for the Union Government of Africa.' The comments of Austin are apposite:

'Here was a vision indeed! But Nkrumah was in a minority of one. The Addis Ababa states drew up a modest 'Charter of the Organization of African States' (sic) which stressed the sovereignty of the individual members, and reached agreement on the principle of non-interference in the territorial integrity of the existing states.'

Instead of utopianism, the practical realism of the protection of state interests was going to govern the relations of African states." – (Robert H. Jackson and Carl G. Rosberg, *Personal Rule in Black Africa: Prince, Autocrat, Prophet, Tyrant*, University of California Press, Berkeley, Los Angeles, London, 1982, p. 204).

There were two strong voices at the first meeting of the Organisation of African Unity (OAU) in Addis Ababa, Ethiopia, in May 1963: Nyerere's gradualist approach to continental unification and Nkrumah's clarion call for immediate unification. Almost all the African heads of state at the conference agreed with Nyerere. Nyerere's realism triumphed over Nkrumah's utopianism.

Disgusted, Nkrumah almost left Addis Ababa. It was only after Emperor Haile Selassie intervened that he agreed to stay. Selassie, as the host and as an elder statesman, asked Sekou Toure to intercede. Toure agreed and went to talk to Nkrumah and told him the Emperor wanted him to stay for the rest of the conference. Nkrumah agreed, although reluctantly, in deference to the elder statesman.

Earlier, before the OAU was formed, Nkrumah was also suspicious of Sekou Toure; he felt that his friend was trying to replace him as the leading champion of African unity. As renowned Ghanaian journalist, Cameron Duodu, stated in his article, "The Birth of the OAU":

"To us in Ghana, the conference that was held in Addis Ababa in May 1963 to give birth to the Organisation of African Unity (OAU) was as exciting as an international football match.

Lined up on one side of the 'pitch' was a group of African states known as the 'Monrovia Group'. Most of its members were drawn from an earlier group called the 'Brazzaville Group' formed in 1960 by mainly French-speaking countries. (Initially, the group was known as the 'Afro-Malagasy Union').

The countries in this 'Brazzaville Group' were

124

Cameroon, Congo-Brazzaville, Cote d'Ivoire (then officially known as Ivory Coast), Dahomey (now Benin), Gabon, Upper Volta (renamed Burkina Faso), Madagascar, Mauritania, Niger, the Central African Republic, Senegal and Chad. Later, the Group was expanded to include Ethiopia, Liberia, Nigeria, Sierra Leone, Somalia, Togo, Tunisia and Congo (Kinshasa).

On the other side of the pitch were the 'Casablanca Group.' The Casablanca Group emerged in 1961 and comprised seven countries: Algeria, Egypt, Ghana, Guinea, Libya (sic), Mali, and Morocco.

Now, it was not only Dr. Kwame Nkrumah who was tremendously disheartened by the existence of the Monrovia and Casablanca Groups in Africa. President Sekou Toure of Guinea (a member of the Casablanca Group) was also unhappy and he linked up with Emperor Haile Selassie of Ethiopia to try and organise a conference of the foreign ministers of the two groups, preparatory to a summit of their heads of state.

Nkrumah heard this and was irritated that his former ally, Sekou Toure, seemed to be trying to steal Nkrumah's thunder as the unacknowledged 'father of African unity.' So he set his own secret diplomatic moves in motion to get the Monrovia and Casablanca Groups to merge and form a common organisation.

He dispatched one of his most trusted aides, Kwesi Armah (better known as Ghana's High Commissioner in London), to Liberia to see President William Tubman, who was widely respected as one of the 'old wise men' of Africa. Tubman had won this respect despite his country's extremely close ties to America.

Nkrumah's message spurred Tubman to convince his fellow members of the Monrovia Group that the pressing issues facing the world and Africa – disarmament, the Cold War, non-alignment, economic co-operation with each other and with other nations, and, above all, how to safeguard the independence recently won by African and

125

Asian nations – could best be addressed in unison. After all, there was the Organisation of American States (OAS) which united North and South America; the Middle East had its Arab League; the Western Powers were bound together in the North Atlantic Treaty Organisation (NATO); while the Soviet Bloc had its Warsaw Pact. Why should Africa not emulate them by forming an organisation that spoke with one voice?" – (Cameron Duodu, "The Birth of the OAU," *Pambazuka News*, 23 May 2013).

In East Africa was PAFMECA (Pan-African Freedom Movement for East and Central Africa) which also played a critical role in the establishment of the Organisation of African Unity (OAU) in Addis Ababa, Ethiopia, in May 1963. It was formed at a conference held in the town of Mwanza on the shores of Lake Victoria in Tanganyika, 16 – 18 September 1958, under the leadership of Julius Nyerere.

The conference was attended by the leaders of political parties from Kenya, Uganda, Tanganyika, Zanzibar and Nyasaland to mobilise forces and coordinate the struggle for independence in those countries. It was expanded in 1962 – not long before the OAU was formed – to include the countries of southern Africa and came to be known as the Pan-African Freedom Movement for East, Central and Southern Africa (PAFMECSA).

Finally, the Organisation of African Unity was formed, bringing together all the African countries under one umbrella in spite of their differences, especially of their leaders, who had the final say on what kind of organisation they wanted to have. The OAU was a product of compromise, embracing gradualists and fast-trackers in the quest for African unity. The gradualist camp, whose *de facto* leader was Nyerere, won. They wrote the OAU Charter. Among fast-trackers, Nkrumah was virtually alone. His dream of immediate continental unification was

126

ignored and rejected by his colleagues at the conference.

Nkrumah also lost to his rival, Nyerere, in another sense. The OAU chose Dar es Salaam, Tanzania's capital, to be the headquarters of the OAU Liberation Committee, the umbrella for all the African liberation movements. He had secretly campaigned to have Accra, Ghana's capital, designated as the headquarters but failed to get enough support for that.

As a consolation, his fellow African leaders chose his capital, Accra, to be the headquarters of the OAU Defence Committee, which was virtually useless but highly significant symbolically because Nkrumah was the first leader who advocated formation of an African High Command to defend the continent. He was also its biggest champion, supported by a few leaders including Nyerere.

Besides being close to the countries of southern Africa still under white minority rule, one of the main reasons other African leaders chose Tanzania to be the headquarters of all the African liberation movements was not only the emergence of Nyerere as a major player on the continental scene but also as a highly principled leader or high moral stature. Let in his career, he came to be acknowledged even by a number of his fellow African leaders as "the conscience of Africa" and as "the OAU minister of foreign affairs."

It was also in the same year the OAU was formed that a major Nigerian newspaper, *The West African Pilot*, taunted Nkrumah stating that he and Nasser were no longer the only stars on the continent; there were others on the rise, in pointed reference to Nyerere without naming him. Before then, "the tournament," as the paper put it, for eminence had been between Nasser and Nkrumah.

The challenge to Nkrumah's eminence as the leading Pan-Africanist was acknowledged by a number of political analysts. Many observers had already noted the rise of Tanzania's president as a leader of continental stature and concluded that the biggest challenge to Nkrumah for leadership in sub-Saharan Africa was none other than Julius Nyerere. Nasser was indeed a major leader on the continent. But he was not such a challenge to black leaders in sub-Saharan Africa because he was primarily seen as an Arab leader dominant in North Africa and in the Arab world in general.

Nkrumah also wanted to eclipse Nyerere as the dominant leader in the liberation struggle in the countries of southern Africa still under white minority rule. He tried to assume control of the liberation movement in Mozambique, a country that borders Tanzania, and whose success in the independence struggle greatly depended on Tanzania as the operational base for the freedom fighters. The liberation movement, FRELIMO, was in fact founded in Dar es Salaam, Tanzania, in 1962 with the help of Nyerere, placing him in a dominant position as the guardian and godfather of the liberation struggle in Mozambique. And there was no way he was going to allow Nkrumah to take control of the struggle in Mozambique.

In an attempt to eclipse Nyerere, Nkrumah even invited a rival group of Mozambican freedom fighters to Ghana, led by Adelino Gwambe, whom he wanted to lead the independence struggle in the Portuguese colony. But he ultimately failed to replace Nyerere as the major leader and supporter of the the struggle not only in Mozambique but in the other countries in southern Africa still under white minority rule.

The earliest attempt Nkrumah made to lead the liberation struggle in the countries of southern Africa was in South Africa itself, the citadel of white supremacy on the continent. Instead of supporting the main liberation organisation in the country, the African National Congress (ANC) founded in 1912, he threw his weight behind a splinter group, the Pan-African Congress (PAC) whose members, led by Robert Mangaliso Sobukwe, broke away from the ANC in 1959 to form the group.

Jordan Ngubane, a South African journalist and writer, stated in his book, *An African Explains Apartheid*, how Nkrumah supported the new rival group. Ngubane knew all the main leaders of the ANC, including the first president of the ANC, John Dube, and P. ka I. Seme, who founded the ANC in Bloemfontein in 1912, as well as Nelson Mandela and Robert Sobukwe. In fact, when Mandela visited Accra, Ghana, in 1962 to seek help for the liberation struggle in South Africa, Nkrumah refused to meet him.

The first country Mandela visited when he left South Africa for the first time in 1962 was Tanganyika. He met Nyerere at his house in Dar es Salaam to seek support for the liberation struggle against the apartheid regime. He had no passport and had to travel to other countries on a document issued by the government of Tanganyika, as instructed by Nyerere. As Mandela states in his book, *Long Walk to Freedom*, the document he travelled on stated: "This is Nelson Mandela, a citizen of South Africa. He has permission to leave Tanganyika and return here."

Nkrumah threw his weight behind the Pan-Africanist Congress because it was a new organisation. He felt he would be able to control it if he provided it with financial and diplomatic support, enabling to become a major player in the liberation struggle in South Africa. He also shared ideological affinity with the organisation because of its emphasis on black unity, unlike the African National Congress whose members included people of all races although it also emphasised the importance of black African solidarity but without excluding non-blacks. In contrast, the Pan Africanist Congress had only black members but also strong credentials as a non-racist organisation.

Yet, in spite his shortcomings, there is no question that Nkrumah was a great leader and a prominent figure in the liberation of Africa as a whole. But when he felt there was a challenge to his position, as the *de facto* continental leader, he became defensive; which partly explains why he tried to discredit and undermine Nyerere who posed the biggest challenge to him.

Another reason why he did not want to be challenged as the main African leader was that since he led the first black African country, Ghana, to independence, he felt he deserved to be acknowledged as the father of the African independence movement; a claim that had some merit, although not all the way. Of equal stature could have been Jomo Kenyatta, the grand old man of the independence struggle on the continent who was acknowledged as the leader of Mau Mau, a group of freedom fighters, mostly Kikuyu, whose military campaign helped to facilitate and speed up the end of British colonial rule in Kenya; although the true leader of Mau Mau was Dedan Kimathi, not Kenyatta. And after independence, Kenyatta did not do anything to support freedom fighters in southern Africa and other parts of the continent.

But as an elder statesman, he preceded Nkrumah in the independence struggle. He started in 1928 when Nkrumah was only a teenager. Therefore, in comparison, Nkrumah was a late comer in the independence struggle.

It was also Jomo Kenyatta who famously said:

"The white man came and asked us to shut our eyes and pray. When we opened our eyes it was too late – our land was gone."

In his book *Towards A Pax Africana: A Study of Ideology and Ambition*, Professor Ali Mazrui attributes that statement to Jomo Kenyatta.

Also, in his novel, *A Grain of Wheat*, Ngugi wa Thiong'o has a character who expresses the same sentiment:

"Kihika from Thabai was one of the speakers who received a big ovation from the crowd....Kihika unrolled the history of Kenya, the coming of the white man: 'We went to their church. Mubia, in white robes, opened the Bible. He said: Let us kneel down to pray. We knelt down. Mubia said: Let us shut our eyes. We did. You know, his remained open so that he could read the word. When we opened our eyes, our land was gone and the sword of flames stood on guard." – (*A Grain of Wheat*, Heinemann Ltd., 1967, 1986; Penguin Books, 2002).

It is a sentiment echoed in other parts of the continent. As Obierika in Chinua Achebe's his classic novel, *Things fall Apart*, also poignantly states:

"The white man is very clever. He came quietly and peaceably with his religion. We were amused at his foolishness and allowed him to stay. Now he has won our brothers, and our clan can no longer act like one. He has put a knife on the things that held us together and we have fallen apart." – (*Things Fall Apart*, pp. 126-7).

But it is Kenyatta who is often identified with the expression of this sentiment because of the role he played in the independence struggle and because of his status as one of the fathers of the African independence movement.

Another elder statesman was Nnamdi Azikiwe, one of the most prominent leaders of the independence struggle in Nigeria and in Africa as a whole who started campaigning for independence when Nkrumah was still a student in the United States.

Nkrumah himself recalls in his book, *Ghana: The Autobiography of Kwame Nkrumah*, that when he left for the United States to enroll as a student at Lincoln University, it was not long after Azikiwe returned to Africa after completing his studies in America. He returned in 1934 and went to work as editor of *The African Morning Post* in Accra, The Gold Coast. Nkrumah left The Gold Coast in 1935.

Still, Nkrumah's role in the liberation of the African continent can not be ignored. He played a very prominent role. He was also unsurpassed in his quest for continental unification even if not entirely for altruistic reasons.

He also made one big mistake. He overlooked or did not acknowledge the formidable opposition he faced from other African leaders in his quest for continental unification.

When the leaders met in Addis Ababa in May 1963 to form the OAU, Nkrumah had already made arrangements to have his book, *Africa Must Unite*, published during that time. He hoped that by doing so, he would be able to convince his colleagues to support his Pan-African scheme to unite the continent, immediately, under one government, obviously under his leadership. But they were not ready to give up power to be ruled by one leader on continental basis. And they believed that Nkrumah wanted to be that leader.

They wanted to stay in power even if it meant Africa had to remain divided.

President Nyerere made that observation back in the sixties when Nkrumah said African countries should "unite now." He made the same point decades later in his speech in Accra, Ghana, in March 1997 where he was invited by President Jerry Rawlings as an official guest to celebrate Ghana's 40th independence anniversary. He also paid great tribute to Nkrumah, stating:

"Kwame Nkrumah was the great crusader for African unity. He wanted the Accra summit of 1965 to establish a union government for the whole of independent Africa. But we failed. The one minor reason is that Kwame, like all great believers, underestimated the degree of suspicion and animosity, which his crusading passion had created among a substantial number of his fellow heads of state. The major reason was linked to the first: already too many of us had a vested interest in keeping Africa divided.

Prior to independence of Tanganyika, I had been advocating that East African countries should federate and then achieve independence as a single political unit. I had said publicly that I was willing to delay Tanganyika's independence in order to enable all three-mainland countries to achieve their independence together as a single federated state.

I made the suggestion because of my fear, proved correct by later events, that it would be very difficult to unite our countries if we let them achieve independence separately.

Once you multiply national anthems, national flags and national passports, seats at the United Nations, and individuals entitled to 21-gun salute, not to speak of a host of ministers, prime ministers, and envoys, you will have a whole army of powerful people with vested interests in keeping Africa balkanized. That was what Nkrumah encountered in 1965.

After the failure to establish the union government at the Accra summit of 1965, I heard one head of state express with relief that he was happy to be returning home to his country still head of state. To this day I cannot tell whether he was serious or joking. But he may well have been serious, because Kwame Nkrumah was very serious and the fear of a number of us to lose our precious status was quite palpable.

But I never believed that the 1965 Accra summit would have established a union government for Africa. When I say that we failed, that is not what I mean, for that clearly was an unrealistic objective for a single summit. What I mean is that we did not even discuss a mechanism for pursuing the objective of a politically united Africa. We had a Liberation Committee already. We should have at least had a Unity Committee or undertaken to establish one. We did not. And after Kwame Nkrumah was removed from the African political scene nobody took up the challenge again."

Although Nyerere and Nkrumah had profound differences on how to achieve African unity, they met in 1963 and talked about their efforts to try to unite African countries and their different approaches to continental unification.

Bill Sutherland, an African American, interviewed Nyerere in the 1990s and asked him about the differences he had with Nkrumah, among other subjects. Sutherland also knew Nkrumah when he lived in Ghana from 1953 – 1961. He left Ghana after falling out with him and went to live in Tanganyika – renamed Tanzania – until the 1990s and came to know Nyerere well through the years. He lived in Dar es Salaam all those years and once worked in the office of Tanganyika's – later Tanzania's – Vice President Rashidi Kawawa. He also worked with other prominent Pan-Africanists including C.L.R. James and George Padmore. As Nyerere stated in the interview:

"My differences with Kwame were that Kwame thought there was somehow a shortcut, and I was saying that there was no shortcut. This is what we have inherited, and we'll have to proceed within the limitations that that inheritance has imposed on us.

Kwame thought that somehow you could say, 'Let there be a United States of Africa' and it would happen. I kept saying, 'Kwame, it's a slow process.'

He had tremendous contempt for a large number of leaders of Africa and I said, 'Fine, but they are there. What are you going to do with them? They don't believe as you do – as you and I do – in the need for the unity of Africa. BUT WHAT DO YOU DO? THEY ARE THERE, AND WE HAVE TO PROCEED ALONG WITH EVERYBODY!'

And I said to him in so many words that we're not going to have an African Napoleon, who is going to conquer the continent and put it under one flag. It is not possible.

At the OAU conference in 1963, I was actually trying to defend Kwame. I was the last to speak and Kwame had said this charter has not gone far enough because he thought he would leave Addis with a United States of Africa.

I told him that this was absurd; that it can't happen. This is what we have been able to achieve. No builder, after putting the foundation down, complains that the building is not yet finished. You have to go on building and building until you finish; but he was impatient because he saw the stupidity of the others.

Bill Sutherland:

You said that you and Nkrumah had one objective, but you differed on how to achieve it. When you thought about a united Africa, did you think that the present nation-states would emerge?

Nyerere:

When I clashed with Kwame, it was when we were very close to a federation of East African states and Kwame was completely opposed to the idea.

He said that regionalization – that's what he called it – was Balkanization on a larger scale.

I said 'Look, Kwame, this is absurd.' I thought that historically there were grounds for different groupings of countries trying to come together. West Africans at one one time – under the British – had a common currency. Basically, the French had two huge colonies – French Equatorial Africa and French West Africa. I thought it was possible to move towards unity by putting those areas together. But even that didn't happen.

I thought that these groups could come together naturally, within the OAU. Then there could be propaganda, an incentive, and the push for greater unity. Kwame thought that we all could just sit down together and come out as a United States of Africa.

I think that Kwame was perhaps over-influenced by the

way the US and the Soviet Union came together. You know the way the thirteen colonies came together, drafted a charter, and then declared the United States of America. I never thought it would work this way, because these African countries had become independent and the mistake was evident in East Africa.

If we wanted to come together, we should have come together before independence, because if you wait until after independence it cannot be done. With four presidents, four flags, four national anthems, four seats at the UN – ahh! It's extremely difficult!

Sutherland:

Didn't you note, about the preamble of the OAU, that it says 'We the heads of state' – it doesn't even say 'We, the People?'

Nyerere:

No, what I said was that the UN Charter has its better: it says 'We the People of the world,' whereas the OAU Charter says 'We the heads of state.'

Sutherland:

Did you not, at a certain time, just shake your head and say that there must be a devil in Africa?

Nyerere:

I said that there is a devil in Africa. I went to Addis and it was an incredible meeting. Here is this continent of young nations coming from colonialism and so forth and the debate is awful, and really what provoked me was the French-speaking countries, you know. With all their French culture, training in rationalization – you can't really argue with those fellows. And I discovered some of these fellows have their visas – THEIR VISAS – signed by the French ambassadors in their own countries! And I said, 'Oh, but I thought you were fighting for freedom?'

I had given up PAFMECA [Pan-African Movement of East and Central Africa]. PAFMECA was 1962, and in '63 the North African and the West African countries had divided themselves between the Casablanca group and the

136

Monrovia group, the radicals and conservatives – really absurd! So I welcomed the idea that we could all be together, rather than have a continent divided along ideological lines.

After the OAU was established in 1963, I allowed PAFMECA to die out. I'm still quietly complaining, because PAFMECA was a movement of people. It was an organization of the liberation movements, and therefore could be a movement of people. 'We the heads of state!' When I hear the African heads of state talking like a bunch of colonials sent by France, of course I get livid!

That's why I said there is a devil in Africa, and that devil is still around. We are still fighting that blessed devil!" – (Julius Nyerere in Bill Sutherland and Matt Mayer, eds., *Guns and Gandhi in Africa: Pan African Insight on Nonviolence, Armed Struggle, and Liberation*, Africa World Press, 2000. The interview was also reproduced, from the book, by Chambi Chachage, "Excerpt from Interview with Bill Sutherland," Centre for Consciencist Studies and Analyses (CENSCA), 5 September 2008).

When Bill Sutherland himself was interviewed on a different occasion, he provided some insights into some of the events which shaped the sixties and the following decades and captured some fascinating moments from that critical period in African history. He was interviewed by Prexy Nesbitt and Mimi Edmunds in Brooklyn, New York, on 19 July 2003. He died on 2 January 2010. He was 91. As he stated in the interview published in a book, *No Easy Victories: African Liberation and American Activists over a half Century, 1950 – 2000*:

Sutherland:
George Padmore (in the UK, where Sutherland stayed for nine months) and an MP (sic) in the (British) Parliament wrote letters to Nkrumah on my behalf, and I

got my permission to go to Ghana, and that's why I ended up there (in 1953).

(March 6, 1957: Ghana becomes Sub-Saharan Africa's first nation to break free from colonial rule and become independent, pushing it to the front of the continental struggle for freedom. Bill Sutherland became an unofficial ambassador for Americans coming through, especially African Americans.)

Sutherland:

I have very often been a bridge between the African American movements and the African movements. People like Martin Luther King, for example, I was instrumental in getting him invited to the independence of Ghana in 1957.

At that time I was a private secretary to the finance minister of Ghana, and I put his name in as one of the invitees to the independence. And then when independence came, there was another African American, Dr. Lee, who was a dentist who had also come to Ghana. He had Martin Luther King and his wife to dinner with Julius Nyerere, who was there at the time.

(At this historical event of Ghanaian independence, Bill Sutherland introduced Kwame Nkrumah and Julius Nyerere to Dr. Martin Luther King. The relationship went both ways across the Atlantic.)

Sutherland:

I got the African liberation movements to sign on to the March on Washington.

Nesbitt:

You hosted Malcolm X, too, right?

Sutherland:

Yes. It was just after he had come back from Mecca. He had passed through (Accra, Ghana). When you say I hosted him, I met him at a party at the Algerian embassy (in Accra), and we got along well, and then I chauffeured him around to his various appointments, and so on, and got to know him fairly well.

Nesbitt:

You really were the kind of people's host for all the African Americans who came through in all those (years) – everybody always said – and I drove your car for a while. And I know that when I drove your car when you were gone, people were always hailing your car, because they thought you were in the car. And then I'd have to explain, no, I'm just borrowing Bill's Peugeot.

Sutherland:

Well, I had my house, I had people there once they had come in and had no place to stay. I had them stay at my house. I guess you could call me an unofficial ambassador.

(It was the 1960s. The African and African American struggles were moving away from nonviolence as a way of achieving liberation and taking a more militant stance. Despite his belief in nonviolence, Bill Sutherland saw the need for the contributions of both Malcolm X and Martin Luther King.)

Sutherland:

But I would say that their roles were complementary. At that time that Malcolm came, he was much more interested in a worldview. He had just come from Mecca, and he had broadened his vision of Islam to include all. Then he went back and he establishes – was in the process of establishing this Organization of African- American Unity.

Martin had been so involved with the American scene that he hadn't done too much about this relationship with Africa. In fact, I saw him in England a few months before he died, and he was saying he wanted to get his organization to come and be more active.

(In Africa the taking up of arms challenged the concept of nonviolence. In the quest for liberation, Bill Sutherland recognized the contradiction and accepted the necessity of armed struggle.)

Sutherland:

I don't think there's any reconciliation. It just is. Facts. But I think that in Africa, that the Sharpeville Massacre was a key turning point for a decision to engage in armed struggle rather than carry on the nonviolent approach. I think I've said in the book that I had talked to this young South African who was active, Philip Kgosana, who said that they were never – he would never go into South Africa again without a rifle in his hands because of what happened there.

We have always believed that the structural violence that apartheid was and certain capitalistic countries have, and so on, that nobody can equate the violence that people use when they're oppressed and down and then that kind of violence and say that they're both the same. This is ridiculous. As far as I was concerned, I always received a lot of criticism from people in America, ultra-leftists, on my pacifist or nonviolent activist approach. But with the revolutionists in Africa, even those who were engaged in armed struggle, they always looked upon me as a comrade and said, you do what you do in terms of your own philosophy, and we're in the same struggle. But they were not the same armchair revolutionists that some of the ultras were in America.

The standard thing that I always said was that if somebody's got the heel of the oppressor on their necks, I'm not going to say wait until I get the proper nonviolent way to take it off. You have to take it off however you can. But I think that as far as the American scene is concerned, the nonviolent revolutionary approach, I think, has been the only way to go.

Edmunds:

What about Nkrumah?

Sutherland:

Well, Nkrumah never pretended or had any pacifist tendency or nonviolence on principle. He was a very pragmatic person. He wrote his book on positive action, having observed what happened in India, and thought that it could be applied in the Gold Coast. But it wasn't – he at no time was a person who was, in any sense, a Gandhian on principle.

I think, when we had the Positive Action Conference in Ghana at the time of the Sharpeville incident, and right after the French exploded the nuclear bomb in the Sahara, he had asked the people who believed in nonviolence to set up the conference. He believed in what was the most practical thing to do in any particular case.

Edmunds:

Are you a pragmatist?

Sutherland:

I'm a person who believes in nonviolence on principle. True nonviolence is a spiritual force that the people can have, which can be the most powerful thing going. But I respect the revolutionist who adopts a violent method, because I think that the most important thing is the revolution.

(Bill Sutherland's friendships with Africa's first leaders reached far and wide.)

Edmunds:

What did Lumumba mean to you?

Sutherland:

Well, I think that he was cut off before he could show what he could do, and that's all.

Edmunds:

Kaunda?

141

Sutherland:

Kaunda? I think that – I feel close to Kaunda on principle.

(In the early 1960s Bill moved to Tanzania where he lived for more than 30 years, earning the friendship of President Julius Nyerere, for whom he worked. Bill also came to know the young Mozambican leaders in their struggle for liberation from Portugal.)

Nesbitt:

You knew Samora?

Sutherland:

Yes.

Nesbitt:

You knew people like Marcelino do Santos?

Sutherland:

I knew Marcelino very well. And it was – Marcelino would have been – he would have put me right in the line with Eduardo. Eduardo, at one time, this was –

Edmunds:

Eduardo Mondlane?

Sutherland:

Mondlane. He told me one time, he says, I know they're going to try to push me aside as this thing goes on. I don't represent the true Marxist position, he said. And I'm ready for that. I know it.

Nesbitt:

Eduardo said that to you?

Sutherland:

Oh, yes. He said it to me right on my own porch, that he realized that they would probably do that to him.

Nesbitt:

"They" would be? Meaning the rest of FRELIMO?

Sutherland:

Well, the Marxists, the Marxist element there. And that they thought he was useful at the stage that the revolution

142

was, but they would not consider him the most reliable person to be head of the state.

Nesbitt:

I often think Eduardo must be rolling over in his grave about what is happening in today's Mozambique.

Sutherland:

Well, I think Eduardo would. I think a lot of people would. I think Nyerere would be very disappointed. Oh, a lot of people would be, because the whole continent has not meant a change for the ordinary people. The ordinary people have not benefited. You know it's an unfinished revolution, that's what it is, throughout. But I have the faith that the revolution will continue.

Edmunds:

If you could say who you think has been the longest-lasting or most impressive leaders of the continent today, who would you give that to?

Sutherland:

I think that Nyerere and, of course, Nkrumah had his vision of a united Africa. But I think Nyerere and Mandela probably to me are the two outstanding people." – (Bill Sutherland in William Minter, Gaily Hovey, and Charles Cobb Jr., eds., *No Easy Victories: African Liberation and American Activists over a Half Century, 1950 – 2000*, New Africa Press, Trenton, New Jersey, USA, 2007).

Nkrumah's and Nyerere's vision of a continental union continues to inspire many people across the continent, especially the younger generation. But the divergent paths they tried to take towards achieving that goal have not been reconciled; and they probably never will.

What is clear is that Africa has taken the gradualist approach advocated by Nyerere and most African leaders, demonstrated by the economic blocs which have been formed on the continent through the years: the Economic Community of West African States (ECOWAS), the East African Community (EAC), the Common Market for

Eastern and Southern Africa (COMESA), and the Southern African Development Community (SADC).

Even after the OAU formally failed to agree on the best way to pursue continental unity but instead agreed on a charter that would maintain the boundaries inherited at independence, Nyerere continued to pursue his dream of trying to unite the three East African countries of Kenya, Uganda and Tanganyika.

It was only a few days after African leaders signed the OAU Charter in Addis Ababa on 25 May 1963 to form the Organisation of African Unity that Nyerere, Kenyatta and Obote met in Nairobi. Kenya, on June 5th to declare that they would unite their countries to form an East African federation before the end the year. The timing, being so close to the signing of the OAU Charter, may have been a coincidence. It, nevertheless, underscored Nyerere's commitment to the gradualist approach in the quest for continental unification.

While Nkrumah's argument for immediate continental unification probably had merit, since it would be very difficult if not impossible to unite later, it is equally true that almost none of the other African leaders agreed with his position. Thus, his Pan-African ambition at the OAU summit in May 1963 for the establishment of a Union of African States under one government was doomed from the start even if Nyerere, who was the most prominent proponent of the gradualist approach, had supported that.

In fact, Nyerere himself had preceded Nkrumah, although on a regional scale, in his call for such an approach in 1960 when he called for immediate unification of the three East African countries – Kenya, Uganda and Tanganyika – before independence so that they could attain sovereign status as a federation since it would be extremely difficult, if not impossible, to unite if they tried to do so after winning independence. Both leaders have been vindicated by history.

As shown earlier, Nkrumah himself was not totally

opposed to formation of region federations, demonstrated by his attempt to form such unions in West Africa and when he tried to unite Ghana with Congo. But when he saw that Nyerere was close to realising his goal of uniting the three East African countries, he worked relentlessly to frustrate Nyerere, contending that such a federation would not only impede continental unification; it would also be discriminatory because it would be impossible for countries such as Ghana, his country, far away in West Africa to join such a union.

Yet when he formed the Ghana-Guinea-Mali Union, he did not say the union was discriminatory since it would be impossible for countries such as Kenya and Tanganyika, which were far away in East Africa, to join it. Instead, he said other African countries were free to join the union in order to unite all the countries eventually under one continental government.

Nkrumah changed his position and embraced immediate continental unification only after his attempt to unite the countries he wanted to unite on regional basis failed.

If the East African federation Nyerere wanted to establish was going to be discriminatory, as Nkrumah contended, since it would be impossible for Ghana and other countries far away from East Africa to join such a union, what made the Ghana-Guinea-Mali Union, established by him, not discriminatory when it was so far away from East Africa?

Was the Ghana-Guinea-Mali union an obstacle to continental unification? If it was, why did he, Nkrumah, together with Sekou Toure and Modibo Keita agree to form such a union? If it was not, why would an East African federation advocated by Nyerere be an obstacle to continental unification? If the Ghana-Guinea-Union would have helped to facilitate continental unification, as Nkrumah said it would, why wouldn't the East African federation championed by Nyerere help to achieve the same goal?

And how realistic was the Ghana-Congo Union, two countries so far away from each other? And how practical was it for Ghana to unite with Guinea and Mali, countries which are also far away from Ghana?

Had the Ghana-Guinea-Mali Union evolved into a functional entity under one government, it is inconceivable that Nkrumah would have denounced it as an obstacle to continental unification. Ghana does not even share borders with Guinea and Mali. Yet Nkrumah was willing to form a political union with them; the latter two share a common border. But when Nyerere tried to do the same thing, form a regional union in East Africa, Nkrumah denounced the move not only as an obstacle to African unity and as discriminatory; he contended it would divide Africa even further, on a grand scale:

"Nkrumah pointed out that his own country could not very easily join an East African federation. This proved how discriminatory and divisive the whole of Nyerere's strategy was for the African continent.

Nyerere treated Nkrumah's counter-thesis with contempt. He asserted that to argue that Africa had better remain in small bits than form bigger entities was nothing more than 'an attempt to rationalize absurdity.'

He denounced Nkrumah's attempt to deflate the East African federation movement as petty mischief-making arising from Nkrumah's own sense of frustration in his own Pan-African ventures.

Nyerere was indignant. He went public with his attack on Nkrumah. He referred to people who pretended that they were in favour of African continental union when all they cared about was to ensure that 'some stupid historian in the future' praised them for being in favour of the big continental ambition before anyone else was willing to undertake it." – (Ali A. Mazrui in his lecture "Nkrumahism and The Triple Heritage: Out of the

Shadows" at the University of Ghana-Legon in 2002; Ali A. Mazrui in Opoku Agyeman, *Nkrumah's Ghana and East Africa: Pan-Africanism and African Interstate Relations*, Fairleigh Dickinson University Press, 1992, p. 16; Ali Al'Amin Mazrui, *Nkrumah's Legacy and Africa's Triple Heritage between Globalization and Counter-Terrorism*, Ghana Universities Press, 2004, p. 35).

Nkrumah had no problem with regional unions, and saw them as viable entities, as long as he was the one who initiated such ventures and as long as he could control and dominate them. But if anybody else tried to do that, then they were "counterproductive" in Africa's quest for continental unification.

Nkrumah also used President Milton Obote to undermine Nyerere in his regional venture to form an East African federation. Obote was a friend of both.

Nkrumah argued that such a federation would not be in the best interest of Uganda because Uganda would be no more than a junior member in a union dominated by Kenya and Tanzania. As Philip Ochieng, a renowned Kenyan journalist and political analyst, stated in his article, "Did Nkrumah Kill Off the First EA Community?," in *The East African*, Nairobi, 28 March 2009:

"In the late 1960s, when Yoweri Kaguta Museveni was the leader of the 'revolutionary' wing of the University of Dar es Salaam's student movement, he and his group militantly rebuked the governments of Uganda, Tanzania and Kenya for failing to federate as they had promised.

The Ugandan leader still appears passionate about that union. Last week, he told a news conference that, instead of fighting over an island smaller than a football pitch, Nairobi and Kampala should fight to make Kenya and Uganda one political entity.

Topical again after a lull of many years, one East

147

African republic was a nationalist, pre-Independence theme. Indeed, a treaty of commitment to it was signed by Jomo Kenyatta, Julius Nyerere and Milton Obote just before Kenya's independence.

So what happened? Why hasn't that great idea panned out for us nearly 50 years after the Uhuru fanfare of the early 1960s? I ask this question because, in truth, Museveni may be in a better position than any of the present East African leaders to answer it....In the Ugandan capital's archives – now controlled by his government – there may lie documents that can enlighten us.

Let me jog the president's memory. He and I were in Dar es Salaam in the late 1960s and early 1970s. He will have heard Obote – whom he still deeply admired – being publicly accused as the chief saboteur of the proposal to federate. Official Tanzania was, of course, mum about this accusation. But it came from top-level academics known to enjoy direct links with Mwalimu's State House. The certainty is that it was Nyerere who was feeding them with the lowdown on Kampala.

What did Mwalimu Nyerere and his Cabinet know about Dr Obote that we did not know? The accusing finger I constantly saw whenever I visited the campus at Ubungo was explicit.

Somebody else – far away from East Africa – was extremely unhappy about an East African union and worked tirelessly – mostly through Kampala – to nip it in the bud, so the story went. No, it was not the British (though they would play a central role in frustrating the federation).

So who could it be? The answer: None other than the great Kwame Nkrumah.

This may sound paradoxical because that redoubtable intellectual and nationalist was the father of the pan-Africanist movement. So you would have expected him to be the chief sponsor of all the regional initiatives that might lead to a pan-African government. That again was

148

paradoxical.

According to the story that I kept hearing, it was because Dr Nkrumah wanted to be the father figure of all the regional initiatives, that he sabotaged the East African chapter....

Nkrumah himself sponsored a West African initiative similar to the proposed East African federation...composed of his Ghana, Ahmed Sekou Toure's Guinea and Modibo Keita's Mali....As long as he was the paramount leader of such an initiative, there was no problem.

In East Africa, Nyerere was also taking serious steps to restructure his society. Tanzania (under Nyerere), indeed, is the African country that has gone farthest in dismantling the political, economic and intellectual pillars of colonialism....

Nkrumah...wanted to be the dominant figure in every regional initiative. Like Joseph Stalin for all of the world's non-Maoist communist parties, Nkrumah wanted to be chief policy-maker and policy implementer for every one of the regional groupings. The probable idea was that, if all those regional groupings decided to unite into a single continental government, no individual would be in a position to vie with the Ghanaian leader to be its first president.

That was why Nkrumah could not trust Mwalimu Nyerere as the intellectual spirit behind the East African proposal. For, although they seemed like ideological comrades, the old Tanganyikan schoolteacher was completely independent-minded and would never have been prepared to act as Nkrumah's regional poodle.

With Nyerere thus dismissed and Mzee Kenyatta accused of having surrendered Kenya as a backyard of corporate Britain, the Ubungo intellectuals explained that, in Nkrumah's eyes, Obote now appeared as the only one not too committed one way or the other. That was why – according to the story – it was Obote that Nkrumah latched onto to frustrate all the plans to federate."

Nkrumah's interference in East Africa to neutralise Nyerere's attempt to form an East African federation was a big mistake and portrayed Nkrumah as a trouble maker who was determined to undermine other African leaders who did not agree with him. As Basil Davidson states in his book, *Black Star: A View of the Life and Times of Kwame Nkrumah*:

"Some, like Julius Nyerere of Tanzania, chastised Nkrumah for his interference. East Africa, Nyerere believed, could best contribute to continental unity by moving first towards regional unity. Although knowing little about East Africa, Nkrumah not only disagreed but actively interfered to obstruct the East African federation proposed by Nyerere.... It was one of Nkrumah's worst mistakes." – (Basil Davidson, *Black Star: A View of the Life and Times of Kwame Nkrumah*, Allen Lane, London, 1973, cited by Geoffrey Mmari, "The Legacy of Nyerere," in Colin Legum and Geoffrey Mmari, eds., *Mwalimu: The Influence of Nyerere*, Africa World Press, Trenton, New Jersey, 1995, pp. 179 – 180).

During the OAU summit conference in Accra in 1965, Nkrumah even had listening devices installed in Nyerere's room and in the rooms of other Tanzanian delegates and those of other African leaders he did not trust or who were a threat to his quest to become the paramount leader of the whole continent. But the director of the Tanzanian intelligence service, Emilio Mzena and his colleagues who accompanied Nyerere to the conference, detected the listening devices. The spying on Nyerere and other delegates from Tanzania by Ghana's intelligence service is one of the subjects addressed by Professor W. Scott Thompson in his book, *Ghana's Foreign Policy 1957 – 1966: Diplomacy, Ideology, and the New State* (Princeton University Press, 1969).

After Nkrumah was overthrown, his espionage activities came to light and were exposed by the new military rulers of Ghana:

"Special attention was devoted to some of these delegates who were thought to be critical of Nkrumah....

Chalet C-4, one of the largest on the grounds of the Star Hotel, also housed Emilio Charles Mzena, a delegate from Tanzania....

At the conference President Nyerere was attended by his personal physician, Dr. A. Nhonoli, who was also an occupant of Chalet C-4." – (*Nkrumah's Subversion in Africa: Documentary Evidence of Nkrumah's Interference in the Affairs of Other African States*, Ghana's Ministry of Information, Accra, Ghana, 1966).

Nkrumah had continental ambitions. He wanted to exert influence on the entire continent. But he also focused on some parts, especially East Africa where he wanted to undermine Nyerere, the most influential leader in the region and one of the most respected across the continent:

"East Africa was high on Nkrumah's list of subversion priorities. At one point, early in 1965, an attempt was made to recruit two sources close to Tanzania's President Julius Nyerere to 'exploit the political contradictions in the East African area.'" – (*Atlas*, a journal, Worley Publishing Company, New York, 1966, p. 22).

As shown earlier, one of them was Oscar Kambona; the other one, probably Kambona's close friend Kassim Hanga. They not only developed their close friendship when they were roommates in London during their student days; they shared high political ambitions.

Kambona, with close ties to Nkrumah, even sent him some money in Conakry, Guinea, where the former Ghanaian leader was living in exile after being overthrown in February 1966.

In his book, *Dark Days in Ghana*, Nkrumah thanked Kambona for sending him the money. Only a small amount is mentioned by Nkrumah in the book. But sources in the Tanzanian government said the amount Kambona sent Nkrumah was large. In fact, when Kambona left Tanzania for Britain in July 1967, he left with a lot of money and was even stopped in Nairobi by the Kenyan authorities who informed the Tanzanian government about the large amount of money he had. But President Nyerere told President Kenyatta to let Kambona go. And when he tried to overthrow Nyerere only two years later, he got a lot of money from other sources to help him achieve his goal. According to *Africa Contemporary Record*:

"The central prosecution witness (in the treason trial) was Potlako K. Leballo, a founder of the Pan-African Congress (Pan-Africanist Congress) of South Africa (PAC), which had its exile headquarters in Dar es Salaam.

The state maintained that seven defendants attempted to enlist Leballo in the plot but that he informed government officials and only appeared to go along with the plot in order to assist in capturing the conspirators.

Leballo testified that he frequently met with Kambona in London and that Kambona had shown him a cache of $500,000 and told him that he could 'get more where that came from' by contacting a U.S. Information Service 'friend' in London (*New York Times*, 19 July 1970, 12).

Leballo further testified that Kambona had an agreement with the South African foreign minister, Hilgard Muller, that South Africa would support the coup." – Colin Legum and John Drysdale, eds., *Africa Contemporary Record: Annual Survey and Documents 1970 – 1971*, London: Africa Research Limited, 1969, pp. 170 - 171. See also Ronald Christenson, ed., *Political Trials in History: From Antiquity to the Present*, Transaction Publishers, Piscataway, New Jersey, USA,

1991, p. 235; and Oscar Kambona in Jacqueline Audrey Kalley, Elna Schoeman, Lydia Eve Andor, *Southern African Political History: A Chronology of Key Political Events from Independence to mid-1997*, Greenwood Publishing Group, 1999, page 594).

Had Kambona succeeded in overthrowing Nyerere, he also would have helped Nkrumah eliminate from the political scene a leader the former Ghanaian leader considered to be his biggest nemesis.

Nkrumah not only had his intelligence service spy on Nyerere during the Accra summit in 1965; he also accused some Ghanaian journalists of trying to undermine his government. When Cameron Duodu returned to Ghana from Tanzania in the early sixties, he was arrested on suspicion of working against Nkrumah when he was in that East African country where he worked as a journalist. He may even have been suspected of working for Nyerere against Nkrumah.

In his article, "Nkrumah's Bequest," published in *West Africa* magazine, March 3 – 9, 1997, Cameron Duodu, stated that Nkrumah "could not get along with many African leaders, including Nyerere."

It was also in the same year of the Accra summit that Nyerere again talked about the imperative for federation in East Africa after the first attempt to unite Kenya, Uganda and Tanganyika failed in 1963. This was again a rebuttal of Nkrumah' thesis that regional federations are an obstacle to continental unification. As Kenya's former vice president, Oginga Odinga who also greatly admired Nkrumah, stated in his book *Not Yet Uhuru: an Autobiography*:

"As late as 8 July 1965, Nyerere said that Tanzania was still ready for East African Federation no matter that outside influences had interfered in the hope of blocking its formation. He said 'If we listen to foreign influence we should be made to quarrel with Kenya and Uganda, but this we will not do.' He had already told President Kenyatta that if his country was ready to unite, Tanzania was also ready." – (Odinga Oginga, *Not Yet Uhuru: An Autobiography*, Heinemann, London, 1967).

This was undoubtedly in response to Nkrumah who had relentlessly worked to undermine Nyerere's efforts to unite the three East African countries.

Yet, in spite of the differences they had, the two leaders worked together and agreed on most things on African liberation and continental unification. As Nyerere said in an interview with Ikaweba Bunting, an African American who had lived in Tanzania for 25 years when he conducted the interview which was published in the *New Internationalist* in December 1998 about one year before Nyerere died:

"Kwame Nkrumah and I were committed to the idea of unity. African leaders and heads of state did not take Kwame seriously. However, I did. I did not believe in these small little nations. Still today I do not believe in them. I tell our people to look at the European Union, at these people who ruled us who are now uniting.

Kwame and I met in 1963 and discussed African Unity. We differed on how to achieve a United States of Africa. But we both agreed on a United States of Africa as necessary. Kwame went to Lincoln University, a black college in the US. He perceived things from the perspective of US history, where the 13 colonies that revolted against the British formed a union. That is what he thought the OAU should do.

I tried to get East Africa to unite before independence. When we failed in this I was wary about Kwame's continental approach. We corresponded profusely on this. Kwame said my idea of 'regionalization' was only balkanization on a larger scale. Later African historians will have to study our correspondence on this issue of uniting Africa.

Africans who studied in the US like Nkrumah and [Nigerian independence leader] Azikiwe were more aware of the Diaspora and the global African community than those of us who studied in Britain. They were therefore aware of a wider Pan-Africanism. Theirs was the aggressive Pan-Africanism of WEB Dubois and Marcus Garvey. The colonialists were against this and frightened of it.

After independence the wider African community became clear to me. I was concerned about education; the work of Booker T Washington resonated with me. There were skills we needed and black people outside Africa had them. I gave our US Ambassador the specific job of recruiting skilled Africans from the US Diaspora. A few came, like you. Some stayed; others left.

We should try to revive it. We should look to our brothers and sisters in the West. We should build the broader Pan-Africanism. There is still the room - and the need."

So, under Nyerere, Tanganyika – later Tanzania – was not only in the forefront of the African liberation struggle; it was, like Ghana under Nkrumah, a leading advocate of Pan-African solidarity transcending continental boundaries to embrace people of Africa descent in the Americas and elsewhere in the diaspora.

Tanganyika was also the first independent African country Nelson Mandela visited in 1962 when he secretly left apartheid South Africa to attend a conference of African leaders in Addis Ababa, Ethiopia, to seek support for the liberation struggle in his country. And the first African leader he met was Julius Nyerere at his house in Dar es Salaam.

It was also in the same year that the Front for the Liberation of Mozambique – FRELIMO – was founded in Tanganyika with the encouragement of Julius Nyerere who urged Mozambican nationalists to bring all their nationalist organizations under one umbrella and form a united front in their struggle against Portuguese colonial rule.

Other liberation movements based in Dar es Salaam included the African National Congress (ANC) and the Pan-Africanist Congress (PAC) of South Africa; the Popular Movement for the Liberation of Angola (MPLA); the Zimbabwe African National Union (ZANU); the Zimbabwe African People's Union (ZAPU); and the South West African People's Organization (SWAPO) of Namibia.

Had Tanganyika not won independence as early as it did, the history of southern Africa may have taken a different course and the liberation struggle would probably have been delayed.

Tanganyika, renamed Tanzania in 1964 after uniting with Zanzibar, played a critical role as an operational base for the freedom fighters until all the countries in southern Africa finally won their freedom after a long, bitter and bloody struggle which, in the case of South Africa, lasted for decades.

It was also in 1961 that the MPLA launched the armed struggle against Portuguese colonial rule in Angola and went on to wage one of the most successful liberation wars in the history of colonial Africa and the entire Third World. It lasted until 1975 when the country finally won independence after 500 years of Portuguese colonial rule.

Another important development in the history of colonial Africa and of the liberation struggle was the release of Jomo Kenyatta from prison.

Acknowledged by many Africans as the Grand Old Man of the African independence movement, and known as Mzee (a Swahili term of respect meaning "Old Man"), Kenyatta was arrested in October 1952 and was later sentenced to 7 years in prison for being the leader of Mau Mau, a charge he denied.

He was sent to a remote, arid region of northern Kenya

to serve his sentence and was released in August 1961.

The release of Jomo Kenyatta was a turning point in the history of one of the countries with the largest number of white settlers on the continent. As he stated on 14 October 1961, about two months after he was released from prison:

"Non-Africans who still want to be called 'Bwana' should pack up and go, but others who are prepared to live under our flag are invited to remain." – (Jomo Kenyatta, quoted by Ali A. Mazrui, *Towards A Pax Africana: A Study of Ideology and Ambition*, op. cit., p. 253.

Kenyatta's admonition caused quite a furor among the white settlers in Kenya especially after Kenyatta went even further in his remarks on 28 January 1962 when he said: "I want Europeans, Asians and Arabs to learn to call Africans 'Bwana'."

He later explained that he was demanding respect rather than servility from whites and other non-blacks in Kenya.

Two years after he was released from prison, he led Kenya to independence. The country won independence from Britain on 12 December 1963 after a bitter struggle. Tens of thousands of Africans, mostly Kikuyu, died during the emergency in the 1950s when the colonial government with the help of the Royal Air Force and ground soldiers fought the Mau Mau insurgents led by Dedan Kimathi. Declassified documents later showed that about 100,000 Africans were killed as a result of this brutal campaign to suppress Mau Mau.

Kenya was the last country in East Africa to win independence. Others were Tanganyika in December 1961, Uganda in October 1962, and Zanzibar on 10 December 1963, only two days ahead of Kenya.

However, Zanzibar's independence was highly controversial. It was bitterly disputed by black Africans in the island nation and elsewhere. They did not accept the leadership of the newly independent nation as being truly representatitve of the majority of Zanzibaris.

The British handed over power to the Arab minority who had ruled the island nation for hundreds of years, thus perpetuating the status quo. Blacks were excluded from the government. It was a recipe for disaster. About a month later, Zanzibar was engulfed in a revolution.

The Zanzibar revolution on 20 January 1964 was one of the most significant events in the history of post-colonial Africa. It had profound implications and repercussions far beyond the borders of the island nation whose ideological orientation under the new revolutionary rulers, and geopolitical considerations of the East and the West during the Cold War, made it a prime target in the rivalry between the United States and the Soviet Union as well as the People's Republic of China.

However, the revolutionary change was enthusiastically supported by the black majority in the island nation since it marked the end of Arab rule and oppression under which they had lived for centuries. The Zanzibar revolution was also celebrated in other parts of Africa as a major achievement in the liberation of the continent.

1962

ONE of the most dramatic events on the African continent during the sixties was the struggle against apartheid in South Africa.

In June 1961, Umkhonto we Sizwe (Spear of the Nation), the armed wing of the African National Congress, had just endorsed armed struggle as a means to achieve its goal of ending apartheid. It was a turning point in the history of South Africa and of the entire continent as other African countries rallied behind the African National Congress and other groups in that country fighting the diabolical regime of apartheid.

On 16 December 1961, exactly one week after Tanganyika won independence from Britain, Umkhonto we Sizwe launched its first attack against some infrastructure, symbols of the apartheid regime's economic power, to send a clear message to the white minority leaders that the struggle for freedom would continue by any means available in spite of the repression the freedom fighters had suffered since the Shaperville massacre and even before then.

The first commander-in-chief of Umkhonto we Sizwe was Nelson Mandela. And the first acts of sabotage against the apartheid state on December 16th were accompanied by a distribution of pamphlets including the manifesto of the armed wing of the ANC. As the manifesto stated:

"Units of Umkhonto we Sizwe today carried out planned attacks against government installations, particularly those connected with the policy of apartheid and race discrimination."

Among the targets bombed were post offices, pass offices issuing pass books and enforcing the notorious pass laws, telephone booths, underground telephone cables and electrical installations.

The armed struggle against apartheid had officially begun.

Another turning point in the history of South Africa and the struggle against apartheid was in January 1962 when Nelson Mandela slipped out of the country to go to Tanganyika, and then to Ethiopia, to seek assistance from the independent African countries for the liberation struggle in his country.

He said when he arrived in Mbeya, a town in the Southern Highlands in the southwestern part of what was then Tanganyika near the border with Northern Rhodesia, now Zambia, that was the first time in his whole life that he felt he was free, in a free African country.

He then flew from Mbeya to Dar es Salaam, the nation's capital, where he met with Julius Nyerere whom he described as "very shrewd," in his book *Long walk to Freedom*.

He also stated in the book that he was very much impressed by Nyerere as "a man of the people" who, although he was the prime minister, lived in a simple house – not in the official residence, the State House –

and drove himself around the city in his simple car, an Austin.

They talked about the situation in South Africa and Mandela said Nyerere was very sympathetic to their cause.

But when he made a request for assistance for the armed struggle against the apartheid regime, he said he was somewhat disappointed when Nyerere told him to wait until Robert Sobukwe was out of prison so that they could coordinate the military campaign against the apartheid state.

In spite of that, Nyerere helped Mandela in other ways and told him he would send a message to Emperor Haile Selassie of Ethiopia asking him to help him. Mandela also said he was given a travel document by the government of Tanganyika, on Nyerere's recommendation, which enabled him to travel to other countries.

He recalls in his autobiography that it was a simple document which simply stated: "This is Nelson Mandela, a citizen of South Africa. He has permission to leave Tanganyika and return here."

After he left Tanganyika, he went to Addis Ababa, Ethiopia, where he attended a meeting of African leaders.

It was a meeting of the Pan-African Freedom Movement for East and Central Africa (PAFMECA) and Mandela addressed the conference. One of the most memorable speeches was delivered by Milton Obote of Uganda who enthusiastically welcomed Mandela to the conference, as did other leaders.

The meeting played a major role in the formation of the Organisation of African Unity (OAU) in the same city of Addis Ababa the following year.

At the meeting in Addis Ababa , Mandela presented his case and made an impassioned plea to African leaders for help to assist their brethren in South Africa in their struggle against apartheid. He was accompanied by other members of the African National Congress (ANC) some of whom were already living in exile.

The leaders of other liberation groups from southern Africa and elsewhere on the continent also attended the conference which lasted until the beginning of February. As Mandela stated in his speech in February 1962:

"The delegation of the African National Congress, and I particularly, feel specially honoured by the invitation addressed to our organisation by the PAFMECA to attend this historic conference and to participate in its deliberations and decisions.

The extension of the PAFMECA area to South Africa, the heart and core of imperialist reaction, should mark the beginning of a new phase in the drive for the total liberation of Africa - a phase which derives special significance from the entry into PAFMECA of the independent states of Ethiopia, Somalia, and Sudan.

It was not without reason, we believe, that the Secretariat of PAFMECA chose as the seat of this conference the great country of Ethiopia, which, with hundreds of years of colorful history behind it, can rightly claim to have paid the full price of freedom and independence.

His Imperial Majesty himself, a rich and unfailing fountain of wisdom, has been foremost in promoting the cause of unity, independence, and progress in Africa, as was so amply demonstrated in the address he graciously delivered in opening this assembly.

The deliberations of our conference will thus proceed in a setting most conducive to a scrupulous examination of the issues that are before us.

At the outset, our delegation wishes to place on record our sincere appreciation of the relentless efforts made by the independent African states and national movements in Africa and other parts of the world, to help the African people in South Africa in their just struggle for freedom and independence.

The movement for the boycott of South African goods

and for the imposition of economic and diplomatic sanctions against South Africa has served to highlight most effectively the despotic structure of the power that rules South Africa, and has given tremendous inspiration to the liberation movement in our country.

It is particularly gratifying to note that the four independent African states which are part of this conference, namely, Ethiopia, Somalia, Sudan and Tanganyika, are enforcing diplomatic and economic sanctions against South Africa.

We also thank all those states that have given asylum and assistance to South African refugees of all shades of political beliefs and opinion.

The warm affection with which South African freedom fighters are received by democratic countries all over the world, and the hospitality so frequently showered upon us by governments and political organizations, has made it possible for some of our people to escape persecution by the South African government, to travel freely from country to country and from continent to continent, to canvass our point of view and to rally support for our cause.

We are indeed extremely grateful for this spontaneous demonstration of solidarity and support, and sincerely hope that each and every one of us will prove worthy of the trust and confidence the world has in us.

We believe that one of the main objectives of this conference is to work out concrete plans to speed up the struggle for the liberation of those territories in this region that are still under alien rule. In most of these territories the imperialist forces have been considerably weakened and are unable to resist the demand for freedom and independence - thanks to the powerful blows delivered by the freedom movements.

Although the national movements must remain alert and vigilant against all forms of imperialist intrigue and deception, there can be no doubt that imperialism is in full retreat and the attainment of independence by many of these countries has become an almost accomplished fact.

Elsewhere, notably in South Africa, the liberation movement faces formidable difficulties and the struggle is likely to be long, complicated, hard, and bitter, requiring maximum unity of the national movement inside the country, and calling for level and earnest thinking on the part of its leaders, for skilful planning and intensive organisation.

South Africa is known throughout the world as a country where the most fierce forms of colour discrimination are practiced, and where the peaceful struggles of the African people for freedom are violently suppressed.

It is a country torn from top to bottom by fierce racial strife and conflict and where the blood of African patriots frequently flows.

Almost every African household in South Africa knows about the massacre of our people at Bulhoek, in the Queenstown district, where detachments of the army and police, armed with artillery, machine-guns, and rifles, opened fire on unarmed Africans, killing 163 persons, wounding 129, and during which 95 people were arrested simply because they refused to move from a piece of land on which they lived.

Almost every African family remembers a similar massacre of our African brothers in South-West Africa when the South African government assembled aeroplanes, heavy machine-guns, artillery, and rifles, killing a hundred people and mutilating scores of others, merely because the Bondelswart people refused to pay dog tax.

On 1 May 1950, 18 Africans were shot dead by the police in Johannesburg whilst striking peacefully for higher wages. The massacre at Sharpeville in March 1960 is a matter of common knowledge and is still fresh in our minds.

According to a statement in parliament made by C R Swart, then Minister for Justice, between May 1948 and March 1954, 104 Africans were killed and 248 wounded by the police in the course of political demonstrations.

By the middle of June 1960, these figures had risen to well over three hundred killed and five hundred wounded. Naked force and violence is the weapon openly used by the South African government to beat down the struggles of the African people and to suppress their aspirations.

The repressive policies of the South African government are reflected not only in the number of those African martyrs who perished from guns and bullets, but in the merciless persecution of all political leaders and in the total repression of political opposition. Persecution of political leaders and suppression of political organizations became ever more violent under the Nationalist Party government.

From 1952 the government used its legal powers to launch a full-scale attack on leaders of the African National Congress. Many of its prominent members were ordered by the government to resign permanently from it and never again participate in its activities. Others were prohibited from attending gatherings for specified periods ranging up to five years. Many were confined to certain districts, banished from their homes and families and even deported from the country.

In December 1956, Chief A J Lutuli, President-General of the ANC, was arrested together with 155 other freedom fighters and charged with treason. The trial which then followed is unprecedented in the history of the country, in both its magnitude and duration. It dragged on for over four years and drained our resources to the limit.

In March 1960, after the murderous killing of about seventy Africans in Sharpeville, a state of emergency was declared and close on twenty thousand people were detained without trial.

Even as we meet here today, martial law prevails

165

throughout the territory of the Transkei, an area of 16,000 square miles with an African population of nearly two and a half million. The government stubbornly refuses to publish the names and number of persons detained. But it is estimated that close on two thousand Africans are presently languishing in jail in this area alone.

Amongst these are to be found teachers, lawyers, doctors, clerks, workers from the towns, peasants from the country, and other freedom fighters. In this same area and during the last six months, more than thirty Africans have been sentenced to death by white judicial officers, hostile to our aspirations, for offences arising out of political demonstrations.

On 26 August 1961 the South African government even openly defied the British government when its police crossed into the neighboring British protectorate of Basutoland and kidnapped Anderson Ganyile, one of the country's rising freedom stars, who led the Pondo people's memorable struggles against apartheid tribal rule.

Apart from these specific instances, there are numerous other South African patriots, known and unknown, who have been sacrificed in various ways on the altar of African freedom.

This is but a brief and sketchy outline of the momentous struggle of the freedom fighters in our country, of the sacrifice they have made and of the price that is being paid at the present moment by those who keep the freedom flag flying.

For years our political organizations have been subjected to vicious attacks by the government. In 1957 there was considerable mass unrest and disturbances in the country districts of Zeerust, Sekhukhuniland, and Rustenburg. In all these areas there was widespread dissatisfaction with government policy and there were revolts against the pass laws, the poll tax, and government-inspired tribal authorities.

Instead of meeting the legitimate political demands of

the masses of the people and redressing their grievances, the government reacted by banning the ANC in all these districts. In April 1960 the government went further and completely outlawed both the African National Congress and the Pan-Africanist Congress.

By resorting to these drastic methods the government had hoped to silence all opposition to its harsh policies and to remove all threats to the privileged position of the Whites in the country. It had hoped for days of perfect peace and comfort for White South Africa, free from revolt and revolution.

It believed that through its strong-arm measures it could achieve what White South Africa has failed to accomplish during the last fifty years, namely, to compel Africans to accept the position that in our country freedom and happiness are the preserve of the White man.

But uneasy lies the head that wears the crown of White supremacy in South Africa. The banning and confinement of leaders, banishments and deportations, imprisonment and even death, have never deterred South African patriots. The very same day it was outlawed, the ANC issued a public statement announcing that it would definitely defy the government's ban and carry out operations from underground. The people of South Africa have adopted this declaration as their own and South Africa is today a land of turmoil and conflict.

In May last year a general strike was called. In the history of our country no strike has ever been organized under such formidable difficulties and dangers. The odds against us were tremendous. Our organizations were outlawed. Special legislation had been rushed through parliament empowering the government to round up its political opponents and to detain them without trial.

One week before the strike ten thousand Africans were arrested and kept in jail until after the strike. All meetings were banned throughout the country and our field workers were trailed and hounded by members of the Security

Branch. General mobilization was ordered throughout the country and every available White man and woman put under arms. An English periodical described the situation on the eve of the strike in the following terms:

> In the country's biggest call-up since the war, scores of citizens' force and commando units were mobilised in the big towns. Camps were established at strategic points; heavy army vehicles carrying equipment and supplies moved in a steady stream along the Reef; helicopters hovered over African residential areas and trained searchlights on houses, yards, lands, and unlit areas.
>
> Hundreds of White civilians were sworn in as special constables, hundreds of white women spent weekends shooting at targets. Gun shops sold out of their stocks of revolvers and ammunition. All police leave was cancelled throughout the country.
>
> Armed guards were posted to protect power stations and other sources of essential services. Saracen armored cars and troop carriers patrolled townships. Police vans patrolled areas and broadcast statements that Africans who struck work would he sacked and endorsed out of the town.

This was the picture in South Africa on the eve of the general strike, but our people stood up to the test most magnificently. The response was less than we expected but we made solid and substantial achievements. Hundreds of thousands of workers stayed away from work and the country's industries and commerce were seriously damaged. Hundreds of thousands of students and schoolchildren did not go to school for the duration of the strike.

The celebrations which had been planned by the government to mark the inauguration of the republic were not only completely boycotted by the Africans, but were held in an atmosphere of tension and crisis in which the whole country looked like a military camp in a state of unrest and uncertainty. This panic stricken show of force was a measure of the power of the liberation movement and yet it failed to stem the rising tide of popular discontent.

How strong is the freedom struggle in South Africa today? What role should PAFMECA play to strengthen the liberation movement in South Africa and speed up the liberation of our country? These are questions frequently put by those who have our welfare at heart.

The view has been expressed in some quarters outside South Africa that, in the special situation obtaining in our country, our people will never win freedom through their own efforts. Those who hold this view point to the formidable apparatus of force and coercion in the hands of the government, to the size of its armies, the fierce suppression of civil liberties, and the persecution of political opponents of the regime. Consequently, in these quarters, we are urged to look for our salvation beyond our borders.

Nothing could be further from the truth.

It is true that world opinion against the policies of the South African government has hardened considerably in recent years. The All African People's Conference held in Accra in 1958, the Positive Action Conference for Peace and Security in Africa, also held in Accra in April 1960, the Conference of Independent African States held in this famous capital in June of the same year, and the conferences at Casablanca and Monrovia last year, as well as the Lagos Conference this month, passed militant resolutions in which they sharply condemned and rejected the racial policies of the South African government.

It has become clear to us that the whole of Africa is unanimously behind the move to ensure effective economic and diplomatic sanctions against the South African government.

At the international level, concrete action against South Africa found expression in the expulsion of South Africa from the Commonwealth, which was achieved with the active initiative and collaboration of the African members of the Commonwealth. These were Ghana, Nigeria, and Tanganyika (although the latter had not yet achieved its independence). Nigeria also took the initiative in moving for the expulsion of South Africa from the International Labor Organisation.

But most significant was the draft resolution tabled at the fifteenth session of the United Nations which called for sanctions against South Africa. This resolution had the support of all the African members of the United Nations, with only one exception.

The significance of the draft was not minimized by the fact that a milder resolution was finally adopted calling for individual or collective sanctions by member states.

At the sixteenth session of the United Nations last year, the African states played a marvelous role in successfully carrying through the General Assembly a resolution against the address delivered by the South African Minister of Foreign Affairs, Mr. Eric Louw, and subsequently in the moves calling for the expulsion of South Africa from the United Nations and for sanctions against her.

Although the United Nations itself has neither expelled nor adopted sanctions against South Africa, many independent African states are in varying degrees enforcing economic and other sanctions against her. This increasing world pressure on South Africa has greatly weakened her international position and given a tremendous impetus to the freedom struggle inside the country.

No less a danger to White minority rule and a guarantee of ultimate victory for us is the freedom struggle that is raging furiously beyond the borders of the South African territory; the rapid progress of Kenya, Uganda, and Zanzibar towards independence; the victories gained by the Nyasaland Malawi Congress; the unabated determination of Kenneth Kaunda's United National Independence Party (UNIP); the courage displayed by the freedom fighters of the Zimbabwe African People's Union (ZAPU), successor to the now banned National

Democratic Party (NDP); the gallantry of the African crusaders in the Angolan war of liberation and the storm clouds forming around the excesses of Portuguese repression in Mozambique; the growing power of the independence movements in South-West Africa and the emergence of powerful political organizations in the High Commission territories - all these are forces which cannot compromise with White domination anywhere.

But we believe it would be fatal to create the illusion that external pressures render it unnecessary for us to tackle the enemy from within. The centre and cornerstone of the struggle for freedom and democracy in South Africa lies inside South Africa itself. Apart from those required for essential work outside the country, freedom fighters are in great demand for work inside the country.

We owe it as a duty to ourselves and to the freedom-loving peoples of the world to build and maintain in South Africa itself a powerful, solid movement, capable of surviving any attack by the government and sufficiently militant to fight back with a determination that comes from the knowledge and conviction that it is first and foremost by our own struggle and sacrifice inside South Africa itself that victory over White domination and apartheid can be won.

The struggle in the areas still subject to imperialist rule can be delayed and even defeated if it is uncoordinated. Only by our combined efforts and united action can we repulse the multiple onslaughts of the imperialists and fight our way to victory. Our enemies fight collectively and combine to exploit our people.

The clear examples of collective imperialism have made themselves felt more and more in our region by the formation of an unholy alliance between the governments of South Africa, Portugal, and the so-called Central African Federation. Hence these governments openly and shamelessly gave military assistance consisting of personnel and equipment to the traitorous Tshombe regime in Katanga.

At this very moment it has been widely reported that a secret defence agreement has been signed between Portugal, South Africa, and the Federation, following visits of Federation and South African defence ministers to Lisbon, the Federation defence minister to Luanda, and South African Defence Ministry delegations to Mozambique.

Dr Salazar was quoted in the Johannesburg *Star* of 8 July 1961 as saying: 'Our relations - Mozambique's and Angola's on the one hand and the Federation and South Africa on the other - arise from the existence of our common borders and our traditional friendships that unite our Governments and our people. Our mutual interests are manifold and we are conscious of the need to cooperate to fulfill our common needs.'

Last year, Southern Rhodesian troops were training in South Africa and so were Rhodesian Air Force units. A military mission from South Africa and another from the Central African Federation visited Lourenzo Marques in Mozambique, at the invitation of the Mozambique Army Command, and took part in training exercises in which several units totaling 2,600 men participated.

These operations included dropping exercises for paratroopers.

A report in a South African aviation magazine, wings (December 1961), states: 'The Portuguese are hastily building nine new aerodromes in Portuguese East Africa (Mozambique) following their troubles in Angola. The new 'dromes are all capable of taking jet fighters and are situated along or near the borders of Tanganyika and Nyasaland'; and gives full details.

Can anyone, therefore, doubt the role that the freedom movements should play in view of this hideous conspiracy?

As we have stated earlier, the freedom movement in South Africa believes that hard and swift blows should be delivered with the full weight of the masses of the people, who alone furnish us with one absolute guarantee that the freedom flames now burning in the country shall never be extinguished.

During the last ten years the African people in South Africa have fought many freedom battles, involving civil disobedience, strikes, protest marches, boycotts and demonstrations of all kinds. In all these campaigns we repeatedly stressed the importance of discipline, peaceful and non-violent struggle.

We did so, firstly because we felt that there were still opportunities for peaceful struggle and we sincerely worked for peaceful changes. Secondly, we did not want to expose our people to situations where they might become easy targets for the trigger-happy police of South Africa. But the situation has now radically altered.

South Africa is now a land ruled by the gun. The government is increasing the size of its army, of the navy, of its air force, and the police. Pill-boxes and road blocks are being built up all over the country. Armament factories are being set up in Johannesburg and other cities. Officers of the South African army have visited Algeria and Angola where they were briefed exclusively on methods of suppressing popular struggles.

All opportunities for peaceful agitation and struggle have been closed. Africans no longer have the freedom even to stay peacefully in their houses in protest against the oppressive policies of the government. During the strike in May last year the police went from house to house, beating up Africans and driving them to work.

Hence it is understandable why today many of our people are turning their faces away from the path of peace and non-violence. They feel that peace in our country must be considered already broken when a minority government maintains its authority over the majority by force and violence.

A crisis is developing in earnest in South Africa.

However, no high command ever announces beforehand what its strategy and tactics will be to meet a situation. Certainly, the days of civil disobedience, of strikes, and mass demonstrations are not over and we will resort to them over and over again.

But a leadership commits a crime against its own people if it hesitates to sharpen its political weapons which have become less effective.

Regarding the actual situation pertaining today in South Africa I should mention that I have just come out of South Africa, having for the last ten months lived in my own country as an outlaw, away from family and friends.

When I was compelled to lead this sort of life, I made a public statement in which I announced that I would not leave the country but would continue working underground. I meant it and I have honored that undertaking.

But when my organisation received the invitation to this conference it was decided that I should attempt to come out and attend the conference to furnish the various African leaders, leading sons of our continent, with the most up-to-date information about the situation.

During the past ten months I moved up and down my country and spoke to peasants in the countryside, to workers in the cities, to students and professional people. It dawned on me quite clearly that the situation had become explosive. It was not surprising therefore when one morning in October last year we woke up to read press reports of widespread sabotage involving the cutting of telephone wires and the blowing up of power pylons. The government remained unshaken and White South Africa tried to dismiss it as the work of criminals.

Then on the night of 16 December last year the whole of South Africa vibrated under the heavy blows of Umkhonto we Sizwe (The Spear of the Nation). Government buildings were blasted with explosives in Johannesburg, the industrial heart of South Africa, in Port

174

Elizabeth, and in Durban. It was now clear that this was a political demonstration of a formidable kind, and the press announced the beginning of planned acts of sabotage in the country.

It was still a small beginning because a government as strong and as aggressive as that of South Africa can never be induced to part with political power by bomb explosions in one night and in three cities only. But in a country where freedom fighters frequently pay with their very lives and at a time when the most elaborate military preparations are being made to crush the people's struggles, planned acts of sabotage against government installations introduce a new phase in the political situation and are a demonstration of the people's unshakeable determination to win freedom whatever the cost may be.

The government is preparing to strike viciously at political leaders and freedom fighters. But the people will not take these blows sitting down.

In such a grave situation it is fit and proper that this conference of PAFMECA should sound a clarion call to the struggling peoples in South Africa and other dependent areas, to close ranks, to stand firm as a rock and not allow themselves to be divided by petty political rivalries whilst their countries burn. At this critical moment in the history of struggle, unity amongst our people in South Africa and in the other territories has become as vital as the air we breathe and it should be preserved at all costs.

Finally, dear friends, I should assure you that the African people of South Africa, notwithstanding fierce persecution and untold suffering, in their ever increasing courage will not for one single moment be diverted from the historic mission of liberating their country and winning freedom, lasting peace, and happiness.

We are confident that in the decisive struggles ahead, our liberation movement will receive the fullest support of PAFMECA and of all freedom-loving people throughout the world."

African leaders who attended the conference, and even those who were not in Addis Ababa, agreed to provide material and financial support to the African National Congress and other liberation movements in countries which were still under colonial or white minority rule.

Mandela also received military training in Ethiopia. He was trained by Colonel Fekadu Wakene. As Penny Dale stated in an article, "The Man Who Taught Mandela to be a Soldier":

"In July 1962, Col Fekadu Wakene taught South African political activist Nelson Mandela the tricks of guerrilla warfare – including how to plant explosives before slipping quietly away into the night.

Mr Mandela was in Ethiopia, learning how to be the commander-in-chief of Umkhonto we Sizwe - the armed wing of the African National Congress (ANC).

The group had announced its arrival at the end of 1961 by blowing-up electricity pylons in various places in South Africa.

Then on 11 January 1962, Mr Mandela had secretly, and illegally, slipped out of South Africa.

His mission was to meet as many African political leaders as possible and garner assistance for the ANC, including money and training for its military wing.

And to be moulded into a soldier himself.

During this trip, he visited Ethiopia twice and left a deep impression on those who met him during his stay in the Ethiopian capital, Addis Ababa.

'Made others laugh'

'Nelson Mandela was a very strong and resilient student, and he took instruction well and was really very likeable,' Col Fekadu said.

'You couldn't help but love him.'

Col Fekadu was a corporal when he trained Mr Mandela. He was a member of a specialist police force - the riot battalion - based in the suburbs of Kolfe, in barracks which are still used today.

He remembers a 'happy, cheerful person' who 'concentrated on the task in hand.'

'He was polite, always happy and you never saw him lose his temper,' he said.

'He laughed easily and made others laugh as well.'

Col Fekadu says he was responsible for training Mr Mandela in sabotage and demolitions and how to stage hit-and-run attacks.

The day's theory lessons were put into practice during night-time exercises.

Mr Mandela was a good student, hardworking and physically strong - but sometimes too robust and too enthusiastic for his own good, the colonel recalls.

'Physically he was very strong and well-built. But sometimes during the training he would get ahead of himself. And while his intentions were good, that could also be dangerous, and sometimes we had to restrain him a bit for safety reasons.'

Col Fekadu had been told to train Mr Mandela by his commanding officer, General Tadesse Birru, the assistant police commissioner who had played a key role in crushing an attempt at the end of 1960 to overthrow Emperor Haile Selassie. He was later executed by the Derg regime of Mengistu Haile Mariam.

Back in 1962, Col Fekadu did not realise the significance of the South African politician he had been instructed to turn into a soldier.

'All we knew was that he was our guest from abroad and that he would spend some time with us,' he said.

'Everything was kept very secret. We were kept in the dark.'

Mr Mandela was in Ethiopia at the invitation of the

emperor, an ardent supporter of Africa's decolonisation and African unity.

At the time, Ethiopia had one of the strongest armed forces on the continent.

Its troops were part of the UN peacekeeping operation during the Congo crisis in 1960 and a decade earlier Ethiopian soldiers had fought in the Korean war.

And the emperor had invited many other African liberation struggle fighters to be trained on Ethiopian soil.

As well as learning how to commit acts of sabotage, Mr Mandela's military training also included briefings on military science, how to run an army and how to use a gun.

He was also taken on long treks carrying his knapsack, rifle and ammunition.

This was one of Mr Mandela's favourite activities during his military training, and he writes about it with affection in his *Long Walk to Freedom autobiography*: 'During these marches I got a sense of the landscape, which was very beautiful... people used wooden ploughs and lived on a very simple diet supplemented by home-brewed beer. Their existence was similar to the life in rural South Africa.'

'Talkative'

Mr Mandela's presence in Addis Ababa was supposed to be top secret. But physically he stood out.

He was much taller and broader than most of the police cadets.

And, as well as going on fatigue marches through the countryside, he would exercise out in the open in the grounds of the barracks.

One person who took a particular interest in the tall stranger in his midst was Tesfaye Abebe, who was working in Kolfe as the head of the battalion's music and drama department.

He recalls Mr Mandela running around a big field in the compound – which today doubles up as a running track and a parade ground.

'He would do squats and jumping jacks. He followed that exercise routine religiously every morning.'

A curious Mr Tesfaye snatched conversations with Mr Mandela when he and his trainer came into the canteen for lunch.

'Security was quite tight and we weren't really allowed to approach him.'

But, he says, Mr Mandela was 'very friendly and talkative' and explained apartheid to him and how the ANC intended to fight it with guerrilla warfare and political activism.

On a couple of occasions, the police band - in which Mr Tesfaye was the pianist - played for Mr Mandela in the officer's club.

'He really enjoyed that. He was really happy when we played for him.'

Mr Mandela's military training in Ethiopia was supposed to last six months - but after only two weeks he was called back to South Africa by the ANC.

He had already spent seven months out of the country - and he was needed back home.

As Mr Mandela left Ethiopia, Gen Tadesse presented him with a pistol and 200 rounds of ammunition - a gun that is thought to be buried somewhere on Lillesleaf Farm, where in 1963 other ANC leaders were arrested and sentenced to life alongside Mr Mandela in the famous Rivionia trial.

Mr Mandela himself had been arrested on 5 August 1962 - for leaving the country illegally, shortly after his return from his trip around Africa - and still in the military fatigues in which he had been trained in Ethiopia." – (Penny Dale, "The Man Who Taught Mandela to be a Soldier," BBC Africa, reporting from Addis Ababa, Ethiopia, 9 December 2013; additional reporting by BBC

Africa's Hewete Haileselassie).

Another interesting aspect of Mandela's secret trip to other African countries after he left South Africa for the first time had to do with his visit to Tanganyika, now Tanzania, which was also the first independent African country he visited:

"Nelson Mandela also visited Tanzania in 1962, staying with the late minister Nsilo Swai, whose wife, Vicky Nsilo Swai, told the BBC about his left luggage:

'On the day Mandela was leaving, he had to leave behind a suitcase because he had too much luggage. In the suitcase was a pair of brown, leather boots. My husband and I ended up keeping them for 33 years.

After my husband retired from politics, we moved from Dar es Salaam to Moshi, near Kilimanjaro – and the boots came with us.

Then, my husband got a job with the United Nations so the boots lived in New York for 15 years.

I kept them in our bedroom in a cupboard. I never polished them, I never cleaned them but I put newspaper in them to keep them firm.

The boots are very strong and the leather is excellent – and when I took them back to Mr Mandela in 1995 they were really like new.

The boots still fitted Mr Mandela and he joked that 'these boots have travelled more than myself'.

A lot of people are surprised why I kept the boots for so long. But I really wanted a man who I saw so dedicated to his country to have a memory of these boots.'" – (Vicky Nsilo Swai, "I Kept Mandela's Boots for 33 Years," BBC Africa, 9 December 2013).

Mandela also underwent military training in Algeria. He also visited other African countries where he was promised support for the liberation struggle in South Africa.

He returned to South Africa in July 1962 and was arrested in Natal on August 5th when he was in a car on his way to Durban from where he would proceed to Johannesburg.

The South African police and intelligence service got information and details about his travels and whereabouts from the CIA. According to *The Washington Post*, November 6, 1990, (p. A18), a CIA officer claimed: "We have turned Mandela over to the South African security branch."

Also, Cox News Service reported in 1990 that a senior CIA officer, Paul Eckel, in a conversation with an unnamed American official, admitted the CIA played a major role in Mandela's arrest. He admitted that just a few hours after Mandela was arrested:

"We have turned Mandela over to the South African security branch. We gave them every detail, what he would be wearing, the time of day, just where he would be. They have picked him up. It is one of our greatest coups."

The CIA officer who provided the information to the South African security officials was Donald C. Rickard working undercover as a consular official at the US Consulate in Durban, Natal. He tipped off the Special Branch of the South African police on Mandela's itinerary and told them that Mandela would be disguised as a chauffeur in a car going to Durban. The CIA agent got the information from an informer in the ANC.

After getting the information, plainclothes policemen and intelligence officers got on Mandela's trail and arrested him at a roadblock outside Howick, Natal, when the police flagged down his car. It was a big victory for the police and for the South African government. Mandela had eluded capture for 17 months and had been able to sneak out of the country during those months.

When he was still in South Africa before leaving to attend the PAFMECA conference in Addis Ababa, he was able to disguise himself and walk around freely without being detected.

CIA's involvement in Mandela's capture had been known right from the beginning. In 1963, at a farewell party for Donald Rickard who had been in South Africa since 1958, the CIA agent said he was, in fact, going to meet with Mandela the night Mandela was arrested but, instead, tipped off the South African Special branch on Mandela's itinerary.

The meeting, which never took place, had been arranged by the CIA informer in the African National Congress. And the farewell party was held at the residence of South African mercenary Colonel "Mad Mike" Hoare who wreaked so much havoc in Congo in the sixties fighting pro-Lumumbist forces on behalf of the pro-Western government in Leopoldville.

Rickard returned to the United States in 1963 and went to live in Pagosa Springs, Colorado, where he was still living n the late 1990s.

Mandela's arrest led to a five-year prison sentence. Then the South African police went on to arrest other ANC leaders and the leaders of other anti-apartheid groups in a crackdown that virtually decapitated the entire anti-apartheid movement in the country. Almost the entire leadership was arrested or fled into exile.

In October 1963, Mandela again, with the other anti-apartheid leaders who had been arrested, went on trial for treason. It came to be known as the Rivonia Trial, named after the highly affluent suburb of Johannesburg where the anti-apartheid leaders had their headquarters at a secret location. That is also where they were arrested when the South African police raided the house in which they were having a meeting.

In June 1964, Mandela was sentenced to life imprisonment together with a number of other anti-apartheid leaders including Walter Sisulu, Govan Mbeki, Andrew Mlangeni, Elias Motsoaledi, Raymond Mhlaba, Dennis Goldberg, and Ahmed Kathrada.

Although the ANC leadership fell in a single swoop, as did some of the leaders of the other anti-apartheid organisations in the country, the struggle against apartheid did not lose its potent although it may have been temporarily interrupted in its activities.

The repressive nature of the apartheid state itself proved to be a catalyst for the liberation movement. It galvanised the movement and helped to propel it, enabling it to go forward and gain momentum as the people became even more determined to end apartheid.

What happened after the leaders were arrested, in terms of mobilisation of forces against the apartheid regime, was that the movement was forced to go deeper underground. It also vigorously sought support from the independent African countries and from its supporters in other parts of the world.

In tandem with what was going on in South Africa was the liberation struggle in the neighbouring Portuguese colony of Mozambique. As the people in South Africa intensified their struggle against apartheid, freedom fighters in Mozambique mobilised forces to fight the Portuguese colonial government in their country.

On 25 June 1962, the Front for the Liberation of Mozambique (FRELIMO) was formed in Dar es Salaam, Tanganyika, bringing together different Mozambican nationalist organisations to form a united front against the colonial forces in their country.

Dr. Eduardo C. Mondlane was elected the first president of FRELIMO. Tragically, he was assassinated in Dar es Salaam only a few years later on 2 February 1969 when he opened a bomb parcel sent to him by the Portuguese secret police. The bomb was hidden in a book of Russian essays, cut out to hide the device. It was mailed from Japan.

Just two years after FRELIMO was formed, the freedom fighters fired their first shots against the Portuguese forces in Mozambique, formally launching the liberation war after 500 years of colonial rule. FRELIMO became one of the most successful liberation movements in the history of the entire Third World.

The guerrilla campaign started on 24 September 1964 in the northern province of Cabo Delgado bordering Tanzania which became an important rear and operational base for the freedom fighters. The guerrilla fighters who first went into action had been trained in Algeria.

Elsewhere on the continent, four countries won independence in 1962.

Rwanda won independence from Belgium on January 1st; Burundi also from the same colonial power on July 1st; Algeria won hers from France on July 3rd after seven years of guerilla warfare in which 1 million Algerians died. And Uganda won independence from Britain on October 9th.

Between 1960 and 1962, a total of 23 African countries won independence; a momentous achievement in so short a time.

It also fuelled rising expectations among the people who believed their lives would get better, much better, now that their countries were being led by fellow Africans. They were right. But they were also wrong, as the history of post-colonial Africa tragically demonstrated.

1963

THE YEAR 1963 started out with some good news for Africa especially for the people of Congo. But it also had some bad news.

Congo was still in chaos. Repression intensified in South Africa as the security forces cracked down on anti-apartheid opponents, arresting most of their leaders. And a government was overthrown in Togo, West Africa, setting a precedent with dire consequences for the continent.

On 13 January, 1963, President Sylvanus Olympio of Togo was assassinated in a military coup. It was the first military coup in post-colonial Africa and was to have profound implications for the rest of the continent in the following decades.

Olympio was assassinated at the gates of the American embassy in the nation's capital, Lome, by a group of Togolese soldiers led by a 25-year-old sergeant, Etienne Eyadema, who later changed his name to Gnassingbe Eyadema.

Eyadema claimed credit for firing the shot that killed Olympio. The president tried to seek refuge at the American embassy when soldiers followed him through the streets of the capital but embassy officials refused to open the gate and let him in.

Olympio's brother-in-law Nicholas Grunitzky became president, but was ousted by Eyadema in a second military coup in 1967 on the fourth anniversary of the first military takeover.

By then, Eyadema had capped his military career in a meteoric rise through self-promotion from sergeant to lieutenant-colonel in less than three years, and to full general less than two years later.

He died in February 2005 after 38 years in power and earned the dubious distinction as the longest-ruling despot in the history of post-colonial Africa. No other leader on the continent had stayed been in power that long. And no other African soldier had gained notoriety before him as a coup maker.

Patrice Lumumba was, of course, the first African leader to be forcibly removed from office in 1960 and was assassinated in January 1961. But his ouster was not a typical military coup; it was part of a larger plot by the West to dismember Congo which turned the heart of Africa into a battleground between two ideological camps: East versus West.

Olympio's assassination drew a sharp response from President Julius Nyerere of Tanganyika. Other African leaders also questioned the legitimacy of such assumption of power by unconstitutional means. As Nyerere stated in a cable to the UN secretary-general, U Thant:

"After the brutal murder of President Olympio, the problem of recognition of a successor government has arisen. We urge no recognition of a successor government until satisfied first that the government did not take part in Olympio's murder or second that there is a popularly elected government." – (Julius Nyerere, in the *Standard*, Dar es Salaam, Tanganyika, 26 January 1963; quoted by Ali A. Mazrui, *Towards A Pax Africana: A Study of Ideology and Ambition*, op. cit., p. 123).

Unfortunately, African leaders made a mistake when they legitimised military coups on the continent by recognising the new government of Togo which came into power by illegitimate means.

Ghana, Senegal and Dahomey (renamed Benin) were the first countries to recognise the military regime. Others recognised it later. Tanganyika, Liberia, Guinea and Ivory Coast denounced the military takeover right away.

But the majority of the African countries eventually recognised the military junta.

Had they taken a firm stand against military coups right from the beginning when the first coup took place in Togo in 1963, the continent may have been spared the agony it went through for decades when military coups became a ritual, and an institution, of African politics. In many countries, assumption of power by unconstitutional means became the norm rather than the exception.

But there was also some good news just two days after Olympio was assassinated, although his assassination continued to haunt Africa and many people were still in mourning.

On January 15th the secession of Katanga came to an end. It was a victory not only for the people of Congo but for the rest of Africa.

Had Katanga succeeded in separating from the rest of the country, it would have set a bad precedent for other countries on the continent. There was a danger that some groups and regions in a number of countries would also try to secede and establish their own independent states.

Therefore Katanga's re-integration into Congo, after the secessionists capitulated to UN forces, was a victory for all African countries which were determined to maintain their territorial integrity. Many of them were already threatened by ethno-regional rivalries as they still are today.

And they were young, fragile nations whose survival depended on the willingness of the members of different ethnic groups to live and work together as one people constituting viable political entities also known as countries.

Fifteen years later, Katanga again posed a serious threat to the security of Congo, then known as Zaire, renamed in 1971 by President Mobutu Sese Seko who also changed his name from Joseph Mobutu in 1972 in pursuit of his policy of authenticity – restoration of African identity.

Again, the imperial ambitions of Western powers led by the United States, and Cold War politics, played a major role in the new conflict, but in a different context of post-colonial Africa in which African countries were more assertive of their independence in practical terms than they were in the turbulent sixties.

The conflict was also different. The Katangese *gendarmes* who threatened Mobutu's government were not puppets of any major power; nor were they surrogate forces of any other country as claimed by the West.

It was in that context that President Nyerere addressed the crisis on 8 June 1978 when he summoned to the State House members of the diplomatic corps accredited to Tanzania. In the audience were Western ambassadors and those of the Eastern-bloc countries as well as others including African diplomats. As he stated in his statement, "Tanzania Rejects Western Domination of Africa":

"I have been very concerned indeed about world reactions to recent events in Africa, and it seems to me to be necessary that I should make Tanzania's position clear. For the events of the past few weeks have once again demonstrated that although our legal independence is officially recognised, our need and our right to develop our countries and our continent in our own interests has not yet been conceded in practice. The habit of regarding Africa as an appendage of Western Europe has not yet been broken.

Soviet Forces in Africa

In Angola the M.P.L.A. did almost all the fighting against the Portuguese colonialists. As independence approached after the Revolution in Portugal, various Western countries – led by the United States of America – decided to try to prevent the establishment of an M.P.L.A. Government in that country. They conspired with South Africa, and gave under-cover finance and arms to rival nationalist movements which had previously been almost inactive.

Faced with this conspiracy and the consequent attacks on Angola from South Africa and across the Zaire border, the M.P.L.A. Government sought help from those who had given support to the Movement during the independence struggle. Cuba and the Soviet Union responded to those requests. With their help the Angolan Government overcame the immediate military threat to its existence, pushed South African troops back across the border into Namibia, and pushed the F.N.L.A. troops back to where they had come from – Zaire.

Cuban troops are still in Angola; and the Soviet Union continues to give military assistance to Angola. The Angolan Government is forced to ask for this assistance to be continued because the threat to the integrity of Angola still exists.

Only last month South African troops entered Southern Angola again, and inflicted heavy casualties upon Namibian refugees. UNITA continues to get outside support. There have been continual attacks made across the Angolan/ Zaire border by F.N.L.A. troops, who are financed and supplied with weapons by external forces and who operate with the active or tacit support of the Zaire Government.

That all this is happening, is known to the Secret Services of South Africa, and of U.S.A., France, and some other western countries. It would not be happening without their connivance and their involvement. It would be incredible if the Governments of those countries did not know what their Agencies were doing.

The history of the ex-Katangese Gendarmes pre-dates the independence of Angola. It was not actions of the M.P.L.A. which took them to Angola; nor were they trained by M.P.L.A. They are a living reminder to Africa of the determined and shameless attempt by the West to dismember the former Congo (Leopoldville) in their own economic interests. When that attempt was defeated, some of these Gendarmes moved into Angola and remained there as refugees.

Now things have changed; the West has a different view of Zaire and is using it to de-stabilise Angola. It would therefore not be surprising if Angola, on its part, felt forced to withdraw the restraints it had been imposing on those Zairean refugees in Northern Angola.

Whether such a policy of retaliation is correct or wise is a matter of judgment; it is nevertheless understandable. But one thing is clear. There is no evidence of Cuban or Soviet involvement in this retaliation. The U.S. State Department was at one time reported to have said as much; the Cubans have persistently and convincingly repudiated such allegations.

So Cuba and the Soviet Union went into Angola and are still in Angola for understandable reasons, at the request of the Angolan Government. There is no evidence at all that they have been involved, directly or indirectly, in any fighting within Zaire.

Cuban and Soviet Forces are also in Ethiopia, at the request of the Ethiopian Government. The reasons •for their presence are well known. They have helped the Ethiopians to defend their country against external aggression. They have not – and nor has the Ethiopian Government – engaged in any fighting outside Ethiopia's borders. And there is some evidence to suggest that the Cuban Government at any rate makes a distinction between the fighting in the Ogaden and the fighting in Eritrea.

Apart from those two countries, where else in Africa are there Soviet or Cuban Forces? There are a few Cuban and Soviet Nationals, and a few Chinese Nationals, helping to train the Freedom Fighters of Southern Africa in the use of weapons Africa gets from Communist countries for the liberation struggle in Rhodesia and Namibia. Apart from vague generalities, and rumours based on the jackets people wear, there is no serious suggestion that these Forces are operating or stationed anywhere else in Africa.

It is, then, on the basis of Soviet and Cuban Forces in two African countries that there is a great furore in the West about a so-called Soviet penetration of Africa. And those Forces are in those two countries at the request of the legitimate and recognised Governments of the countries concerned, and for reasons which are well known and completely understandable to all reasonable people. Yet Western countries are objecting, and are holding meetings ostensibly about how to defend the freedom of Africa against what they call Soviet Penetration.

Let me make it quite clear. Tanzania does not want anyone from outside Africa to govern Africa. We regret, even while we recognise, the occasional necessity for an African government to ask for military assistance from a non-African country when it is faced with an external threat to its national integrity. We know that a response to such a request by any of the Big powers is determined by what that Big Power sees as its own interests. We have been forced to recognise that most of the countries acknowledged as World Powers do not find it beneath their dignity to exacerbate existing and genuine African problems and conflicts when they believe they can benefit by doing so.

We in Tanzania believe that African countries, separately and through the O.A.U., need to guard against such actions. But we need to guard Africa against being used by any other nation or group of nations.

The danger to Africa does not come just from nations in the Eastern Bloc. The West still considers Africa to be within its Sphere of Influence and acts accordingly. Current developments show that the greater immediate danger to Africa's freedom comes from nations in that Western Bloc.

A Pan-African Security Force

It might be a good thing if the O.A.U. was sufficiently united to establish an African High Command, and a Pan-African Security Force. If, having done so, the O.A.U. then decided to ask for external support for this Force, no-one could legitimately object. But the O.A.U. has made no such decision. It is highly unlikely that the O.A.U. meeting in Khartoum will be able to agree unanimously on the creation of such a military Force, or – if it did – that it would be able to agree unanimously on which countries to ask for support if that was needed.

Yet until Africa, at the O.A.U., has made such a decision, there can be no Pan-African Security Force which will uphold the freedom of Africa. It is the height of arrogance for anyone else to talk of establishing a Pan-African Force to defend Africa. It is quite obvious, moreover, that those who have put forward this idea, and those who seek to initiate such a Force, are not interested in the Freedom of Africa. They are interested in the Domination of Africa.

It was from Paris that this talk of a Pan-African

Security Force has emanated. It is in Paris, and later in Brussels, that there is to be a meeting to discuss this and related matters pertaining to the 'freedom' of Africa. The O.A.U. meets in Khartoum in July; but we are told that African freedom and its defence is being discussed in Paris and Brussels in June.

There is only one reason why the idea of Europe setting up, or initiating, a Pan-African Security Force – or an African Peace Force – does not meet with immediate and world-wide amazement and consternation. It is the continuing assumption that Africa is, and must always remain, part of the West European 'Sphere of Influence'. This assumption is hardly being questioned yet. Even some African states take it for granted.

We all know the facts of power in the world. But we cannot all be expected to accept without question this new insult to Africa and to Africans. We may be weak, but we are human; we do know when we are being deliberately provoked and insulted.

The French have troops in many countries of Africa. In Chad, in Western Sahara, in Mauretania, and now also in Zaire, French Forces are engaged in combat against Africans. France continues to occupy Mayotte. But there are no meetings in Washington, or even in Moscow, to discuss the threat to Africa's freedom by the French Penetration of Africa. Nor should there be. But not even Africa, in Africa, discusses the question.

The reason is very simple. It is the continued assumption that it is natural for French troops, or Belgian troops, or British troops, to be in Africa, but it is a threat for troops from any Non-member of the Western Bloc to be in Africa. A threat to whom? To African freedom, or to the domination of Africa by ex-colonial powers and their allies, operated now through more subtle means and with the help of an African Fifth Column?

The answers to those questions are very obvious. There have been continued incursions by South Africa and

Rhodesia into Angola, Botswana, Zambia, and Mozambique. The West has not shown much concern about these; nor have their new-found surrogates in Africa.

When the U.S.S.R. sent its troops into Czechoslovakia in 1968 Tanzania was one of the many countries which protested. Is it expected that we should not protest when Western Powers send their troops into an African country? These 'rescue operations' almost always seem to result in the death of a lot of innocent people and the rescue of a Government. But that is apparently not regarded in Europe as interference in African affairs. Instead, the same country which initiated the military expedition then calls a meeting to discuss, they say, the freedom of Africa!

There should be no mistake. Whatever the official Agenda, the Paris and Brussels meetings are not discussing the freedom of Africa. They are discussing the continued domination of Africa, and the continued use of Africa, by Western Powers. They are intended to be, taken together, a Second Berlin Conference.

The real Agenda, inside and outside the formal sessions of these meetings, will be concerned with two things. It will be concerned with neo-colonialism in Africa for economic purposes – the real control of Africa and African states. That will be led by the French. It will be concerned also with the use of Africa in the East-West conflict. That will be led by the Americans. These two purposes will be coordinated so that they are mutually supportive, and the apportionment of the expected benefits – and costs – will be worked out. It is at that point – the division of the spoils – that disputes are most likely to occur.

But the costs may also be higher than the participants anticipate. Tanzania is not the only nationalist country in Africa. There are nationalists everywhere. Sooner or later, and for as long as necessary, Africa will fight against neo-col0nialism as it has fought against colonialism. And eventually it will win. western Block countries which try to resist the struggle against neo-colonialism need to recognise that it will not only be African countries which will suffer in the process.

Nor will the whole of Africa acquiesce in being used in the East-West confrontation. We are weak, but weak countries have before now caused a great deal of embarrassment and some difficulty for Big Powers. If the West wants to prove, either to the Russians or to their own people, that they are not soft on Communism they should direct their attention to where the Soviet tanks are, and the Soviet front-line is. They should not invent an excuse to bring the East-West conflict into Africa. For if they succeed in doing that Africa will suffer, and African freedom will suffer; but it may also turn out to be very expensive for those who choose Africa as another site for East-West confrontation.

The African people have the same desire as every other people to be free and to use their freedom for their own benefit. They have the same determination to work and to struggle to that end. They know that no-one else is interested in their freedom. This talk in Europe about a Pan-African Security Force is an insult to Africa, and a derogation of African freedom.

It makes little difference if the European initiators of this plan find Africans to do their fighting for them. There were Africans who fought with the colonial invaders; there were Africans who assisted in the enslavement of fellow-Africans; and there were Africans who fought against the freedom movements. But we ask those African Governments which may have. agreed to participate in this plan to consider well be fore they go further.

We have the O.A.U. With all its faults and its incapacities, it is the only Pan-African organisation which exists and which is concerned with African freedom. Do not let us split it – and Africa – between those who are militarily allied with the West and those who may in consequence find themselves forced to seek assistance from elsewhere against the African-assisted neo-colonialism. – (Julius Nyerere, in a statement, "Tanzania Rejects Western Domination of Africa," to members of the diplomatic corps, at the State House, Dar es Salaam, Tanzania, 8 June 1978; reproduced in *Tanzanian Affairs*, London, Britain-Tanzania Society, Bulletin of Tanzanian Affairs No. 6, July 1978).

Back in the sixties, not long after Katanga was reunited with the rest of the country in January 1963, Africa witnessed another major step towards unity.

From 23 – 25 May 1963, African heads of state and government met in Addis Ababa, Ethiopia, and formed the Organisation of African Unity (OAU) to promote cooperation among African countries in different areas and work towards continental unity.

One of the cardinal principles enshrined in the OAU was the acceptance and maintenance of the national boundaries inherited at independence.

The resolution to maintain the territorial borders established by the colonial rulers was introduced by Julius Nyerere, the president of what was then Tanganyika, who feared that any attempt to change the boundaries would plunge the continent into chaos. As he stated in "Reflections," one of his last speeches – it was an impromptu speech – at an international conference at the University of Dar es Salaam, Tanzania, on 15 December 1997:

"The OAU was founded in 1963. In 1964 we went to Cairo to hold, in a sense, our first summit after the inaugural summit. I was responsible for moving that resolution that Africa must accept the borders, which we inherited from colonialism; accept them as they are. That resolution was passed by the organisation (OAU) with two reservations: one from Morocco, another from Somalia.

Let me say why I moved that resolution. In 1960, just before this country became independent, I think I was then chief minister; I received a delegation of Masai elders from Kenya, led by an American missionary. And they came to persuade me to let the Masai invoke something called the Anglo-Masai Agreement so that that section of the Masai in Kenya should become part of Tanganyika; so that when Tanganyika becomes independent, it includes part of Masai, from Kenya.

I suspected the American missionary was responsible for that idea. I don't remember that I was particularly polite to him. Kenyatta was then in detention, and here somebody comes to me, that we should break up Kenya and make part of Kenya part of Tanganyika. But why shouldn't Kenyatta demand that the Masai part of Tanganyika should become Masai of Kenya? It's the same logic. That was in 1960.

In 1961 we became independent. In 1962, early 1962, I resigned as prime minister and then a few weeks later I received Dr. Banda. *Mungu amuweke mahali pema* (May God rest his soul in peace).

I received Dr. Banda. We had just, FRELIMO had just been established here and we were now in the process of starting the armed struggle.

So Banda comes to me with a big old book, with lots and lots of maps in it, and tells me, 'Mwalimu, what is this, what is Mozambique? There is no such thing as Mozambique.'

I said, 'What do you mean there is no such thing as Mozambique?'

So he showed me this map, and he said: 'That part is part of Nyasaland (Malawi was still Nyasaland at that time). That part is part of Southern Rhodesia, that part is Swaziland, and this part, which is the northern part, Makonde part, that is *your* part.'

So Banda disposed of Mozambique just like that. I ridiculed the idea, and Banda never liked anybody to ridicule his ideas. So he left and went to Lisbon to talk to Salazar about this wonderful idea. I don't know what

Salazar told him. That was '62.

In '63 we go to Addis Ababa for the inauguration of the OAU, and Ethiopia and Somalia are at war over the Ogaden. We had to send a special delegation to bring the president of Somalia to attend that inaugural summit, because the two countries were at *war.* Why? Because Somalia wanted the Ogaden, a *whole* province of Ethiopia, saying, 'That is part of Somalia.' And Ethiopia was quietly, the Emperor quietly saying to us that 'the whole of Somalia is part of Ethiopia.'

So those three, the delegation of the Masai, led by the American missionary; Banda's old book of maps; and the Ogaden, caused me to move that resolution, in Cairo in 1964. And I say, the resolution was accepted, two countries with reservations, and one was Somalia because Somalia wanted the Ogaden; Somalia wanted northern Kenya; Somalia wanted Djibouti."

As Nyerere stated, Morocco was the other country which – together with Somalia – voted against his resolution on retaining the borders inherited at independence in order to avoid disintegration of African countries and conflicts over inter-territorial borders. And he was vindicated by history.

Morocco did not like the resolution because it had expansionist ambitions. Twelve years later, after the 1964 OAU summit, Morocco annexed the former Spanish colony of Western Sahara. It was known as Spanish Sahara when it was ruled by Spain.

The people of Western Sahara are still fighting for their right to self-determination after being forcibly incorporated into Morocco by King Hassan II.

In 1964, Somalia declared war on Ethiopia in an attempt to reclaim the Ogaden ceded by the British to the Ethiopian emperor. And in 1977, the two countries fought the bloodiest war in which both sides suffered heavy casualties. But Ethiopia emerged victorious and almost wiped out the entire Somali army of more than 30,000 troops. Somalia also lost most of its army tanks and other weapons and conceded defeat.

Earlier in the sixties, Somalia also clashed with Kenya over the northeastern district of Kenya – then known as the Northern Frontier District – which, like the Ogaden in Ethiopia, is inhabited mostly by Somalis. Somalia claimed both in an attempt to establish a Greater Somalia.

Had both Morocco and Somalia voted for the resolution introduced by Nyerere at the OAU summit in Cairo in 1964 asking African countries to retain the boundaries inherited at independence instead of trying to change them or redraw the map of Africa, all those conflicts could have been avoided. When the OAU was founded in 1963, one of its main objectives was exactly that: avoid or help resolve such conflicts.

So, the mere fact that African leaders agreed on the imperative need for such an organisation to foster cooperation, facilitate efforts towards regional and continental unity, help resolve conflicts and support the liberation struggle against white minority rule, was by itself a major achievement in 1963; as was the re-integration of Katanga into Congo earlier in the same year, bringing an end to a secessionist movement which posed the greatest threat to the survival of one of Africa's biggest and potentially richest countries.

The Organisation of African Unity (OAU) itself went on to play a major role in the course of events during the post-colonial period more than any other single institution in Africa and thus changed destiny of the continent.

The most important role it played was in supporting the liberation struggle against white minority rule in southern Africa and in the Portuguese colony of Guinea, later renamed Guinea-Bissau, in West Africa. The liberation movements waged the armed struggle, complemented by diplomatic offensives, under the auspices of the OAU Liberation Committee and with the help of the independent African countries in varying degrees of commitment. Some did more than others.

All that changed the course of African history in the post-colonial era especially in the countries still under white minority rule. The OAU facilitated the armed struggle and helped to speed up the decolonisation process.

Had it not been for the role played by the OAU and the independent African countries, the countries still under white minority rule in southern Africa would not have won their freedom and independence when they did. The struggle would have taken much longer. And it would have been much harder for the people in those territories if they had to fight on their own without the coordinated help and support they got from other African countries.

Decolonisation was hardest, most complicated, and took the longest in the countries of southern Africa. And it required a concerted effort on a continental scale to bear fruit. Independent African countries waged a coordinated campaign on all fronts to support the liberation movements.

It is a pivotal role which was one of the most important, and most positive, developments on the continent in the post-colonial period.

African countries may not have been able to play that role had they not worked together to create the Organisation of African Unity.

The establishment of the OAU also coincided with the publication of Nkrumah's book, *Africa Must Unite*, in May 1963. Nkrumah deliberately made arrangements to have his book released around the same time African leaders were meeting in Addis Ababa, Ethiopia, to establish the OAU. It was a challenge and an inspiration to encourage African leaders to seriously consider forming a continental government before it was too late, as he passionately argued in his book and in his other speeches and writings through the years. And he was vindicated by history.

But his approach towards African unity, demanding immediate continental unification, without *first* laying the foundation for it, may have been unrealistic.

However, his Pan-African ideals were noble, inspiring and worthy of serious consideration, and his book urging African countries to unite stimulated and fuelled discussion and debate on this important subject for decades.

Nkrumah became the most controversial and most well-known leader on the continent during his time. Even today, more than 40 years after death – he died of cancer in a hospital in Bucharest, Romania, on 27 April 1972 – his Pan-African ambitions to liberate and unite the continent continue to ignite debate.

In 2000, a survey conducted by the BBC among its African listeners found that Nkrumah was considered to be the most influential African leader the continent has ever produced. He was voted Africa's "Man of the Millennium." And probably some of the people who voted for him also read or knew about his book *Africa Must Unite* published in 1963. Tragically, he was overthrown three years later in a military coup engineered and masterminded by the CIA.

Nkrumah also was one of the African leaders, together with Nyerere and a few others, who enjoyed a lot of support among many African Americans. Also Nkrumah and Nyerere were some of the leading founders of the Organisation of African Unity (OAU).

And during the civil rights movement in the United States in the sixties, African governments took strong interest in the struggle for racial equality in the US and issued a formal statement condemning racial injustice against people of African descent in other parts of the world but especially in the United States.

The statement was in the form of a resolution linking racial discrimination in the United States to apartheid in South Africa and was issued by the African heads of state and government who met in Addis Ababa, Ethiopia, in May 1963, to form the Organisation of African Unity. It was incorporated into the OAU Charter:

"The Summit Conference of Independent African States meeting in Addis Ababa, Ethiopia, from 22 May to 25 May 1963; having considered all aspects of the questions of apartheid and racial discriminations; unanimously convinced of the imperious and urgent necessity of co-ordinating and intensifying their efforts to put an end to the South African Government's criminal policy of apartheid and wipe out racial discrimination in all its forms,...expresses the deep concern aroused in all African peoples and governments by the measures of racial discrimination taken against communities of African origin living outside the continent and particularly in the United States of America,...intolerable mal-practices which are likely seriously to deteriorate relations between the African peoples and governments on the one hand and the people and Government of the United States of America on the other."

The end of 1963 was marked by celebration when another country, Kenya, a British colony, won independence on December 12th. It was the only country on the entire continent that won independence in 1963.

A few months later, a major event took place in the island nation of Zanzibar and changed the continent's political landscape.

It led to the birth of a new nation, the only one of its kind in Africa as a product of a merger of two independent states. The macronation was Tanzania.

Without the Zanzibar revolution, the two countries of Tanganyika and Zanzibar would not have united when they did, if at all.

1964

THE ZANZIBAR REVOLUTION was one of the most significant events in the history of post-colonial Africa.

It was a victory in the struggle for African liberation; it brought fundamental change in Zanzibar; and it helped pave the way for the political union between Tanganyika and Zanzibar which was a major political transformation in the history of the continent.

On 12 January 1964, the Arab rulers of Zanzibar were overthrown in a revolution which went down in history as one of the bloodiest conflicts up to that time in Africa since the end of colonial rule and involving change of government by unconstitutional means.

The armed uprising was led by John Okello, a self-styled field marshal originally from Uganda who had lived in the island nation, on Pemba island, since 1959. He was born in Uganda in 1937 and also lived in Kenya for a few years.

After he moved to Pemba, he became a policeman and joined the Afro-Shirazi Party (ASP) led by Sheikh Abeid Amani Karume. He moved from Pemba to Zanzibar in 1963 where he started preparing secretly for a revolution to end Arab rule.

During the revolution, Okello led a group of about 300 men to seize power from the Arab rulers and overthrew Sultan Sayyid Jamshid bin Abdullah. Jamshid Abdullah, 35, ascended the throne after his father died. Okello was 26.

The people he recruited for the revolution were young men who were also members or supporters of the Afro-Shirazi Party which resented Arab domination. He had been meeting with some of them secretly for some time to prepare for the revolution. And they made history the following year.

In 2002, I got in touch with one of the people who used to live in Zanzibar and who witnessed what happened on the island when the revolution took place. He did not tell me back then exactly who or what he was when he was in Zanzibar until I found out later. He said he was not a Zanzibari or a Tanzanian but an American – that is all he said to me in terms of his identity – and explained the following in "The Zanzibar Revolution" which he also made publicly available:

"On the night of January 12, 1964 a band of some 300 people violently seized the Island of Unguja. They were led by a little known man named John Okello, who had lived on Pemba, having come to the islands some years earlier from Uganda.

In Zanzibar he developed a popular following among a core of young, tough men, many of whom were the Stevedores and Porters who worked the ships coming in and out of Zanzibar Harbor.

His group met in secret. He promised changes to these men, fellows long used to working together, in sometimes dangerous settings, and ready to follow orders of any 'captain' who could pay their fee. Theirs became a rebellion looking for a home.

Political unrest had been increasing on Zanzibar and Pemba since the death of Sultan Khalifa in 1960. He had reigned in Zanzibar for almost 50 years, since 1911.

After much jockeying for constituencies and coalitions the main political parties had narrowly split the two general elections of 1961 to the satisfaction of none. The British were leaving, their troops, including a contingent of Irish Guards, stationed near the golf course at the edge of Stone Town, pulled out in early 1963.

When the new Sultan, Jamshid, hoisted the flag of the independent nation of Zanzibar, on December 10, 1963, he marked the departure of the last British Resident, (Governor) of Zanzibar and the end of the colonial period.

Another election in late 1963 had given a slim majority to a coalition of two political parties, the ZNP (the Zanzibar Nationalist Party) and the ZPPP (the Zanzibar and Pemba Peoples Party). The ASP (the Afro-Shirazi Party) was to be in the minority in a British style parliamentary system with the sultan serving as the reigning but not ruling 'monarch.'

This nation, a full member of the British Commonwealth and a newly enrolled sovereign member of the United Nations was destined to last only 33 days.

Political debates raged and street demonstrations were not uncommon in those days.

I remember bicycling to school through crowds chanting the names of political leaders and traveling in the country past road-blocks manned by British soldiers.

The various factions debated everything; rights versus privileges, new-comers versus old-established families, capitalism vs socialism, merchants vs landowners, Zanzibaris vs Pembans, Asians vs Arabs, Swahilis vs Mainlanders, and all this against the backdrop of the Cold War and the other nationalistic and de-colonial movements abounding in Africa at that time.

John Okello didn't have answers to these thorny issues, but he did have the insight to realize that all of these competing interests presented an opportunity for a man of action like himself. After all, a few hundred determined

205

men might be able to seize the few local centers of communication and the three police barracks.

Once he had those under his control and possessed the weapons stored there, who on the islands could throw him out?

Would the politicians join together to denounce and oppose his illegal actions? Or as he hoped, would they continue to distrust each other, to suspect that one or another of themselves must have put him up to it?

Would not they want to make a deal with him, quick, before someone else did? On that January night he rolled the dice.

The ASP leaders, though surprised by Okellos' actions, (many were not even on the island at the time) moved quickly to embrace the rebels.

Hundreds of party followers were whipped into a frenzy by those eager to seize this opportunity to cut the Gordian knot of democratic debate and go straight to the prize of ruling. They sought to gain the chance to remake society in accordance with their own ideals. Ideals were a dime a dozen in those days. Humanity was to become a much more costly item.

Having seen just how vulnerable a government could be, and not trusting their own mixed record in open elections, it was clear to some ASP leaders that drastic measures were warranted to secure the survival of what was now being called 'The Revolution.'

The mobs were unleashed. Law and order disappeared from the streets of Zanzibar. Landowners and merchants were dragged from their houses and shops, looting and killing spread throughout Stone Town. The city literally sacked itself.

Arabs and Asians, who had supported the other parties in large numbers, were killed indiscriminately. In a single night uncounted lives were lost and over the next few days thousands more fled the islands with only what they could carry.

John Okello established for himself the rank of 'Field Marshal' and, with his mob-battalions, established a reign of terror on the islands. He broadcast bizarre threats and promises of death to all who might oppose him....

When the dust settled the multi-cultural diversity of the islands was radically altered. A one-party state was decreed. Still nervous regarding the possibility of resurgent opposition from their now exiled opponents, the 'revolutionaries' further secured their positions by signing an agreement of confederation with mainland Tanganyika. This would allow thousands of mainland political allies to intervene in any future struggle.

The police forces on the isles were virtually replaced by mainland police loyal to the party and an isolationist curtain fell over the isles which was destined to persist for more than 20 years."

Although the revolution was carried out by only a few hundred people, it had popular support among the majority of black Africans. Thousands of Arabs were killed and thousands more fled the island nation. Sultan Jamshid Abdullah first sought refuge in Mombasa, Kenya, but was denied entry.

He sailed back and went to Dar es Salaam, Tanganyika, where he and his family and others on the vessel were allowed into the country. He later left Tanganyika and went to live in Britain.

The exact number of the people killed in the Zanzibar revolution has never been officially acknowledged but estimates put the figure at least in the thousands. Some say about 17,000 – 20,000 people, mostly Arab, were killed. Other sources, including an American diplomat, Donald Petterson who was in Zanzibar during that time, say 5,000 Arabs were killed. As Petterson stated:

"The population (of Zanzibar) included about 250,000 Africans....In addition to the Africans, Zanzibar had

50,000 Arabs, and about 20,000 Asians of Pakistani and Indian origin. During the revolution, some 5,000 people were killed. Almost all of these were Arabs. That's one tenth of the Arab population. By the time I left the island near the end of 1965, the number of Arabs was less than 25,000....The Asian population was also down by half or more by that time. As the government of Zanzibar became more and more repressive, Asians wanted out, and those who could, left.

Karume, despite a lot of good qualities, became increasingly dictatorial. I didn't see the worst of it during my time and I got along very well with him, as did Frank (Carlucci)....My own relationship with him, and again, this was before he really got bad, was quite good because of the friendship we had established when I was a vice consul, and because I continued to deal with him in his own language, and, of course, treated him with a proper measure of respect." – (Ambassador Donald Petterson, "The Association for Diplomatic Studies and Training Foreign Affairs Oral History Project," interviewed by Charles Stuart Kennedy and Lambert Heyniger; initial interview date: December 13, 1996, pp. 50, and 55).

Probably the most controversial figure in the Zanzibar revolution was John Okello. He played the most important role in the upheaval in spite of attempts by the main leaders of Zanzibar to write him out of history. He is the one who launched and led the revolution. He is the one who was directly responsible for the downfall of the Arab regime in the island nation. The revolution was not led by Karume, Babu or Hanga. They were not even in Zanzibar when the revolution took place. They were in Dar es Salaam, Tanganyika.

When I was growing up in Tanzania, it was John Okello who was the most well-known leader of the Zanzibar revolution. He was acknowledged as the leader of the uprising. The revolution took place when I was 14 years old. And as Petterson explained:

"As the afternoon wore on, a phone call from the rebels finally came. It was from Aboud Jumbe, one of the ministers in the new government, who said that he wanted to come over and take Picard to the revolutionary headquarters. In due course he arrived in an open Land Rover with armed people in it. Jumbe himself was heavily armed.

Fritz and I, along with Jim Ruchti and the executive officer, got into the Land Rover and were driven to Raha Leo (about a mile away), the site of the radio station and the African community center. Raha Leo was now the command headquarters of the revolution. There was electricity in the air when we neared Raha Leo. Hundreds of Africans who were in a very fierce mood ringed the place, many or most armed with everything from sticks to old swords; an occasional rifle was seen.

As we approached the headquarters, better-armed revolutionaries came into sight. They carried police rifles, and a few had automatic weapons. We saw Arab prisoners, some of them bloodied, some lying near the entrance to the revolutionary headquarters, all looking despondent. The crowd was so excited because they knew that at that moment, or soon thereafter, Ali Muhsin, whom they hated, would be brought in....

It was so tense as they began to swarm toward the Land Rover, that Aboud Jumbe yelled at them in Swahili (he had a bullhorn) to get back or he would open fire. They obliged, and a way was cleared for us. We got out of the Land Rover and waited for somebody to come out of revolutionary headquarters.

After a while, a figure emerged, a man dressed in a semi-military uniform. He had on dark shorts and a dark blue shirt, a peaked cap, knee socks in the British style. He approached us, went up to the executive officer, pulled a revolver out of his holster, stuck it right at the exec, either in his ribs as I remember it, or in his face as Jim Ruchti remembered it, and said, 'How do you do? I'm John Okello.'

With that, he put his revolver back in the holster and said there was going to be some target practice behind revolutionary headquarters. Would we like to join in? Well, figuring that the targets might well be some of the captured Arabs, we declined.

He escorted us into Raha Leo. We went up the stairs into a meeting room, where after another wait we were ushered into the room.

Sitting there behind a table with Okello were Abeid Karume, leader of the Afro-Shirazi Party and now the president of the new government, Babu, Hanga, and several others.

Back from Dar es Salaam. Karume had come back to Zanzibar by boat early that morning with Babu and Hanga. The British high commissioner had met with them just before we did, and as he left we entered.

The discussion began. Fritz, first of all, told Okello (who had put his revolver on the table with the barrel pointing at Fritz) that we would not negotiate at gunpoint. Okello made no reply, but picked up and reholstered his weapon. He didn't say much during the ensuing discussion, in which Fritz made the request for an evacuation.

Babu replied angrily, so did Hanga; Karume was uncomfortable. They were angry that the Americans had brought in this warship. And it seemed to us, as we thought about it a bit later, that they didn't know whether the Manley might open fire. In any case, they really didn't care for the evacuation. They didn't want to see it happen, but they agreed to it, fearing there might be consequences otherwise.

Finally, Karume indicated that he would not oppose the request. Then he turned to Okello and said, 'It's your decision.'

Okello sort of shrugged and said, 'All right.'

This made it clear to us there that Okello was indeed of great importance. I say this because later on there were those who belittled Okello's role in the revolution. In fact, the official history of the revolution barely mentions him. But he was the force that pulled it off. Weeks later, others with more political sagacity took control...." – (Ibid., pp. 37 – 38).

Petterson went on to state:

"I formed a friendship with Karume as a result, because I was the only American who spoke Swahili and my Swahili was getting better and better all of the time. We carried out our conversations in Swahili. I was very deferential to him; Fritz was not. Fritz, unfortunately, was a bit patronizing with Karume....

Now Babu was a factor to be reckoned with. He was not an African. He didn't belong to the Afro-Shirazi Party, but his followers, many of whom had been trained in Cuba or other Communist countries, had automatic weapons. They had more firepower than Okello's people, and therefore were a factor to be reckoned with. Babu was the Zanzibar government's foreign minister. I chatted with him, and we agreed we would talk later on. I was told to go back to my own house, which I did.

That began a period of five weeks, during which I was the only American in Zanzibar, pretty heady stuff, a junior Foreign Service officer in charge of the embassy!....

I formed a relationship...also with Babu, who was a very charming guy, a militant left-winger, to say the least, and very shrewd, very intelligent.

Karume was a stolid man, not nearly as bright as Babu, but a man of very real native intelligence. I don't mean to use that term in a derogatory sense at all. He was a very able man in many ways, but impressionable and unsophisticated. As time would go by the results of that

211

would be harmful to Zanzibar...." – (Ibid., pp. 40, 42).

Petterson further stated:

"In the early part of '64,...by this time, Okello had been eased out of power. He was simply not up to the skills of people like Babu and Karume. He had embarrassed them during the revolution. He had been on the radio giving very inflammatory announcements about who would be killed and who would be boiled in oil and all sorts of grisly comments, which embarrassed some Zanzibaris and terrified others.

But as much as Karume and others in the Afro-Shirazi Party leadership and Babu and his followers feared Okello for a time, they must had known that they would be able to get rid of him at some point. He had no political base. All he had was some mainly very unsophisticated people with weapons. Okello was not clever enough to see that disarming these people, which Karume had inveigled him into doing, and putting them into new military units would remove his base of power.

Sometime in March, he went over to the mainland, and when he came back to Zanzibar, Karume met him at the airport and said, 'You can't get off the plane.' Karume flew with him back to Dar es Salaam, where he stayed for a while before being ejected from Tanganyika.

He was a Ugandan who had gone to Kenya when he was a young man, worked as a laborer, then as a mason, and learned construction skills that he took with him to Pemba in 1959....

He ended up in Uganda. From Dar es Salaam, he went to Kenya, where he was expelled. Nobody wanted this man around. He had a fearsome reputation. People were afraid that wherever he went, he might foment a revolution. He had trouble with immigration authorities and was either expelled from places or put in jail.

Finally he returned to Uganda, where he was

212

imprisoned. In 1971, he was seen with Idi Amin shortly after Amin came to power. Then John Okello disappeared from the face of the earth, no doubt killed by Amin." – (Ibid., pp. 49 – 50).

Petterson went on to say:

"In the meantime, Karume was concerned about Babu and his people, who had close relations with the Chinese and who were very well armed. Karume feared that they wanted to take over the revolution. So did Julius Nyerere on the mainland.

Nyerere and Karume decided that they would unify their two countries to undercut Babu. This they did, telling only a very few trusted advisors. Their decision, when announced, came as a complete surprise.

Babu was out of town. As Zanzibar's foreign minister, he was in Pakistan on an official visit. When he heard about the union, he was furious. He later denied that he was upset and said, untruthfully, that he knew in advance about the plan for union. When he came back, he found a new political dispensation. The government of Tanzania, the name chosen for the country later, was in the process of being formed.

Babu was given a post in the Tanzanian government, which was located in Dar es Salaam, since it was the new country's capital. In time, other Zanzibaris who were deemed as possible security threats were transferred to mainland jobs or sent off as diplomats. Babu was effectively stripped of his political power. From then on, he was bitter toward Karume and, especially, Nyerere. With Babu's departure from Zanzibar, Karume's power increased.

The marriage between Tanganyika and Zanzibar was a marriage of convenience. It had strains from the very beginning. As time went on the relationship became more strained as Zanzibar wanted to run its own foreign affairs, have its own military, and control its own foreign exchange. But the union continued. Nyerere wanted it and Karume wanted it, if on his own terms." – (Ibid., p. 50).

There are those who contend that the union was a product of the Cold War, formed at the behest of the United States and Great Britain, especially the United States, to contain or neutralise communist elements in Zanzibar who supported the Zanzibar revolution.

What is deliberately ignored or overlooked by the proponents of this view is Nyerere's commitment to African unity. More than any other East African leader, he relentlessly sought to unite the countries in the region and even offered to delay the independence of Tanganyika so that the three countries of Kenya, Uganda and Tanganyika would emerge from colonial rule on the same day and form a federation under one government.

Just months before the Zanzibar revolution, the leaders of Kenya, Uganda and Tanganyika – Jomo Kenyatta, Milton Obote and Julius Nyerere – met in Nairobi, Kenya, and signed a declaration on 5 June 1963 which explicitly stated that the three countries would form a federation before the end of the year and invited Zanzibar to join the union after the island nation won independence.

The federation was never formed. But that did not discourage Nyerere from pursuing unity on a smaller scale with Zanzibar.

Some observers have questioned why Nyerere did not inform his colleagues – the leaders of Kenya and Uganda – about the impending union or invite them to join the merger since he was so determined to unite the countries in the region.

Informing them or inviting them to join the union would not have served any purpose in terms of regional unification. The three East African countries of Kenya,

214

Uganda and Tanganyika had failed to unite just the month before, December 1963, which they had set as the deadline to form a federation that year when the leaders of those countries met in Nairobi in June and signed a declaration stating that they would unite their countries before the end of the year.

Therefore, Nyerere inviting his colleagues to join the smaller union would not have convinced them of the merits of unification anymore than the earlier attempt to do so – which failed – did. They were simply not interested; not as much Nyerere was in forming an East African federation.

So, Nyerere made the next move, which was to pursue a merger of Tanganyika and Zanzibar.

It is also worth remembering that even as far back as the mid-fifties, Nyerere worked closely with the leaders of Zanzibar in the quest for independence and to bring the two countries even closer than they already were. And prominent leaders of the party in Tanganyika – Tanganyika African National Union (TANU) – which was campaigning for independence on the mainland – went to Zanzibar to help the Afro-Shirazi Party (which came into power after the revolution) to mobilise the masses for the independence struggle in the island nation. One of those prominent figures was Bibi Titi Mohammed, a fiery campaigner and an effective mobiliser of the masses even in Tanganyika itself.

The two – TANU and the Afro-Shirazi Party – were already sisters parties even before the revolution. Therefore it was only natural that their leaders went a step further and decided to unite their countries which were already bound by historical, cultural and linguistic ties; in fact, Africans in Zanzibar were inextricably linked to the mainland. That is where they originated.

All those ties, which facilitated unification of the two countries, had nothing to do with the Cold War or pressure exerted on Nyerere by the United States and Great Britain to force him to form the union.

Even without pressure from the United States and Britain on Nyerere to form the union in order to eliminate a communist threat from the island, Nyerere would have pursued the goal, anyway, to unite the two countries because of the indissoluble ties between them and his Pan-African commitment in pursuit of African unity.

The United States and Great Britain may indeed have wanted the two countries to unite in order to prevent communist leaders in Zanzibar from turning the island nation into a communist state or into "another Cuba" in collusion with Eastern-bloc countries. But Nyerere also wanted to form the union for his own reasons in pursuit of African unity.

Therefore a more compelling argument is that the interests of the United States and Great Britain – to prevent a communist threat in the island nation by placing Zanzibar under the control of Tanganyika – coincided with the interests of Nyerere who wanted to unite the two countries in fulfillment of his Pan-African commitment even if there was no such threat; a goal he had been pursuing long before the Zanzibar revolution.

Pan-Africanism was not a product of the Cold War. It preceded the Cold War. As a philosophy and ideology of decolonisation and unification, it started way back in the 1900s. It did not start after World War II, although it found concrete expression during that period, especially in the fifties and sixties, which became the era of decolonisation on the African continent.

The Cold War argument, competition between the East and the West as the driving force behind the merger of Tanganyika and Zanzibar to protect Western interests in the region and in Africa as a whole, is refuted even by the CIA itself which was active in Zanzibar – and in Tanganyika – according to some of its declassified documents.

While it is true that the United States and Britain

wanted to contain Zanzibar to make sure it did not fall into communist hands, hence the imperative need for unity with Tanganyika which would enable Nyerere and his colleagues on the mainland to control radical elements on the island nation, there is no question that Nyerere pursued unification of the two countries on his own initiative.

He already had a track record of trying to unite African countries, first by forming an East African federation of Kenya, Uganda and Tanganyika, which would have become a reality had his colleagues in Kenya and Uganda shared his passion for unity. According to a CIA declassified report on the Zanzibar revolution, "Zanzibar: The Hundred Days' Revolution," 21 February 1966:

"Toward the end of 1956, Julius Nyerere, Tanganyika's foremost African nationalist and the founder of the Tanganyika African National Union (TANU), is reported to have come to Zanzibar t o urge Africans and Shirazis to stand against the Arabs and to form a political party based on pan-Africanism. On hisi initative, the Afro-Shirazi Party (ASP) was formed in 1957....

In late 1963 Mohammed Shamte, the leader the ZPPP (Zanzibar and Pemba People's Party) and the Chief Minister of Zanzibar's coalition government, stated privatelty that Nyerere and Kambona were basically unfriendly to the present government of Zanzibar 'including Zanzibar Africans like myself.' He expressed bafflement, saying he could not figure out what 'I or any Zanzibar Shirazi had ever done to the Tanganyikans.'

TANU leaders themselves usually advanced two basic reasons for their support of the ASP; first, their close feeling of kinship with the African element in Zanzibar and, second, their fear of Communisin or proto-Communism in the ZNP (Zanzibar Nationalist Party), especially people like Babu. Although there was no talk of alliance or annexation, it no doubt was even then the view of the   Tanganyikan leaders that Zanzibar ought to be associated closely with Tanganyika.

Three other non-bloc countries, besides Tanganyika, are known to have supported the ASP (Afro-Shirazi Party) before the revolution in 1964.

Ghana was, perhaps, rather slower than Tanganyika in coming out openly in favor of the ASP, but by at least 1961 the die was cast. In that year, the Ghana Bureau of African Affairs sent over $15,000 to assist the ASP in the election; later that year, Ghanaian legal assistance was afforded the ASP in defense of individual Africans accused of offenses committed during the election riots; at the end of 1962 the ASP opened an office in Accra; and in early 1963 the High Commissioner of Ghana in Uganda held private discussions with ASP leaders on the subject of financial assistance for the ASP.

Prior to the independence of Zanzibar, the Ethiopian Government also provided financial assistance to the ASP, on the grounds that it represented the majority and was the only predominately (sic) African political party. Haile Selassie, who was under considerable pressure from Egypt, was particularly sympathetic to the ASP's concern about Arab influence in Zanzibar. He was reportedly delighted when the coup ousted the Arab-dominated government in January 1964, and the Ethiopian Government was among the first to recognize the new regime.

While the ASP maintained liaison with these several ruling African parties and with Israel, the ZNP (Zanzibar Nationalist Party) found its major international ally in Egypt....

Sometime in mid-1963, probably soon after the June elections, a group of ASP leaders, including Hanga, went to Tanganyika to ask for money and arms in support of their revolutionary plan. Tanganyikan complicity with the ASP has been well established. Although President Nyerere may not have been aware of the extent to which Tanganyikan Defense Minister Kambona was involved in supplying arms and money to the Zanzibar revolutionaries, he obviously knew and approved of the general plan for the revolution.

Apparently, the coup was planned for March or April 1964. The most important figure in the plot was Hanga; Karume personally was never involved; it is doubtful that Othman Shariff knew of the plan....

Although Zanzibar's union with Tanganyika was in his interests – inasmuch as it got Babu off the island – Karume apparently was not initially enthusiastic about the idea; certainly, he was not as strongly in favor of the union as Hanga, who claims that he and Kambona agreed when they were students together in London that Tanganyika and Zanzibar should be united one day.

The idea of a union was not a new one. Nyerere probably had it in the back of his mind when he first became involved in Zanzibar politics, beginning around 1956. For years, he had looked forward to the time when an African government would come to power in Zanzibar, at which time he planned to merge the two countries. His feeling of urgency about the union in March and April 1964 was probably a reflection of his concern that Babu was well on his way to consolidating his position in Zanzibar and his belief that only decisive action taken in time could save Zanzibar's African revolution from Arab control.

There is evidence that Nyerere was concerned about the excessive degree of Communist influence in Zanzibar, but press and other comment in the West was probably wrong in emphasizing this as Nyerere's chief concern. It seems that the Tanganyikan President deliberately exeaggerated his fears that Zanzibar was falling under Communist control; it was an argument that he could use most convincingly in the West to win support for his move to absorb Zanzibar into Tanganyika.

Whereas in private conversations with Westerners, Nyerere has always emphasized the anti-Communist line as the main rationale for the union, in public he has taken the position that the the union was simply a natural step toward African unity.

The important point is that the union of Tanganyika and Zanzibar *was a Tanganyikan initative* (italics not in the original text; added by me – Godfrey Mwakikagile). Although the idea had occurred to Western officials as the obvious solution to the Zanzibar problem, the subject was never officially discussed with the Tanganyikans. Thus, it appears that the move to form the union was strictly African in origin, without British or American inspiration; the news of the event caught all of the major world powers by surprise.

For more than a month, Nyerere and his representatives had been conducting secret negotiations with Karume and other Zanzibari leaders. Although they had suceeded in convincing several of them – including Hanga and Twala – that it was in their best interests to follow the Tanganyikan guidance, Karume was not immediately persuaded.

Finally, Nyerere's threat to recall the Tanganyikan police contingent had the force of an ultimatum. Faced.with the prospect of being deprived of the support he needed against Babu, Karume agreed to the union.

As an independent nation, Zanzibar had lasted just one hundred days. In its brief and turbulent career as a sovereign state, it had faced a bitter internal struggle for power, near economic collapse, and an intensive Communist offensive. It is not surprising that its new African leaders should have found it impossible to preserve their independence against these odds. Zanzibar was not really equipped for independence. To preserve the integrity of the African revolution they had just won, its leaders had to sacrifice the independence they had just been given. Zanzibar's future had always seemed in the long run to lie with Tanganyika. It was only surprising that this should have been realized so quickly....

During March and April Nyerere frequently invited

Karume to Dar es Salaam for private talks, where he would be away from the influence of Babu and Hanga. Reportedly, the Tanganyikan President was very worried about what was happening in Zanzibar and was anxious to bolster Karume. In their, Nyerere first broached the subject of a Tanganyika-Zanzibar merger to Karume. Although it was not his sole reason for the union, he definitely believed that a merger would strengthen Karume's power position in Zanzibar. His feeling of urgency about the matter was probably due to his concern to ensure Karume's dominance as soon as possible.

Before the union, the main thing that kept Karume in power was the Tanganyikan police force contigent, which Nyerere s e n t to the island as a measure of protection for Karume against Okello and his armed followers. After Okello's departure, Karuine kept the police as protection against Babu and the pro-Communist elements that were attempting to secure position of power in the government. Although they were nominally under the control of Karume, they took their orders from Nyerere. Without such concrete support from Nyerere, Karume would probably not have been able to stay in power in Zanzibar....

Even before the revolution, the affiliation of Zanzibar with Tanganyika had been under discussion in the context of a larger East African Federation. Nyerere, Karume and Hanga were on the record as favoring the Federation; Babu was opposed. It had never been a question of a union between Tanganyika and Zanzibar alone, however; that possibility arose as a direct result of the revolution.

As noted earlier, it was Nyerere who initiated the negotiations leading to the union. Much has been written about his reasons for wanting a Tanganyika-Zanzibar union. Press comment in the U.S. and other Western countries has tended to emphasize the cold war aspects of the situation....He has said on a number of occasions that he was personally furious with the way the American and

British press treated the union....

On the question of the 'African revolution' Nyerere is deeply emotional. The possibility that Babu and his Arab followers might come to dominate the Government of Zanzibar was anathema; to Nyerere, it would have been a repudiation of the Zanzibar revolution.

By late March or early April, Babu had consolidated his position to the point where a take-over by the Arabs appeared imminent. Nyerere could have been expected to do anything and everything in his power to prevent such an eventuality. His solution was the union. As the best way to guarantee the integrity of the Zanzibar revolution, he decided on a union of the two countries in which the Zanzibar Arabs would be absorbed by an overwhelming African majority.

In the case of Zanzibar, Nyerere's natural concern to safeguard the 'African revolution' everywhere in Africa was closely bound up with Tanganyikan national interests. For years, Tanganyikans, including Nyerere, had had the idea that Zanzibar was really a part of T anganyika. They had looked forward to the time when an African government would come to power in Zanzibar, at which time they planned to merge the two countries. It may well have been his interest in a Tanganyika-Zanzibar union that prompted Nyerere to become involved in Zanzibar politics in the first place, beginning in 1956....

Besides Nyerere, Defence Minister Kambona is reported to have long believed that Tanganyika should absorb Zanzibar. Although the union was reportedly a Nyerere initiative and Nyerere remained in full control of the negotiations, this is one instance in which Kambona worked in complete harmony with the President....

Hanga was probably the most receptive to the Tanganyikan initiative. He has stated privately that he and Kambona agreed that Tanganyika and Zanzibar should unite when they were students together in London. Nyerere has also commented that Hanga favored the union even more than Karume. In July URTZ (United Republic of Tanzania) Foreign Affairs parliamentary secretary Tambwe said that

Nyerere was 'paticularly pleased with Hanga because he is, above all, an African nationalist who really supports the union'....

The U.S. Government did not have any earlier indication that a union between Tanganyika and Zanzibar was being negotiated....

By all reports, Karume and Nyerere are determined to see the union through.

Nyerere and Kambona and other Tanganyikan officials have said that they will never, under any circumstances, accept its dissolution, that they are prepared to maintain it at all costs – even to the point of armed intervention. So far, they have avoided anything resembling a showdown with the Zanzibaris, but apparently they are prepared to do everything, including intervene (sic) with force, before they see the union crumble. All indications are that the union is here to stay." – ("Intelligence Study – Zanzibar: The Hundred Days' Revolution (ESAU XXX), No. 18, RSS No. 0013/66," 21 February 1966, pp. 1 – 2, v, xiii – xv, 9 – 10, 63 – 64, 118 – 119, 120 – 121, 122, 123, 125, 136).

In forming the union, Nyerere emphasised the imperative need for unity among African countries, even on a small scale as happened in the case of Tanganyika and Zanzibar. Even a communist like Hanga who strongly supported the union from the beginning did so for the same reason. Had he wanted to establish and consolidate a communist base for himself and fellow Marxist-Leninists in Zanzibar, he would not have agreed to unite Zanzibar with Tanganyika. And had the union been a product of Western powers to neutralise communists in Zanzibar, he would not have supported a merger which was deliberately intended, by Westerners, to destroy him politically.

Hanga was widely known as an uncompromisng African nationalist and gave an emotional speech in the Zanzibar Revolutionary Council urging his compatriots to approve the merger of the two countries. He supported the union, not to serve Western interests but to advance the cause of Pan-

Africanism and the wellbeing of Africa. If he committed political suicide by supporting the union, he did so for the sake of Africa, not the West. And as Nyerere himself, the driving force behind the union, stated in his speech to a special session of the Tanganyika National Assembly on 25 April 1964 concerning the merger:

"The union between Tanganyika and Zanzibar has been determined by our two Governments for the interests of Africa and African Unity. There is no other reason.

Unity in our continent does not have to come via Moscow or Washington. It is an insult to Africa to read cold war politics into every move towards African Unity. Africa has its own maturity and its own will.

Our unity is inspired by a very simple ideology – unity. We do not propose this Union in order to support any of the 'isms' of this world. We propose it in order to support and strengthen Africa, and our particular part of Africa....

We shall work for African Unity and African Freedom, and we shall remain non-aligned in world power struggles which do not concern us. Each international issue will be determined on its own merit and our friendship towards all nations will be affected only by their actions towards us. We shall not allow our friends to choose our enemies for us." – (Julius K. Nyerere, *Freedom and Unity: Uhuru na Umoja*, Dar es Salaam, Tanzania: Oxford University Press, 1969, p. 292).

There is no question that the Zanzibar revolution provided an impetus for unification of the two countries: Tanganyika and Zanzibar. But is was not the sole or even the prime determinant, as demonstrated above. It only facilitated the merger, and at a faster pace than would otherwise have been the case involving gradual consummation of the union of the two countries.

The successful revolution led to the establishment of Zanzibar as a republic under the leadership of the Afro-

Shirazi Party (ASP). Sheikh Abeid Amani Karume, leader of ASP, became president; Kassim Hanga became prime minister, and Abdulrahman Mohamed Babu, minister of defence and external affairs.

Babu was the leader of Umma, meaning the Party of the Masses, whose members defected from the Arab-dominated Zanzibar Nationalist Party (ZNP) to whom the British transferred power on attainment of independence on 10 December 1963.

The People's Republic of Zanzibar and Pemba, as the new nation was officially known, was ruled by a Revolutionary Council composed of 30 members. It was the new government. Zanzibar became a one-party state and land and other assets including major means of production were nationalised in pursuit of socialist transformation of the country.

The Zanzibar revolution was hailed as a victory for the oppressed masses who had endured oppression including slavery under Arab domination for centuries and was supported by many people across Africa and in other parts of the world, especially in the Third World and socialist countries.

Among African leaders who were the strongest supporters of the revolution were Nyerere and Nkrumah. Other African leaders who supported and defended the revolution included Emperor Haile Selassie, Nigerian Prime Minister Abubakar Tafawa Balewa, and Nigerian Foreign Affairs Minister Jaja Wachuku.

Castro also supported the Zanzibar revolution, as did East Germany, the People's Republic of China and the Soviet Union.

One of the leading figures in the Zanzibar Revolutionary Council, Sheikh Thabit Kombo, stated years later in one of his speeches to the members of Tanzania's ruling party – Chama Cha Mapinduzi (CCM) which means Party of the Revolution or the Revolutionary Party – that besides Nyerere, Nkrumah also helped to

225

finance the Zanzibar revolution. As Andrew Nyerere, President Nyerere's eldest son, stated in his letter in 2004 in response to a number of questions I asked him when I was working on the second edition of my book about his father, *Nyerere and Africa: End of an Era*:

"As you look at the history of Mwalimu Nyerere and his contemporaries, you see that they were like a team who were born at the same time for the purpose of liberating the country from British imperialism.

So we do well to find out the truth about what these men did. We see, for example, that there is evidence that Kwame Nkrumah financed the Zanzibar Revolution.

In a speech to the Party, Sheikh Thabit Kombo gives an account of it. He explains how during the election in Zanzibar, there had been great carnage and many Arabs were killed. And Nkrumah had financed this. He says it was not the fault of the Arabs that the disturbances started. They had masterminded it, and started the trouble.

But it is just modesty to say that the Arabs made no mistakes because this was a government which was based on slave trading.

So, during this election, there was a lot of trouble and many Arabs were killed, and Thabit Kombo and Mr. Karume fled to Dar es Salaam. They decided that they should go to Nyerere to discuss this with him, to find out what was his opinion.

And when they met Nyerere, they discussed this and he told them to go back, and said, 'I will send you money, I will send you guns.'

They went back and there was a trial. A white judge came from London. And Karume was asked by the prosecutor, 'Do you know, Mr. Karume, when you started that fracas, 75 Arabs died?' And Mr. Karume made a very memorable statement. He spoke out in exasperation. He asked, 'Who did you want to die?'

This is a statement which all the oppressed people of

the world should remember. It is all on tape. I made copies of it and sent it to quite a few people."

Tanganyika under Nyerere provided both financial and material support including security forces to restore order soon after the revolution. About three months later, Zanzibar united with Tanganyika to form Tanzania, the first union of independent states ever formed on the continent and which still exists today more than 50 years later.

One of the most dramatic pictures from that period shows Abdulrahman Mohamed Babu rowing a canoe reportedly from Zanzibar to Dar e Salaam, Tanganyika – although that was never confirmed. The new government under the Zanzibar Nationalist Party (ZNP) to whom power had been transferred by the British was getting ready to arrest him before he fled to Dar es Salaam, reportedly in a canoe. He later became one of the most prominent members in the union cabinet and one of the most influential leaders in Africa and in the entire Third World.

He died in London on 5 August 1996. He was 72. The government of Tanzania under President Benjamin Mkapa paid for the funeral and to bring his body back home from London. He was given an official burial – not a state funeral – in spite of the fact that he had not been a cabinet member since 1972.

He was buried in Zanzibar at a funeral attended by many Tanzanian leaders and others. And he will always be remembered as one of the main architects of the Zanzibar revolution.

It is a revolution that had an impact beyond Zanzibar and the rest of East Africa. In some fundamental respects, its impact was continental in scope in terms of ideological influence and political re-alignment of allies. And as the former Zanzibar resident cited earlier and who was in the island nation during the revolution stated elsewhere in

"Nine Hour Revolution":

"Zanzibar is well known for it's 'Shortest War in History.' A 19th Century battle that lasted only about 45 minutes but served to demonstrate for all time the Iron fist beneath the pre-colonial European domination of East Africa.

What is less well known is the 20th Century record Zanzibar set for similar brevity in the Zanzibar Revolution of 1964.

In this Revolution a government with over a century of continuity was toppled in less than a day. Essentially a settler society, with well-defined Arabic, Indian, Swahili, Comorian and indigenous elements, and ruled by an hereditary sultan, the newly independent nation of Zanzibar vanished in astounding suddenness.

That night was full of suspense and surprise, courage and despair. It began at 3 a.m. on the day just before a large religious holiday.

The holiday prompted large numbers of people to congregate in and around Stone Town. They set up tents or just sleep under the palms while awaiting the opening of the festivities in the morning. Among the crowds were large numbers of young men; some of these men were followers of a minor politician named John Okello.

Just how many men actually followed Okello into revolutionary battle is of some dispute.

It is clear that by the end of that fateful day thousands had joined the revolutionaries but this was after the results were known.

It's also true that Field Marshal Okello talked of having had 4 'battalions' in the field against the government forces that night, but how men many were really there when it counted?

Okello reported that the revolution began when he marched in the dead of night on the Ziwani Police Barracks (and Armory) at the head of the 250 men of his

'4th Battalion.' At 3:00 a.m. he ordered his men to cut the wire surrounding this fortified compound.

That was the first real revolutionary act and it served to 'separate the men from the boys.' Okello said of his men at the time, 'The enormity of our predicament was suddenly obvious to them: we, armed with pangas, spears and a few motor car springs were going to face the risk of close combat with men armed with automatic rifles...' All but 40 men deserted or refused to crawl through the wire.

These 40 men seized the island of Zanzibar and toppled a dynasty that had ruled the islands through 12 Sultans for over 133 years.

The revolutionaries crawled to within 25 meters of the Barracks building. Inside, asleep were scores of paramilitary police. However like most sensible people on Zanzibar they slept on the upper floors of the building, where cooling ocean breeze could ventilate the hot tropical nights. Only two men were awake and on guard duty below.

John Okello and his men rushed at these guards. Automatic fire rang out and three of the 4th battalion men went down. However one of sentries also fell, downed by an arrow shot by a revolutionary named Albert. By then Okello had closed on the remaining sentry. It was here that the deciding moment of the revolution occurred. The two crashed together. The Field Marshall tells us that 'I got hold of the gun, we fought and I managed to hit him in the cheek with the gun butt.' The firing stopped.

His men were now at the gates of the armory where hundreds of modern weapons and thousands of rounds of ammunition were locked up. The police above, who were unarmed, (in keeping with standard peacetime practice, all weapons were locked away 'for safekeeping' when the officers were off duty), attempted to storm down the single exterior staircase and enter the fray.

However, the 4th Battalion men unleashed a rain of spears, arrows and stones on the stunned troops and they piled up upon themselves on the narrow staircase. Okello's liberated rifle, which had only three bullets left, decided the issue with a short burst of fire. The police retreated back upstairs to look for ropes to lower men out of the windows.

It was too late. The doors of the armory gave way and the 4th Battalion rushed in. Soon every man was armed with a modern automatic rifle. The 'Freedom Fighters' who had started the night armed with sharpened automobile springs now were the best equipped force on the island. They poured a fuselage of fire into the upstairs rooms and very shortly the surviving police surrendered.

The sultan's forces made one serious attempt to counter attack the rebels. The 'flying squad' arrived on the scene about an hour after the defeat of the Ziwani garrison. These 75 or so men had only light duty firearms and were no match for the now heavily armed Battalion ensconced in the fortified Armory.

The rebels allowed the sultans' paramilitary police to approach and then poured an overwhelming storm of fire into them. The firing was so intense that the surrounding bush caught fire and the police retreated in despair.

With their new base secure, guns were distributed to the other three battalions (who had encircled but not yet attacked other key sites). In short order the few other police posts and the communications centres were overrun and captured. The most serious resistance was offered by the Malindi Police Station, where firing could still be heard in the late hours of the morning.

However, by noon, the Sultan had fled. The rest is history."

There are many conflicting reports about what actually happened on that day. But there is no question that neighbouring Tanganyika supported the revolution; so did Ghana under Nkrumah according to the testimony of one of the leading figures in the Zanzibar Revolutionary

Council, Sheikh Thabit Kombo, which became the government after the revolution.

Regardless of the different interpretations on what happened in Zanzibar during that period, and why the revolution took place, what is clear to black Africans in Zanzibar and to many other Africans elsewhere, and to thoughtful non-African observers, is that the revolution was not a spontaneous uprising. It was a product of cumulative suffering blacks had endured for centuries under Arab domination.

It was a powerful response to such oppression and exploitation, as clearly shown by the overwhelming support the revolution got from the vast majority of black Africans in the island nation. The revolution was also an integral part of the nationalist tide sweeping the continent during the era of decolonisation.

A lot has been said about the Soviet Union, the People's Republic of China, East Germany, Cuba and other socialist countries and their involvement in Zanzibar during those turbulent times. What is overlooked or deliberately ignored in all this is the nationalist aspirations of the black African majority in the island nation. They wanted to be free.

And it was not just the socialist countries which got involved in Zanzibar. The United States also had a strong interest in what was going on and looked at Zanzibar from an American perspective influenced by the Cold War to secure American geopolitical interests in the region and neutralise Soviet and Chinese influence.

The policies of both ideological camps were dictated by Cold War imperatives with regard to most parts of the Third World. And Zanzibar was no exception. Before the revolution, Zanzibar was not high on the American agenda of Cold War politics. But the revolution changed all that, prompting American officials to draw up contingency plans on what to do in case they had to intervene in Zanzibar.

Unfortunately, their perception of Zanzibar was refracted through the prism of the Cold War to the exclusion of any other interpretation which would have been more rational and realistic than what they had.

Declassified documents from the US State Department that were made available in 1999 a few years after the end of the Cold War precipitated by the collapse of the Soviet Union shed some light on what American leaders thought should be done about Zanzibar because of the revolution that had taken place in the island nation.

According to these documents, on 7 February 1964, the US State Department prepared a report for President Lyndon Johnson which stated:

"The crux of the Zanzibar matter is to prevent its takeover by the Communists. The new regime is an uneasy coalition of African nationalist and pro-Communist elements, each struggling for power. We are gravely concerned that the role of the nationalists may be deteriorating.

The elements of preventing a Communist takeover include:

1. Elimination or control of 'Field Marshal' Okello and armed thugs, who represent a continuing threat to order and stability.

2. Development of an independent nationalist government probably built around President Karume, leader of the Afro-Shirazis.

3. Political containment of any pro-Communist force, including Babu and Hanga, if they are unwilling to work with Karume. Babu and Hanga have had strong ties with Peiping and Moscow. Nevertheless Nyerere believes in the showdown they are African nationalists who can be and must be worked with. This is questionable.

4. Support and strengthening of Nyerere in Tanganyika and Kenyatta in Kenya.

...The U.K. has a military capability in the area to

disarm Okello and his followers and to maintain order. It would do this on its own initiative if British nationals were endangered. Otherwise, understandably, it would desire a written GOZ request from Karume. Only the British can act militarily with adequate effectiveness.

...Every effort must be made to induce the British to take effective action. Since any definitive U.S. action would be based on the extent and type of action by the British, alternative measures the U.S. might take diplomatically, covertly or through economic or technical assistance would best be considered in light of the British program.

Despite the short-term stability which the U.K. military presence probably will insure, basic problems will remain, making British disengagement extremely difficult. Dependable African security forces cannot quickly be developed.

At the same time, East Africa's leaders will be under mounting domestic pressure to seek early U.K. withdrawal. Domestic and general African pressures could lead to a British withdrawal before internal security forces have been adequately strengthened." – (*Foreign Relations of the United States 1964 - 1968*, pp. 610 – 611).

Because of the revolutionary nature of the Zanzibar regime which was perceived to be anti-West, the United States assumed a more active role in African affairs and did everything it could to contain the revolutionary elements in Zanzibar. When Zanzibar united with Tanganyika, American officials hoped that President Nyerere would have a moderating influence on the revolutionary government in Zanzibar.

However, he did little to please the West. Tanzania under his leadership was non-aligned and went on to establish strong ties with many countries in the socialist camp – while also maintaining ties with the West – and adopted policies for socialist transformation of the country along African lines in pursuit of African socialism; what Nyerere called *ujamaa*, a Kiswahili term meaning "familyhood," based on the traditional African communal way of life.

The revolutionaries in Zanzibar had, of course, already embraced socialism although of a more radical kind with some of them espousing Marxist principles.

Although the Zanzibar revolution had an impact beyond its borders, it was not engineered, orchestrated or manipulated by external forces and elements. It was an indigenous phenomenon and a military expression of the political aspirations of the oppressed black African majority.

Arabs and other non-blacks who supported the revolution also wanted a new society restructured along egalitarian lines in which rule by an oligarchy of whatever stripes would have no place under the new dispensation. And that is what gave the revolution its transcendent and nationalistic character as a non-racist uprising, getting full support from some Arabs like Abdulrahman Mohamed Babu who was a nationalist more than anything else.

Whatever happened in the island nation, and regardless of the different interpretations which are still being given today by many people including politicians, scholars and laymen alike, there is no question that the revolution was a momentous upheaval of cataclysmic proportions in the context of Zanzibar and changed the island nation forever. Zanzibar was never to be the same again.

The revolution also played a critical role in the consummation of the union of Tanganyika and Zanzibar on 26 April 1964. Both leaders, Nyerere of Tanganyika and Karume of Zanzibar, wanted their countries to unite. But the union would probably not have taken place when it did had it not been for the Zanzibar revolution.

The revolution provided an impetus towards unification for a number of reasons. Black Africans in Zanzibar were afraid that their former Arab rulers would try to come back and re-institute Arab domination of the island nation. To prevent that, they sought protection from Tanganyika, a much bigger country that was also predominantly black, by forming a union under one government.

Nyerere and other leaders of Tanganyika were also concerned that instability in Zanzibar – possibly leading to anarchy – would have a direct impact on the mainland and negative consequences which should be avoided before it was too late. Unification of the two countries would be the best way to avert such a catastrophe. It would also enable Nyerere to control some of the far more radical elements in the government of Zanzibar.

Some observers contend that the union of Tanganyika and Zanzibar was a product of the Cold War. They argue that the United States wanted to neutralise communist influence in the island nation. And a union with Tanganyika would provide such a solution.

Frank Carlucci, who was the American consul in Zanzibar during the revolution and who later became director of the CIA and US secretary of defence, said he is not sure whether motivation for the union came from Nyerere or the American government. But he admits that there was concern in the American government that if the situation in Zanzibar was not contained, the island nation would become a communist stronghold.

A number of American officials said they feared Zanzibar would become another Cuba or the Cuba of Africa. And the Zanzibari leader who was feared the most as the spearhead of such communist penetration was Abdulrahman Mohamed Babu.

Babu was a subject of discussion in many circles. For example, in Nigeria, American Ambassador Averill Harriman asked Nigerian leaders what they thought about Babu. Nigerian Foregin Minister Dr. Jaja Wachuku assured Harriman that he had known Babu for many years and that Babu was an African nationalist more than anything else.

It is true that the United States denounced Zanzibar as "the Cuba of Africa" after the January 1964 revolution led by John Okello who toppled the Arab-dominated regime and transferred power to the predominantly black majority and their allies including a number of Arabs, Iranians (originally from Shiraz in Iran), and others. But it is also true that the people who led the revolution were not interested in substituting one master for another – capitalist or communist – and their uprising was not communist-inspired.

The communist threat in Zanzibar was overly exaggerated. Even the leaders who could have established communism on the isles dismissed the threat. They were explicit in their intentions and would not have shied away from acknowledging that they were going to establish communism in Zanzibar – which would have been an open secret, anyway, sooner rather than later.

They included Abdulrahman Mohammed Babu, the most prominent leader with communist leanings on the islands and whom the CIA followed closely, as it did all the other leaders including Abdullah Kassim Hanga. According to one of the declassified documents in the US Archives written from Nigeria by the American diplomat and statesman Averell Harriman (he was a trip to Nigeria as a special envoy) to President Lyndon B. Johnson and Secretary of State Dean Rusk on March 25, 1964:

"In long talks with Prime Minister Abubakar (Tafawa Balewa) and Foreign Minister (Jaja) Wachuku,...both minimized concern I expressed for Communist takeover in Zanzibar, assured me that Karume was sensible and Babu was primarily African nationalist and would not permit Communist takeover. When I pressed Wachuku, he firmly insisted he could guarantee Babu whom he had personally known a long time." – (Averell Harriman, Johnson Library, National Security File, International Meetings and

236

Travel File, Africa, Box 31, Harriman's Trip, 3/64. Confidential; Priority; Exdis. Passed to the White House. See also, US Diplomatic Archives: Nigeria (1964 - 1968), *Foreign Relations of the United States 1964 - 1968, Vol. XXIV)*.

The dispatch from Nigeria by Harriman was followed by other reports on the potential for communist penetration of Africa during the early years of independence in the sixties.

Ambassador Harriman himself in another report to President Johnson on 28 October 1964, about nine months after the Zanzibar revolution and just one day before the Union of Tanganyika and Zanzibar was renamed Tanzania (on October 29, 1964), conceded:

"Not a single new African nation has succumbed to Communist domination."

The report is one of the declassified documents published in *Foreign Relations of the United States 1964 – 1968*. The document has also been been cited by other people including Kevin Kelly, "How Communism Affected US Policy in East Africa," in *The East African*, Nairobi, Kenya, 6 December 1999, the same year the declassified documents from the US State Department were released.

Officials in the Johnson Administration were convinced that communists had played an active role in the Zanzibar revolution on 12 January 1964, according to released documents contained in the 850-page volume of *Foreign Relations of the United States 1964 – 1968*. As one US State Department background paper, 7 February 1964, asserted: "There was obvious communist involvement in Zanzibar."

Yet, the same officials admitted that disturbances in other parts of East Africa – the army mutinies in

Tanganyika, Kenya, and Uganda in January 1964 –
around the same time did not appear to be communist-
inspired.

In fact, President Nyerere himself resolutely
maintained:

"(There was) no evidence whatsoever to suggest that the
mutinies in Tanganyika were inspired by outside forces –
either Communist or imperialist." – (Julius Nyerere,
quoted in the East African Standard, Nairobi, Kenya, 13
February 1964; cited by Ali Mazrui, Towards A Pax
Africana, op. cit., p. 153).

The army mutinies started in Tanganyika on 20 January
1964 and spread to Kenya and Uganda within two days.
The mutineers demanded higher salaries and expulsion of
British army officers whom they said should be replaced
by African officers. But there was also potential for a
military coup in each of those mutinies.

In Tanganyika, the involvement of union labour leaders
Christopher Kasanga Tumbo and Victor Mkello who had
close ties to the mutineers created strong suspicion that the
mutiny was an attempt to overthrow the government.

There was also a common logic that linked the
mutinies to the Zanzibar revolution. The revolution was an
African uprising against Arab domination and had a
distinct racial component (it was also a class conflict
between dispossessed blacks and the merchants and
landowners who were mostly Arab and Indian), as was
clearly demonstrated during the revolution in which many
Arabs and Indians, as well as some Comorians, but mostly
Arabs, were massacred.

The highest figures of those who were killed – 13,000
to 20,000 – come mostly come from the supporters of the
old Arab regime who, even today, are still opposed to the
union of Tanganyika and Zanzibar.

The army mutinies in Tanganyika and in the other two

East African countries (Kenya and Uganda), partly inspired by the uprising in Zanzibar, also had a racial dimension. In addition to demanding an increase in salaries, the mutineers also demanded the replacement of British army officers with African ones to Africanise the armed forces all the way to the highest level in a true spirit of independence by eradicating the last vestiges of colonialism.

The mutiny in Tanganyika was not only the first one among the three in East Africa; it was also the most successful in terms of "usurpation" of power as the only mutiny that almost ended up in a military coup, according to the evidence gathered from an analysis of records and documents contained in the archives of the East Africana Collection at the University of Dar es Salaam, Tanzania. As Professor Ronald Aminzade states in "The Politics of Race and Nation: Citizenship and Africanization in Tanganyika":

"(The) abortive military mutiny on January 20, 1964, (was) motivated by demands for higher pay and the replacement of British officers by Africans.

The six-day mutiny, which began at Colito Barracks (renamed Lugalo Barracks) in Dar es Salaam and spread to troops atationed at Tabora (and Nachingwea), appears to have been well-planned. After arresting their British officers, soldiers built roadblocks at strategic points throughout the city, seized the State House (the president's official residence, although Nyerere did not live there but in a simple house on the outskirts of the city in Msasani, and used the State House, popularly known as Ikulu, only for official functions), police stations, airport, radio station, and railway station, and placed guards at critical postal, telegraph, and bank buildings.

The Tanganyikan mutiny sparked similar uprisings in the Ugandan and Kenyan armies as well as the looting and pillaging of Asian shops in Dar es Salaam.

Hundreds of people were arrested during the looting in the commercial areas of the capital. Local forces of order were weakened by the government's earlier decision to send the Dar es Salaam Field Police (known by the acronym FFU - Field Force Units), a contingent of 300 men, to Zanzibar to help restore order on the troubled island.

The fear that racial violence might escalate was linked to the revolution in Zanzibar, which took place in the preceding week and was accompanied by race riots, the murder of hundreds of Arab and Asian shopkeepers, and the mass exodus of Asians to the mainland.

Field Marshal John Okello, who had seized power in Zanzibar, declared: 'We are friends of all Europeans and other foreigners. It is only the Ismailis and certain other Indian groups and people of Arab descent we do not like.' (*Tanganyika Standard*, January 17, 1964).

The racial antagonisms behind the army mutiny were evident in the behavior of the mutinous soldiers stationed in the town of Tabora, who beat up all Europeans and Asians who crossed their path. (Listowel, 1965: p. 433). During the looting of Asian shops in Dar es Salaam, 17 people were killed and 23 seriously injured. (*Tanganyika Standard*, January 22, 1964). Rumors spread throughout the capital that Nyerere had fled the country and a general strike was imminent. Nyerere, while still hiding, broadcast a radio message on the second day of the rebellion, to reassure the country that he was still in power.

Had they moved quickly, the mutineers could probably have seized control of the government, but the rebellious army units had no plans to launch a coup d'etat. Rebellious soldiers negotiated with Minister of Defence Oscar Kambona and agreed to release the 30 captured European (British) officers, who were quickly flown out of the country.

Kambona had offered to replace all European officers with Africans and discuss wages, provided the troops

240

release the officers and return to their barracks.

Nyerere's first public act, after he emerged from hiding on January 22, was to tour the city on foot, visiting the areas of looted Asian shops to express his condolences to Asian shopkeepers who had been targets of violence. (*Tanganyika Standard*, January 23, 1964).

Only after the mutineers began to negotiate with militant leaders of the trade union movement did the government reluctantly ask the British to intervene (the British were soon replaced by Nigerian troops at Nyerere's request at an urgent OAU summit he called in Addis Ababa, Ethiopia, to deal with the crisis). Trade union leaders hoped to take advantage of the situation and turn the mutiny into a coup d'etat.

The two most prominent proponents of Africanization, trade union leaders Christopher (Kasanga) Tumbo, who had returned from Kenya, and Victor Mkello, met in Morogoro to plan a new government. (Listowel, 1965: pp. 437 - 38). On January 25, British troops quickly took control of the barracks and disarmed the rebels, killing five African soldiers in the confrontation.

The army mutiny proved to be a great embarrassment for the government, which was forced to call on troops of the former colonial power to restore public order. Yet the uprising also provided the occasion to move decisively against those who had continued to press for Africanization.

After the abortive mutiny, the government arrested 50 policemen implicated in the uprising, reorganized the military (while Nigerian troops sent to Tanganyika by the Nigerian Federal Government provided defence for the country), and replaced British officers to defuse the issue of Africanization.

It used Preventive Detention Law, rarely invoked since its passage in 1962, to order the arrest of more than 200 trade union leaders, many of whom were released after questioning.

Fifteen soldiers were sentenced to prison for their role in the mutiny. The trade union movement was brought firmly under the control of the government by the dissolution of the Tanganyika Federation of Labour (TFL) and establishment in its place of the TANU-controlled National Union of Tanganyika Workers (NUTA).

Several days after the suppression of the mutiny, on January 28, 1964, Nyerere announced the appointment of a presidential commission to pursue the plans that had been announced earlier to create a single-party state,
"
subsequently instituted in the constitution of 1965. – (Ronald R. Aminzade, "The Politics of Race and Nation: Citizenship and Africanization in Tanganyika," in Diane E. Davis, ed., *Political Power and Social Theory, Vol. 14*, Amsterdam: Elsevier Science, 2001, pp. 53 – 90; Ronald Aminzade, "The Africanization Debate, The Failed Army Mutiny, and a Restructured State," in Ronald Aminzade, *Race, Nation, and Citizenship in Post-Colonial Africa: The Case of* Tanzania, New York: Cambridge University Press, 2013, 79 – 89).

Professor Aminzade of the sociology department at the University of Minnesota conducted his research in Tanzania, published on 2 December 1998.

Reports on the mutiny in Tanganyika were also published in the *Tanganyika Standard*, Dar es Salaam, 22 – 23 January 1964.

In spite of all the speculations about the spectre of communism looming over East Africa, especially Tanganyika and Zanzibar, we see that from all available evidence, it is clear that communism – or any form of external involvement or manipulation – was not a factor in the army mutiny in Tanganyika or those in Kenya and Uganda; three inter-related incidents in a chain reaction that almost plunged the three countries into chaos during those fateful days in January 1964.

Probably more than anything else, even more than salary demands, the mutinies were inspired by black nationalism and were a military expression of indigenous political aspirations; so was the Zanzibar revolution, although it transcended race and included some Arabs and people of Persian origin in the vanguard in the quest for racial justice.

But since the oppressive regime that was overthrown was Arab, oppressing and exploiting black people more than anybody else, the revolution assumed a racial dimension as an indigenous expression of the political and economic aspirations of the black majority – who did not need communism to wake them up to reality and show them that they were being oppressed and exploited by the Arabs because they were weak and black. Experience is the best teacher.

Although all three governments – under Nyerere in Tanganyika, Jomo Kenyatta in Kenya, and Milton Obote in Uganda – survived and remained in power, there is no doubt that the mutinies had a profound impact across the continent and helped change the course of African history during the post-colonial era.

The mutinies not only demonstrated the power of the armed forces to extract concessions from national leaders and governments; they also showed, probably more than anything else, that soldiers in any African country had the power to overthrow governments without fear of retribution or any kind of punishment against them. Governments were too weak to stop or punish them, except in cases of abortive coup attempts.

Within a few years, military coups became a continental phenomenon, although not all of them could be attributed to the mutinies in East Africa. The coup in Togo is a good example. It took place in January 1963, almost exactly one year before the army mutinies in East Africa.

But like their counterparts in the three East African countries who mutinied in January 1964, soldiers in other parts of Africa knew on their own that they could storm out of the barracks, force national leaders to bow to their demands, and even overthrow them at will.

They knew the military was the strongest institution in Africa. Civilian governments were at their mercy and remained in power because soldiers allowed them to. The people were powerless to stop such intervention even if some of the governments which were being overthrown were popular and had been democratically elected.

The army mutinies in the three East African countries not only helped inspire military coups on the continent when soldiers in other countries saw how they could use guns to extract concessions from civilian governments and even overthrow them if they wanted to; they were also some of the earliest manifestations of the intrusive power of the military in African politics as a continental phenomenon, and of what was yet to come in an even more violent way: coups and assassinations spanning four decades.

The events in Tanganyika and Zanzibar in January 1964 – the Zanzibar revolution and the army mutiny on the mainland – were soon followed by another major development unprecedented anywhere else in Africa: formation of a political union of two independent states, Tanganyika and Zanzibar, to create Tanzania on April 26th in the same year.

One of the best analyses of the consummation of this union came from the late Professor Haroub Othman (he died on 28 June 2009 at the age of 68) of the Institute of Development Studies, University of Dar es Salaam, Tanzania. A Tanzanian from Zanzibar, he had the following to say in his analysis published in three parts from April 26th – 28th in 2004 in the *Guardian*, Dar es Salaam, Tanzania, on the union's 40th anniversary, entitled "Tanzania: Forty Years of the Union: Is it Withering Away?":

"'If I could tow that island out into the middle of the Indian Ocean, I'd do it.' - Julius Nyerere.

At a dinner party in Dar es Salaam a year or two before independence, Nyerere had remarked that he thought one of Tanganyika's biggest problems in later years would be Zanzibar:

'No, I'm not joking....I fear it will be a big headache for us.'

Historical Links

In the last forty years, Tanzanians have prided themselves in having the only union of independent states in Africa; and even though no other states have followed their example, they have not been discouraged by this lack of interest in forging larger units in Africa; nor do they think there were any lessons to be drawn form the failures of such attempts elsewhere.

But now cracks are appearing, without any obvious prodding form outside. The international community is bound to raise eyebrows, and to ask itself what is happening.

Situated a few miles away in the Indian Ocean, Zanzibar is mainland Tanzania (Tanganyika)'s closest neighbour to the east. The two countries have had a close relationship that dates back to several centuries before Christ.

It is believed that the indigenous population of Zanzibar, consisting of Wahadimu and Watumbatu, must have originated from the mainland.

The Persian and other explorers and merchants who visited these parts in the 7th century A.D. made Zanzibar their main centre among the city states in the East Coast of

Africa.

The Arab rulers who came to these areas in the early 18th century extended their rule and influence on the mainland through Zanzibar; and European explorers and missionaries, who appeared on the scene in the 19th century, used Zanzibar as a base to launch their penetration into the African hinterland.

The slave trade made Zanzibar an important centre of this human merchandise. Thousands of people captured on the mainland were sent to Zanzibar to be sold before they were shipped to Mauritius, Reunion, Arabia and other places as slave labour.

And when the clove plantation economy replaced the slave trade as the main economic activity of the islands, it was farm hands acquired from the mainland that came to the islands to open up virgin lands, till them and plant clove trees. Until the late 1950s, people form Tanganyika used to come to the islands in large numbers for seasonal employment in clove picking.

Political Relations

The two countries of Tanganyika and Zanzibar were administered separately during all the time of the colonial rule. When Tanganyika fell into German hands as a result of the Berlin Conference of 1884 - 1885 that carved up Africa amongst the European powers, Zanzibar had already fallen under Arab rule.

Sultan Said of Oman moved his capital to Zanzibar in 1832 and established the Al-Busaidy dynasty in the islands. As a result of the inter-imperialist rivalry in the region, Seyyid Said's son, Seyyid Ali bin Said, accepted British protection, and so the islands formally became a British protectorate on 4th November, 1890.

When Germany was defeated in the First World War, its colonial possessions were divided amongst the victor powers, and Tanganyika became a British-administered

246

territory under the League of Nations mandate (and later the United Nations Trusteeship System).

But even when the two countries were ruled by the same colonial power their administrations were different. The British Governor in Tanganyika was reporting directly to the Colonial Office in London, and periodically the British had to make a reporting to the League of Nations (and the United Nations). In the case of Zanzibar, even though the British Resident was answerable to the Colonial Secretary in London, in his decisions he had to take into consideration the sensitivities of the Arab Sultan.

This in no way indicates, as has been suggested by some writers, that Zanzibar during this period was under dual power. Britain was the ultimate colonial power.

A number of ethnic and cultural organizations were established by the peoples of the two countries to deal with their social, religious and cultural concerns. In 1929 an African Association was founded in Tanganyika mostly as a social and cultural organization of the African elite in Dar es Salaam and other urban areas. A branch of this Association was established in Zanzibar in 1934 with its membership mostly Zanzibaris of mainland origin.

The struggles for national independence raging throughout Africa did not fail to affect East Africa as well. In Kenya nationalist agitation had already started, culminating in the formation of the Kenya African Union (KAU); and when the demands for independence were not having any effect on the white settler community and the colonial authorities, the Kenyans took up arms in the Mau Mau uprising.

In Uganda nationalist organizations had already begun to form. Tanganyika African National Union (TANU), an organization that was to be the political vehicle of the people in voicing their demands for independence, was founded on 7th July 1954.

In Zanzibar, the Zanzibar Nationalist Party (ZNP) was founded in December 1955 and the Afro-Shirazi Party

(ASP) was established on 5th February 1957.

Prior to the formation of these nationalist parties in Tanganyika and Zanzibar, semi-political organizations and trade unions had already been operating: the Tanganyika Territory Civil Servants' Association was established in 1922, and a decree legalizing the formation of trade unions was passed in Zanzibar in 1931. The ports of Dar es Salaam and Zanzibar had experienced their major dockworkers' strikes in 1947 and 1948 respectively.

Unlike in other colonial possessions outside Africa where nationalist movements did not form continental or regional organizations to coordinate their struggles against colonialism, in Africa most nationalist movements, especially those founded after the Second World War, recognized the need for waging common struggles.

Starting with the 5th Pan-African Congress held in Manchester in 1945, and attended by Kwame Nkrumah of Ghana and Jomo Kenyatta of Kenya among others, the African peoples have focused their struggles not only on the independence of their own individual countries but also the complete eradication of colonialism in the continent and for the achievement of total African unity.

It was no wonder, therefore, that nationalist organizations in Eastern and Central Africa came together in September 1958, at the invitation of TANU, in the lake city of Mwanza, to exchange views and experiences and to forge unity. The ZNP and ASP from Zanzibar were also there.

It was at this conference that the Pan-African Freedom Movement for East and Central Africa (PAFMECA) was founded. Later the organization was to include nationalist movements from Southern Africa, and its name was changed to the Pan African Freedom Movement of Eastern, Central and Southern Africa (PAFMECSA).

The nationalist organisations of these three regions of Eastern, Central and Southern Africa in December of that year attended an All-African Peoples' Conference that was held in Accra, Ghana, at the invitation of Kwame Nkrumah's Convention People's Party (CPP).

One of the recommendations at the Mwanza Conference was that in an area where more than one nationalist organization existed, they should try and merge, and if that was not possible, then they should at least coordinate their activities. Zanzibar was one case in point.

The ZNP and ASP agreed to coordinate their activities, and a coordinating body was formed. This point was also stressed at the Accra conference at a meeting of Zanzibari leaders especially convened by Kwame Nkrumah.

These efforts succeeded for a time; but soon tension flared up again, because, as TANU President Julius Nyerere pointed out at the time "... politically the (Zanzibar) parties all agreed to one objective but they opposed each other because of race". Kanyama Chiume of Malawi and Francis Khamisi of Kenya were dispatched to Zanzibar by PAFMECA to help, to no avail. Things became more unsatisfactory when in 1959 the ASP split, and a new organization, the Zanzibar and Pemba People's Party (ZPPP), emerged.

Independence of Tanganyika:
The 'Mecca' of Africa's Liberation Emerges

Tanganyika was the first country in Eastern, Central and Southern Africa to gain its independence, on 9th December 1961 (African nationalists and most of progressive humanity had never recognized the 'independence' of South Africa). Like Ghana before it, Tanganyika felt that its own 'independence was meaningless until the whole of Africa was free.'

It therefore helped, with all the resources available, other peoples in the region to gain their independence: it opened its borders to patriots from other areas running away from persecution; it allowed its territory to be used

249

for the training of freedom fighters who would launch armed struggles to end colonial rule in their countries; it made possible the establishment of offices by the nationalist organizations so that they could reach the international community for support; and it gave its diplomatic and political support to all those fighting racism and colonialism everywhere.

It was no doubt this commitment to Africa's liberation together with its geographical position at the time vis-à-vis the colonial territories of the region that won Tanganyika the honour, in 1963, of becoming the headquarters of the OAU Liberation Committee, a body that was to coordinate Africa's and international support for the nationalist movements fighting colonialism, racism, apartheid and white settler supremacy in Africa.

Zanzibar presented TANU and its government with a dilemma. There was the Afro-Shirazi Party (ASP), claiming to represent the indigenous and migrant African population of Zanzibar, who were the majority, and at whose founding Mwalimu Julius Nyerere was present. (And it should be remembered that the ASP was a merger of the Shirazi Association and the African Association that was established in 1934 in Zanzibar as a branch of the Tanganyika African Association - the very association that transformed in 1954 into TANU).

On the other hand, there was the ZNP, which in rhetoric, seemed to challenge the colonial regime, and was very radical in its demands and programmes. But it was preaching non-racialism: would this ensure an African majority government in Zanzibar? ZNP was also embracing the monarchy: would an Arab Sultan be able to survive African nationalism in the area? TANU, in any case, decided to give its full support to the Afro-Shirazi Party (ASP).

Tanganyika as A Political Issue in Zanzibar: The Mainlanders Are Coming

The decision of the TANU leadership to give its full support to the ASP became an issue in Zanzibar politics. This support was not only political but material as well. Some children of ASP members in Zanzibar (including the former Zanzibar President Dr. Amin Samour) were sent to Tanganyika for education; ASP had an office in Dar es Salaam; and several ASP leaders who could not get travel documents to travel abroad used to sneak to Dar es Salaam where they were provided with travel documents.

At times of Zanzibar elections, TANU leaders such as Bibi Titi Mohamed and Ali Mwinyi Tambwe went to Zanzibar to campaign openly for ASP. This was the background against which the Zanzibar Nationalist Party (ZNP) made the accusation that should the Afro-Shirazi Party (ASP) win the elections it would sell Zanzibar to Tanganyika. ASP, of course, retorted by saying that a NZP victory would bring back the slave trade into those islands, given the fact that a number of prominent ZNP leaders were of Arab origin and the party had fully identified itself with the royal family and maintained strong ties with the Arab world.

Zanzibar's Independence:
Arab Dynasty Legitimised?

Zanzibar's road to independence was a bumpy one. While in Tanganyika TANU enjoyed overwhelming support of the population, in Zanzibar the two major political parties had almost even support. In the 1957 elections, the first of its kind in Eastern and Central Africa, ASP stormed through, winning five out of six seats in the Legislative Council; but in the subsequent elections of January and June 1961 and July 1963, the party maintained the lead in the number of votes it captured, but was unable to translate that into a majority of seats in the Legislative Council.

In Tanganyika the struggle for independence went on peacefully, in Zanzibar the June 1961 elections were disrupted by explosive riots that resulted in 68 deaths, 400 injured and 1,000 arrests. A year later, a prominent Zanzibari politician, Abdulrahman Babu, who was at the time secretary-general of the Zanzibar Nationalist Party (ZNP), was sent to jail after a libel case. Certainly the June riots were an indication of what was to come: the 1964 Zanzibar Revolution. Violence was being accepted as a way of solving political conflict.

When the dust had settled, physical wounds healed and tempers cooled, a constitutional conference was held in London between 19th March and 6th April 1962, attended by all the political parties in the Legislative Council, with the Colonial Secretary chairing. At the conference the ZNP/ZPPP alliance and the ASP showed very divergent views on future constitutional development.

While they both reaffirmed their loyalty to the Sultan and the throne and their desire that the dynasty should continue, they had different ideas on the programme of taking Zanzibar into internal self-government and independence.

On 24th January 1963 Zanzibar became an internally self-governing territory, and new elections were held. It was clearly understood by all that these were to be the last elections before independence, and that the government that was to be formed would lead the country to independence.

The elections were held from 8th to 15th July 1963 for a legislature of 31 members. The ZNP/ZPPP alliance won 18 seats, and the ASP 13. As indicated above, the ASP won the majority of votes cast but not a majority of seats. While the ZNP had a fall in in the percentage of votes cast from 35.0% in 1961 to 29.8% in 1963, the ASP increased its share of the votes from 49.9% in 1961 to 54.3% in 1963. The ZNPPP made an increase from 13.7% in 1961 to 15.9% in 1963.

Once more the ASP and its supporters felt cheated in the whole election exercise. After all in the January 1961 elections as well, the party had won 10 seats against ZNP's 9 and ZPP's 3.

ASP could not understand why the British Resident did not call upon its leader to be the Chief Minister, given the fact that with the three ex-officio British civil servants, namely the Chief Secretary, the Financial Secretary, and the Attorney-General, in the Legislative Council, the party would have had a working majority.

But the British argued that a party must have its own majority before counting on the support of the ex-officio members. Meanwhile, the ZPPP split itself, with one member joining the ASP and the other two allying themselves with the ZNP.

Thus new elections had to be called in June; and meanwhile, a coalition government of all the parties with the Chief Secretary acting as the Chief Minister operated in the interim period.

Independence was attained on December 10th, 1963, with the Sultan as the head of state, with power also to nominate his successor. Thus, as Michael Lofchie stated, Arab rule had not only survived the introduction of representative institutions, but had acquired a degree of legitimacy under constitutional democracy.

The Revolution:
Class Struggle or Racial War?

What surprised many people outside the islands was how there could occur a 'sudden' revolution barely one month after Zanzibar attained its 'flag independence.' James Cameron, writing on Zanzibar in 1960, said: "Today this sleepy place holds little to help us in our search for the African Revolution." But hardly four years after those words were written, Zanzibar experienced a revolution that not only overthrew the ZNP/ZPPP coalition

253

government, but immediately abolished the monarchy.

With the establishment of a republic and a new coalition of classes in power, a radical change of circumstances occurred. Indeed, it has been remarked that 'with the possible exception of (Sekou Toure's) Guinea, no country in tropical Africa changed so radically in so short a time.'

The first action of the revolutionary government was to abrogate the Independence Constitution of 1963 and proclaim a 'Constitutional Decree No.5' that provided for 'Constitutional Government and Rule of Law.'

Although the revolutionary government allowed itself a period of one year to call a Constituent Assembly to adopt a constitution, such a body was never called, and Zanzibar only came to have a written constitution 15 years later, in 1979. In fact the first President of Zanzibar, the late Abeid Karume, no doubt remembering how ASP had suffered in elections in the past, had warned that there would be no elections for sixty years!

The revolution has been consistently described as a racial one and as a culmination of the struggle between the minority Arabs and the African majority. But that is only half the truth, and a distorted one as well. If we accept Lenin's definition that every political struggle is a class struggle, we can see that behind the 'racial revolution' there was a class war. The point about pre-revolution Zanzibar is that racial differentiations went parallel with class differentiations.

The 1964 upheaval can be characterised as a revolt of the landless peasantry and the labouring masses against the landed aristocracy and political oligarchy. As Duggan has remarked, the revolt appeared to be a classic one, having been staged 'in an area where political, economic and social conditions favoured its institution and guaranteed its success.' And as Michael Lofchie observed in his book *Zanzibar: Background to Revolution*:

254

'The revolution set as its objective to transform Zanzibar into a wholly egalitarian society...[and] undertook measures to bring about a fairer distribution of the arable land. [It] also sought to eliminate from Zanzibar all symbolic vestiges of racial clubs and organizations and sought to infuse the society with radical socialist methods stressing class and national solidarity rather than race.'

Union of Tanganyika and Zanzibar: African Initiative or Cold War Rivalry?

Since the 1920s the countries of East Africa, namely Kenya, Tanganyika, Uganda and Zanzibar, had developed common services and joint institutions. Matters such as posts and telecommunications, harbours, railways and currency were run jointly. There was also a body to coordinate the development of Kiswahili.

This, no doubt, was easy in view of the fact that all the four countries were neighbours and under one colonial power. The white settlers in Kenya had at one time pressed the British Government for a federation of the East African countries on the lines of that of Central Africa (Northern Rhodesia, Southern Rhodesia, and Nyasaland).

But people in Tanganyika and Uganda feared that if that was to happen it would throw their countries into the hands of white supremacists in Kenya, in the same way that the peoples of Central Africa found themselves under the white supremacists of Southern Rhodesia at the time of the Central African Federation (whose capital was Salisbury, now Harare). And so this idea was opposed at the time.

But as the countries were approaching independence and because of the close cooperation among the nationalist organizations, the idea of federation re-emerged.

Nyerere, in a statement made in Addis Ababa when Tanganyika's independence was imminent, said that he was prepared to delay his country's independence if the four countries of East Africa could come to independence at the same time and form a federation.

But with independence each country retreated into its own national shell, and what was agreed was the formation of the East African Common Services Organisation that later in December 1967 was transformed into the East African Community.

When, therefore on 26th April, 1964, the People's Republic of Zanzibar and the Republic of Tanganyika announced that they had merged to form a Union, the international community felt that Zanzibar and Tanganyika had succeeded where the four East African countries together had failed. But was it the ideals of Pan-Africanism that brought Zanzibar and Tanganyika together?

Was the Union the result of an African initiative or was it propelled by cold war rivalry? The circumstances in which the Union was formed raised a lot of questions, many of which are still unanswered, and some have been at the centre of continuing debates and controversies in Tanzania in the last twenty years. Have the fears of ZNP that Zanzibar would be 'taken over' by Tanganyika been proven true?

In later years, the Union was to haunt the Zanzibar politicians for a long time, with each of them playing the "Union card" either for legitimacy on the mainland or for support at home.

Nyerere stated that he casually proposed the idea of the Union to Karume when the latter visited him to discuss the fate of John Okello. According to Nyerere, Karume immediately agreed on the idea and suggested that Nyerere should be the President of such a Union.

In a New Year message to the Nation on 2 January 1965, Nyerere implied that even if the ASP had come into power through constitutional means and not as a result of a revolution, the Union would still have taken place.

But Amrit Wilson's research has revealed that there

was a very strong Western pressure, especially from the United States, for the Zanzibar Revolution to be contained because it was felt that it held the threat of the spread of communism in the East African region.

The Untied States, Britain and the then West Germany, which Tanganyika was heavily dependent on at the time, viewed the revolutionary government in Zanzibar as either a surrogate of the communist powers or dancing to their tune.

The international press had already started to characterize Zanzibar as the 'Cuba of Africa', though to be fair to Duggan, he had referred to Zanzibar as "Tanganyika's Cuba" far back in July 1963 when he had interviewed Nyerere in Washington during the latter's state visit to the US.

In a cable message to US embassies in Dar es Salaam, Nairobi and Kampala, the US Secretary of State Dean Rusk instructed his diplomats to urge Nyerere, Kenyatta and Obote to explain to Karume the dangers involved in his dependence on Babu and:

'The danger Babu represents... to the security of Zanzibar and East Africa generally... they should recognize here that the big problem is that Karume himself has great confidence in and dependence on Babu... also that Nyerere has said that Karume needs Babu who, despite his background, can and must be worked with.

Kenyatta and Joseph Murumbi on the other hand appear to regard Babu as undesirable and the chief threat to Karume.

Would it be useful to liaise with Nyerere, despite his previous objection, the idea of a Zanzibar-Tanganyika Federation as a possible way of strengthening Karume and reducing Babu's influence? Such action at this time may also help Nyerere's own position.'

In an interview with Amrit Wilson in 1986, Frank

Carlucci, the US Consul in Zanzibar at the time of the Union who was later thrown out of Zanzibar because of CIA activities (and who later rose to become the Director of CIA and US Secretary of Defence), confessed that there was United States' pressure on Nyerere. Susan Crouch in her book *Western Responses to Tanzanian Socialism 1967-1983* reveals that:

'To this end the American Central Intelligence Agency was active in trying to create the conditions for union, fanning antagonisms among Zanzibar's revolutionary leaders, and creating a fear of Zanzibar as a communist threat among East African leaders.'

Was the Union then, as is indicated in U.S. State Department papers, dictated by cold war considerations first and the questions of pan-African ideals of unity were secondary to ideological factors and questions of personal survival?

It has also been suggested that Karume wanted a Union with Tanganyika as a means of warding off his Marxist and left-wing colleagues. What seems to be the case is that after the electoral defeat of July 1963 Karume's leadership within the ASP parliamentary group was shaky.

There was a schism in it, with Karume being challenged by Othman Shariff, and some of the party's MPs calling for a government of national unity that would bring together in government all the political parties in parliament.

After the revolution, Umma Party radical elements in the government (Babu, Khamis Abdalla Ameir, Ali Sultan Issa, Ali Mahfoudh, Salim Rashid, Badawi Qullatein, etc) were forging links with the ASP leftists (Abdallah Kassim Hanga, Abdulazizi Ali Twala, Hassan Nassor Moyo, etc.), and this might have scared Karume and other moderate elements within the regime. At the same time, the radical way in which the revolution was surging ahead might have

258

alarmed the regime in Dar es Salaam.

It should not be forgotten that within days of the revolution in Zanzibar, an army mutiny took place in Tanganyika (later repeated in Kenya and Uganda); and even though we know now that there was no link between the revolution and those mutinies, it was difficult to see it that way at the time.

As a result of the army mutiny in Dar es Salaam, Tabora and Nachingwea, there was virtually no government in Tanganyika for three days, anarchy prevailed, and Nyerere was forced to request British military intervention to bring the country back to normalcy.

The West, particularly the Untied States, perceived developments in Zanzibar in the context of East-West rivalry, and given the leftist credentials of the Umma Party and some of the ASP leaders that were prominent in the Revolutionary Council, it was assumed that a Cuba-type situation was evolving.

The best way of averting it, short of direct military intervention a la Playa Giron (though this was thought of and preparations made), was to try an "African initiative'. And it worked.

Legitimacy of the Union: The 'Absence' of the Attorney-General and The Question of A Referendum

Many questions continued to be raised regarding the legal basis of the Union: whether the two presidents on their own had the powers to sign such a Union Agreement; why the Zanzibar's Attorney-General, as the principal legal advisor to the government, was not consulted; why there was no referendum; and whether in joining such a union Zanzibar was not in fact 'swallowed' and 'annexed' by Tanganyika.

Discussions on the union were conducted very secretively. From the archival materials and the statements of those who were in the 'corridors of power' at the time, it would appear that not many people in the Tanganyika government or the Zanzibar Revolutionary Council knew what was happening.

Apart from Nyerere and Karume, the only other people who might have been privy to those discussions were Rashidi Kawawa, Oscar Kambona, Job Lusinde, Abdallah Kassim Hanga, Abdul-Aziz Ali Twala and Salim Rashidi.

When these discussions were at an advanced stage, Nyerere is said to have called in his Attorney-General at the time, British expert Roland Brown, and asked him to draft a Union Agreement without anybody knowing.

In the case of Zanzibar, the Attorney-General, Wolfgang Dourado, is said to have been sent on a one-week 'leave' and instead a Ugandan lawyer, Dan Nabudere (accoding to his own account which was corroborated by Babu), was brought in to advise Karume on the draft submitted by Tanganyika. Both Brown and Nabudere were present in the Karume-Nyerere discussions.

One can speculate that one reason why Dourado was not involved was because he was 'inherited' from the previous ZNP/ZPPP regime and the revolutionary government was hesitant to involve him in such a sensitive matter.

Under both the 1962 Republic of Tanganyika Constitution and the Zanzibar Presidential Decree No.5 quoted above, the two Presidents had the powers to enter into international agreements on behalf of their governments.

What is also important is that the Union Agreement was ratified by both the Tanganyika Parliament and the Zanzibar Revolutionary Council. Contrary to what some writers have said, the Nyalali Commission was satisfied that the Revolutionary Council met to ratify the 'Articles of Union'.

Both Abdulrahman Babu and Khamis Abdallah Ameir, the two former Umma Party leaders who were in the

Revolutionary Council at the time, have confirmed that the matter was discussed in the Council, and while there were reservations on the part of some members, these were 'quashed' by Abdallah Kassim Hanga who made an emotional intervention to support the Union.

Once the 'Articles of Union' had been ratified by the two legislative bodies in Tanganyika and Zanzibar, there was no further requirement in law to make them enforceable. The question of referendum would not have arisen because under the Commonwealth legal tradition, in which the two countries were brought up, the notion of a referendum was unknown.

The referendum was introduced as a legal requirement under British law in the 1970s during the heated debate in the United Kingdom on the question of its entry into the European Economic Community.

To have also expected the Zanzibar revolutionary government to call a referendum on the Union, four months after it came into power through unconstitutional means, was like expecting the French revolutionaries of 1789 to have invited King Louis XVI for dinner after they had overthrown him.

Should ASP have conducted a referendum to ask Zanzibaris whether or not to stage a revolution? In law, therefore, the Union Agreement, as both Prof Issa Shivji and Dr Kabudi have pointed out, is valid.

Articles of Union: 1 + 1 = 3

The Union Agreement, signed by Karume and Nyerere in Zanzibar on 22 April 1964, is known as the 'Articles of Union'. When this agreement was announced the following day many people inside the two countries, and outside too, were taken by surprise.

The strong feeling was that the West had won in their intention to containing the Zanzibar Revolution; in fact there were military preparations by both Britain and the

United States in case there was a violent reaction in Zanzibar against the Union.

What the Tanganyika leadership wanted at the time was to play down the whole event. In a cable message of 23 April 1964 to the U.S. Secretary of State, the U.S. Ambassador in Dar es Salaam, William Leonhart, informed:

'Mbwambo, Chief protocol, has just telephoned a personal request ..... that, to the maximum extent, any US public statements on Tangovernment-Zanzibar union be avoided. Situation over the next few days in Zanzibar could be very critical and both the Soviet and Chinese reaction is undetermined.'

In an address later to the National Assembly requesting the ratification of the 'Articles of Union', Nyerere insisted that the move was inspired by the ideals for an African unity. 'Unity in our continent does not have to come via Moscow or Washington,' he insisted.

The 'Articles of Union' have been given different interpretations and characterised as federal, quasi-federal, an interim arrangement towards one government, etc. Some have seen the Union as similar to the relationship between the United Kingdom and Northern Ireland.

Those who were close to the scene at the time also differ as to what type of relationship it is.

The U.S. Ambassador in Dar es Salaam, in a cable message to his government on 22nd April, 1964, the day the 'Articles of Union' were signed by Karume and Nyerere, stated:

'Like the relationship between Northern Ireland and Britain, the union of Zanzibar and Tanganyika gave the island limited regional administrative autonomy ... but ensured overall power ... was held by the centre at Dar es Salaam.'

But Frank Calucci, reporting from Zanzibar the next day, said that Karume was 'still under the impression that he is agreeing to a federation of two autonomous states, not a centralised union envisaged under the present articles.'

Attwood, the U.S. Ambassador in Kenya at the time, says he was informed by Dustan Omari, Nyerere's Permanent Secretary then, 'that the major power would rest in the centre ... but that Zanzibar would retain its own internal governmental affairs.'

While I have difficulty in accepting some of the assertions of some of the writers on the character of the Union for reasons that I will advance later, I would only want to agree with the notion that the 'Articles of Union' are the Grundnorm, the fundamental law of the United Republic, on which the Constitutions of Tanzania and Zanzibar, and other laws, have to be based and from which they derive their legitimacy. Like any supreme law in any other legal system, no other law or constitutional act can be in conflict with it.

'Articles of Union' provide for matters that would be under the Union arrangement. From the original 11 items in 1964, the list has now expanded to 23. Some people question the validity of such an expansion, though one must admit that there was nothing that was added into the list unconstitutionally.

The 'Articles of Union' also provide for the existence of two governments: One for the whole Untied Republic for all Union matters and for non-Union matters in Tanganyika, which, under the 1977 Union Constitution is referred to as Tanzania Mainland, and one for Zanzibar in all matters that are non-Union.

According to Nyerere, Karume wanted a total union, but he (Nyerere) cautioned against it, saying that such a move might be construed by Zanzibaris and others as meaning that Zanzibar had been swallowed up, annexed, incorporated into or taken over by Tanganyika. He insisted that Zanzibar's identity must be maintained.

There is no way one can construe the 'Articles of Union' as a basis for a federal set-up. Nor can they be seen as an interim arrangement towards one government. They intended to create a single state with two authorities, but with one of those authorities having a limited geographical jurisdiction. The intention was to retain the identity of the smaller unit.

By this event, Tanganyika has not been lost; in fact it has been enlarged. Even if it is accepted that the Union was a Western conspiracy against the Zanzibar Revolution, the effect of the intention was to deny Zanzibar the capacity to be an international actor, not to interfere with what was happening inside the country. To be able to change the internal course of events would have entailed changing the regime.

What might have confounded some of the law experts looking at the relationship between Zanzibar and Mainland Tanzania was the fact that no such example existed in the Anglo-Saxon legal system. The closest they could think of then was that of the United Kingdom and Northern Ireland.

The Consolidation of the Union:
Popular Approval of the "Swallowing Up"

At the time of the union, Zanzibar and Tanganyika were ruled by different political parties, ASP and TANU respectively. The 'Articles of Union' did not require the formation of a single political party for the whole United Republic.

Thus in the period 1964-1977 each party operated within its own geographical area, though at the approach of every general election, the two parties held a joint congress where they nominated a join presidential candidate for the elections.

Only in 1977, after a national survey of members of both parties, did the two parties merge to form Chama Cha Mapinduzi (CCM) with authority over the whole country.

But why did Zanzibaris agree to such a merger? Nyerere had always expressed surprise when recalling the radiant faces he saw and the jovial mood of the Zanzibaris the day CCM was proclaimed at the Amani Stadium in Zanzibar.

The fact is that Zanzibaris were celebrating not only the birth of CCM but also the demise of ASP. By that time the general feeling in the islands was that the ASP had outlived its usefulness.

The revolution which it had championed had stooped so low as to devour its own sons: most of the leaders were busy amassing wealth; prison and death were the only options open to political dissent; and political thugery was a virtue.

One matter that was added in 1984 to the list of Union items was that of national security. This happened at the time when Ali Hassan Mwinyi was President and Seif Shariff Hamad the Chief Minister of Zanzibar in 1984-85, commonly known as the Third Phase Government.

Not having much confidence in the security personnel they inherited, who might have had personal allegiance to Jumbe and Seif Bakari, the new Administration sought the extension of the National Security Act of the Mainland to Zanzibar. In that case it was possible to transfer the security personnel in Zanzibar to the Mainland and vice versa.

So from the above one can see the following: First, Zanzibaris wanted a merger of the parties, and for the united party to have authority all over the country, in the hope that it would rescue them from a regime that was no longer able to inspire confidence and instil enthusiasm; and second, a 'consolidation' of the Union in this regard was necessary for one faction of the leadership to ward off any possible challenge by the other.

The long-term effect of the parties' merger was to have matters that were entirely within Zanzibar's jurisdiction, and that were not Union matters, decided by a pan-territorial political party where Zanzibari representation was not decisive.

This became clear in 1984 when Aboud Jumbe was forced to resign as Zanzibar President: it was the party's NEC which appointed Ali Hassan Mwinyi as an Interim President and later nominated him for election as the President of Zanzibar.

Since NEC's Zanzibari membership is no more than a third of the total, this means therefore that a Zanzibar President could be chosen by a forum which is predominantly non-Zanzibari. And this was further evidenced with the nomination by CCM's NEC of the present President of Zanzibar.

A number of other measures were taken to consolidate the Union, particularly in the constitutional realm. A permanent constitution was put in place in 1977 instead of an interim one that had been in existence since 1964.

Zanzibar's Identity in the Union

In the 'Articles of Union,' Zanzibar is allowed to retain its autonomy and pursue its own policies in all matters other than those stipulated as Union matters.

In this case, the power to decide is left to the Zanzibar organs such as the House of Representatives, the Revolutionary Council and the President of Zanzibar and Chairman of the Revolutionary Council.

The Union Constitution stipulates that constitutional amendments require the approval of two-thirds of Zanzibaris sitting in the Union Parliament and the same proportion of Mainlanders.

In order to avoid a clash in the legislative functions of the two sides of the Union, it has been provided that if the House of Representatives enacts any law which should be

266

under the jurisdiction of the Union Parliament that law will be null and void, and also if the Union Parliament enacts a law on any matter under the jurisdiction of the House of Representatives that law will be null and void.

The Constitution also provides for effective Zanzibari representation in the Union Parliament. It also guarantees a separate judiciary system for Zanzibar which has jurisdiction over Zanzibar alone. Even though the Court of Appeal of the United Republic is a Union organ, it has no power to decide on a case involving a dispute between the Union Government and the Zanzibar Revolutionary Government.

However one might view the circumstances that made Zanzibar merge with Tanganyika in 1964, the fact of the matter is that Zanzibar was not annexed or forcefully incorporated. It agreed on the Union out of its own free will and as a result of decisions made by its own organs. The argument that within the Union Tanganyika has lost its identity has no basis.

If anything it has enlarged its territory. It is Zanzibar's autonomy and identity that must be maintained lest, as Nyerere himself has pointed out several times, an impression is created that the larger and more populous Tanganyika has swallowed Zanzibar.

Such a situation is not new even in the most centralized states. In China, despite the fact that the country has a centralized authority and no federal traces of any kind, yet because of certain historical, political or cultural reasons, certain areas are conferred autonomy, and are constitutionally given the status of autonomous regions.

As will be pointed out later there are entities in present-day Europe that enjoy full autonomy within one state. To entertain the thought that the 'Articles of Union' are a temporary arrangement, and that ultimately the intention should be to create one government is to manifest 'big brother chauvinism.'

Debates on the Union:
The Polluted Political Atmosphere

In 1983/84 and 1990/92 extensive political and constitutional debates took place in the country that deeply probed the question of the Union. The debates of 1983/84 resulted in major amendments to the 1977 Union Constitution and the formulation of a new Zanzibar Constitution in 1984.

But they also resulted in the forced resignation of Aboud Jumbe from all his state and party positions, the sacking of a Zanzibar Chief Minister and the serious warning given by the ruling party to a number of prominent Zanzibar figures.

The debates of the 1990/92 period resulted in the Nyalali Commission making major recommendations on the structure of the Union. In between the two periods also another Zanzibar Chief Minister was sacked, and several leading Zanzibar politicians were dismissed form the ruling party.

As stated above, the question of Zanzibar being 'sold' to the Mainland was an issue in pre-revolutionary Zanzibar. And if one remembers that the political parties were almost evenly divided, then one can assume that almost half of the Zanzibar population was already biased against the Mainland even before the Union.

The post-revolution politics in the islands did not help matters much. Karume went into a Union to save himself from his Marxist and left-wing colleagues; and since Jumbe was not considered to be the 'heir apparent' before Karume's assassination in 1972, he was not thought of as the natural successor when he took over.

It has been speculated that the Revolutionary Council had Col. Seif Bakari in mind, but Nyerere advised that since Karume was killed by an army officer, Seif Bakari taking over might be construed as a military coup. Jumbe, feeling that he had not much support within the

268

Revolutionary Council, depended very much on Nyerere's and Mainland's support.

It is no wonder then that it was during his presidency that much of the consolidation of the Union took place, with the most items added to the Union list. It is significant too that the merger of the parties took place then. But this dependency on the Mainland was costing him much popular support at home.

Either as a way of outflanking his opponents or because of genuine problems he found in the Union (after all he was for a long time a Minister for Union Affairs before he became President of Zanzibar), he first raised the question of restructuring the Union in a speech seven years before the 1983/84 debates.

Other politicians in Zanzibar too have used the Mainland as a trump card either to crush their opponents or to climb the political ladder. Seif Shariff Hamad, Khatib Hassan, Shaaban Mloo and others accused Jumbe in 1984 of planning to break up the Union, and thus forced Jumbe to resign from his political posts then. They in turn faced the same accusation from their opponents in 1988 and were dismissed from the party.

The issues that were raised in both the 1983/84 and 1990/92 debates centred on the following:

1. Whether the 'Articles of Union' of 1964 provided for a federation, that is three governments (one of Tanganyika, the other of Zanzibar, and a third a federal one) or only two governments as presently existing;

2. As the Union Government is also the government for the Mainland in non-Union matters, does this not give the impression that Mainland is the Union?

3. Does Zanzibar get a fair share in the distribution of benefits coming form the Union?

4. Is Zanzibar well represented in the diplomatic service?

5. Does it get a fair share of foreign aid coming to

Tanzania?

6. Since the people of Zanzibar were not consulted at the time of the formation of the Union, should there not be a referendum now to ascertain whether the people wanted the Union or not?

Most of these questions, as can be seen, were coming from Zanzibar, and what surprised many people at the time of the 1983/84 debate, was that they were being aired in the state-owned-and-controlled official mass media.

No such strong feelings were voiced on the Mainland during the debates. Many people who made submissions to the Nyalali Commission said hardly anything about the system of governments that the Union should have.

It was only after the opening up of the political system and the establishment of more political parties that one began hearing very strong views coming form the Mainland on the question of the Union; some of those going even further than anybody in Zanzibar had ever contemplated.

Nyalali Commission on the Union: Agreed to Disagree

One of the major recommendations of the Nyalali Commission was for the replacement of the present Union set-up with a federal one. This was one of the areas that bought about a very heated debate within the Commission and which necessitated members of the Commission having to vote.

Later those who were opposed to the federal idea had to append their own Dissenting Opinion to the main report to explain their position.

But the division in the Commission on this issue almost came to a Mainland/Zanzibar division. Of the 11 members from Zanzibar, 7 wanted the present Union set-up, with some major changes, to remain; 3 wanted a federal and 1

270

was undecided. Of the same number from the Mainland, 9 wanted a federal set-up and 2 wanted the present arrangement to continue.

What is important is that both sides agreed that there were problems within the Union. Even though at the time the complaints form the Mainland were not so loud compared to Zanzibar, it would have been wise if those complaints were addressed and resolved.

The majority of members of the Commission felt that in a federal set-up, both Tanganyika and Zanzibar would retain their identity, federal areas would be clearly defined and the responsibilities of each would be understood, and the federal entity would be distinct from the national ones.

Those holding the minority opinion, on the other hand, were of the view that there was nothing in the 'Articles of Union' to suggest that their framers had a federal set-up in mind; that a federation would be a step backward and might be a prelude to the dissolution of the Union; that corrective measures could be taken, if there is political will, which would define Union matters, list Union institutions and apportion the responsibility of each side on those matters.

Examples were provided from the two Scandinavian countries of Denmark and Finland where entities (Faroe Islands, Aaland Islands and Greenland) have full autonomy in a number of areas that they exercise within a non-federal state. The Dissenting Opinion in the Nyalali Report pointed out:

* Greenland and Faroe Islands, both of which are part of Denmark, have full autonomy in many matters. For example, a parliament that is not subject to interference form the central government of Denmark, and all political and economic matters agreed upon and even in international relations. The islands of Faroe have their own flag hoisted in all government buildings and on ships registered in Faroe islands. Also Faroe Islands authority

issues passports;

* Denmark had agreed to join the European Economic Community. So did Greenland. But later, Greenland withdrew from the Community. Therefore, all EEC agreements and conditionality accepted in Denmark did not apply in Greenland. Similarly, the Islands of Faroe are not a member of the EU.

* In regard to Finland, the islands of Aaland have their own parliament and government. The islands of Aaland also have their own 'identity' for persons born in the islands and who have not lived abroad consecutively for five years or more. The islands have their own flag, issue their own stamps and its citizens are not subject to military service. The islands of Aaland are a demilitarized zone. The Central Bank of Finland must consult the government of Aaland before it takes measures that might harm the economy of Aaland. This, despite the fact that they share a common currency;

* The islands of Aaland, as is the case for Greenland and Faroe, are, on their own right, represented in the Nordic Council that consists of Denmark, Finland, Sweden, Norway and Iceland.

Conclusion:
Whither the Union?

As pointed out above, there have been historical links between Zanzibar and Tanganyika long before the coming of the colonialists in East Africa; and colonialism did not in fact stop such interactions from continuing. During the struggle for national independence, the two main political parties in the two countries cooperated though there is nothing to suggest that the two parties were thinking of merging into a Union of this kind after they came into power.

What they had in mind was to form a federation with Kenya and Uganda. Until the elections of July 1963, ASP still thought that it would win power through the electoral process; and it would appear that their main supporters, TANU, thought likewise.

Now the Union is a fact. Despite a lot of problems, it has brought stability and peace in the region. It is difficult to speculate what would have happened to the Zanzibar Revolution without the Union: whether Zanzibar would have advanced faster or whether a counter-revolutionary force would have taken over and embellished a dictatorship worse than anything the islands have actually experienced especially during the first phase government.

What is clear though is that the Union has brought the two peoples much closer together.

I do not believe that the unity of the two peoples can be strengthened by restructuring the present set-up into a federation.

I see movement from the present set-up to a federation as a step towards the dismemberment of the Union; and I do not think that that is to the short- or long-term benefit of the people of Tanzania.

The present problems can be resolved if there is a strong political will on the part of our political class and if the people are told the truth about those problems.

Only when corrective measures are taken, would it be possible to sustain and strengthen the Union. Otherwise if the difficulties inherent in the 'Articles of Union' and the problems arising from implementation are only emphasized and not resolved, the tendency would be towards the withering away of the Union.

In this era of multipartism and openness, it is even more important that matters are discussed and solutions founded on popular will. Of all the political parties that have been established since the abolition of the one-party system, only one, the Democratic Party led by Reverend

Christopher Mtikila, has come out strongly against the Union and called for its dissolution.

Others are prevaricating between 'referendum', 'federation' and modifications within the present set-up. The CCM and its governments which seemed earlier on to strongly accept the Dissenting Opinion in the Nyalali Report, now seems to be torn apart, with a strong group calling for a federal set-up.

The national language, the ethics of equality and human dignity, and the Union of Tanganyika and Zanzibar are what overcame the ethnic hatred, religious bigotry, regional parochialism and national differences and forged national cohesion and unity.

It is these that have made Tanzania an example in a continent beset with secessionism, ethnic violence and religious pogroms. One hopes that there is capacity, honesty and patriotism within Tanzania that will look beyond the sectarian interests. The alternative is too horrendous to contemplate."

The union of Tanganyika and Zanzibar may still have been consummated but probably at a later date had the revolution not taken place at all in the island nation. And the impact it had on the African continent is still felt today in many areas.

It influenced political and diplomatic relations between and among countries and changed the course of history. It was even a factor in the super-power rivalry between the United States and the Soviet Union during the Cold War. It also became a major subject of intellectual and ideological debates in and outside Africa for many years. And it continues to stimulate debate even today.

Problems faced by the union have also served as a warning to other African countries which may contemplate uniting, although this is a remote possibility on a continent where nationalism transcends Pan-Africanism despite professions to the contrary.

274

Not far from Zanzibar was another major development in 1964 involving the liberation struggle in Africa, thus changing the destiny of the continent.

It took place in Mozambique, a country bordered by what was then Tanganyika. In fact, a number of people who went on to play a major role in the liberation struggle in Mozambique had lived in Zanzibar and Tanganyika. And together with their brethren from Mozambique, Nyasaland (now Malawi), Southern Rhodesia (renamed Zimbabwe), and Kenya, met in Dar es Salaam, Tanganyika, to form a liberation organization, FRELIMO, in June 1962 under the leadership of Dr. Eduardo Mondlane.

It was this organization which started in 1964 to transform Mozambique into a fundamentally different country from what it was before.

The liberation struggle in Mozambique was one of the most significant developments in the history of the continent. What FRELIMO did in 1964 was a turning point in the 500-year history of Portuguese colonial rule in that country and in the other Portuguese colonies on the continent.

On 25 September 1964, the Front for the Liberation of Mozambique (FRELIMO) launched an armed struggle against the Portuguese colonial rulers in one of the oldest colonies in Africa. It was guerrilla warfare.

The guerrilla fighters were trained in Algeria and went on the offensive in Cabo Delgado, a province bordering Tanganyika, what is now Tanzania mainland. The liberation war had officially begun.

As the fighting intensified, it spread to Niassa province by 1965, and in 1968, the freedom fighters launched attacks in Tete province. By that time, FRELIMO claimed control of one-fifth of the country. The Portuguese colonial rulers were on the defensive, forcing them to pour more troops and resources into the country in a desperate attempt to stem the nationalist tide, to no avail.

Independence was only seven years away. The rest, as they say, is history.

The liberation struggle in Mozambique got a boost from, and intensified when, neighbouring Tanganyika won independence in 1961 and other countries in different parts of the continent also won their freedom from Britain and France. President Nyerere encouraged the Mozambican freedom fighters to form a united front and provided them with operational bases in Tanganyika.

He also invited Dr. Eduardo Mondlane to Dar es Salaam, Tanganyika, to unite the various nationalist organizations and promised him support. Dr. Mondlane was then working at the United Nations and agreed to move to Tanganyika.

What happened in Mozambique had a profound impact on the liberation struggle in the rest of the countries in southern Africa still under white minority rule and changed the course of African history. Victory in Mozambique was critical to what would happen in the rest of the region in terms of liberation.

Mozambique was the first country in southern Africa to win independence by armed struggle, and its victory had an enormous impact on all the other liberation movements in the region in terms of morale. Mozambique's geographical location as a neighbour of some of the countries still under white minority rule also proved to be of great strategic value in the success of the liberation struggle in those countries.

Besides Tanzania, Malawi and Swaziland, all of which were independent when FRELIMO started fighting, Mozambique is also bordered by Zimbabwe, what was then Rhodesia, and by South Africa, both of which were still under white minority rule when Mozambique won independence.

Throughout its military campaign, FRELIMO was based in Tanzania, its operational base, where it had guerrilla training and refugee camps. President Nyerere strongly believed that success in Mozambique was critical to the liberation of the other countries still under white minority rule in the region. It would inspire the people in those countries in their quest for freedom; it would also speed up their liberation.

Mozambique itself, like Tanzania and Zambia, played a critical role as a rear base for the freedom fighters in Rhodesia (now Zimbabwe) and in apartheid South Africa in the seventies and eighties and when the liberation struggle was most intense, until Zimbabwe won independence in April 1980, and the apartheid regime in South Africa collapsed in May 1994. As Nyerere told Bill Sutherland, an African American who lived in Tanzania from the late 1950s until the 1990s and who was still living there when Nyerere died:

"When you win, the morale of the African freedom fighters will go up and the morale of their opponents throughout southern Africa will go down. I said that's what we should do, demonstrate success, which we did." – (Julius Nyerere, in an interview with Bill Sutherland, in Bill Sutherland and Matt Mayer, *Guns and Gandhi in Africa: Pan-African Insights on Nonviolence, Armed Struggle and Liberation in Africa*, Trenton, New Jersey: Africa World Press, 2000).

The success was best demonstrated in Mozambique when the country became the first in southern Africa to win freedom by armed struggle after 500 years of Portuguese colonial rule. FRELIMO also became one of the most successful liberation movements in history.

While FRELIMO had just launched guerilla warfare in Mozambique against the Portuguese colonial rulers, and many people were celebrating the Zanzibar revolution, another uprising was going on elsewhere on the continent.

Almost exactly one year after Katanga surrendered on 15 January 1963, ending the secession of this mineral-rich province, followers of Lumumba launched a rebellion in Kwilu Province in the western part of the country in an attempt to replace the western-backed government in Leopoldville.

The rebellion started on 22 January 1964 under the leadership of Pierre Mulele, Lumumba's minister of education and heir-apparent, coincidentally in the same month, and the same year, the Zanzibar revolution took place a few hundred miles east of Congo.

And like the leaders of the Zanzibar revolution, Pierre Mulele and his colleagues were socialist-oriented and had the support of socialist countries including Cuba, the Soviet Union and the People's Republic of China. Lumumba's followers in Congo also had the support of neighbouring Tanzania, their strongest supporter among all the African countries. Tanzania was also used a conduit for sending weapons and other forms of material assistance to the Congolese nationalist forces inspired by the martyred Lumumba.

The rebellion in Kwilu Province started almost exactly a year after the secession of Katanga Province ended in January 1963. Moise Tshombe went into exile in Spain and there was some hope that the country would start enjoying relative peace and stability after so much fighting had taken place since independence. But that was not the case. And that was because of what happened to Lumumba and the fiasco that followed his assassination. His followers were not ready to give up the fight.

The Kwilu rebellion quickly spread to other parts of the country, mainly eastern Congo, Lumumba's political stronghold and his home region. The leader of the rebellion in eastern Congo was Gaston Soumialot.

Before the rebellion started in the east, Soumialot was living in Congo-Brazzaville where the National Liberation Council – Conseil National de Liberation (CNL) – was based. It was an umbrella organisation of nationalist groups following Lumumba's ideals and was opposed to the western-backed national government in Leopoldville, the nation's capital.

In January 1964, Soumialot was sent by the CNL to Burundi to mobilise forces and launch a rebellion in eastern Congo which would be coordinated with the uprising in Kwilu to topple the regime in Leopoldville.

When he moved to the east, he was able to mobilise thousands of recruits in eastern Kivu, a region bordering Burundi in the eastern part of Congo. Many people joined the rebellion because they were disgusted with the leadership in Leopoldville that was riddled with corruption and paralyzed by incompetence. The uprising in eastern Congo came to be known as the Simba rebellion, with Stanleyville, Lumumba's political stronghold, as its nerve centre.

The 1964 rural insurgency in Congo received extensive coverage during that period. And many observers have offered thoughtful insights into this phenomenon in a larger national context to explain how and why it happened. According to Herman Kinder and Werner Hilgemann in *The Anchor Atlas of World History, 2:*

"From January to August 1964, rural insurgency engulfed five *provincettes* out of twenty-one and made substantial inroads into another five, raising the distinct possibility of a total collapse of the central government.

The extraordinary speed with which the rebellions spread among the rural masses attests to the enormous insurrectionary potential that had been building up in previous years.

Prolonged neglect of the rural sectors, coupled with the growing disparities of wealth and privilege between the political elites and the peasant masses, inefficient and corrupt government, and ANC (*L'Armée Nationale Congolaise*) abuses, created a situation ripe for major uprising.

Further aggravating the frustration of the rural masses,

279

the promise of a life more abundant made at the time of independence had remained unfulfilled. It seemed to many, especially disaffected youths, that nothing short of a 'second independence' would bring them salvation.

Among the several factors that combined to precipitate rebellion, none was more consequential than the dissolution of parliament in September 1963, a move spurred by the incessant divisions and bickering among deputies. The immediate result was to deprive the opposition of the only remaining legitimate avenue for political participation.

Faced with this situation, several deputies affiliated with the MNC-Lumumba, among them Christophe Gbenye and Bocheley Davidson, decided to move to Brazzaville, in the former French Congo, and organize a National Liberation Council (*Conseil National de Liberation*--CNL). In time the CNL became the central coordinating apparatus for the eastern rebellion.

Another major factor behind the insurrection was the anticipated withdrawal of the UN forces by June 30, 1964. The prospective elimination of the only reliable crutch available to the central government acted as a major incentive for the opposition to mobilize against Adoula.

Finally, with the arrival in the Kwilu area of Pierre Mulele in July 1963, a key revolutionary figure entered the arena. Once affiliated with Antoine Gizenga's PSA, Mulele traveled widely in Eastern Europe before reaching China, where he received sustained training in guerilla warfare.

Upon arriving in Kwilu, Mulele proceeded to recruit a solid phalanx of followers among members of his own ethnic group, the Mbunda, as well as among Gizenga's kinsmen, the Pende, both of whom had long been the target of government repression.

The Kwilu rebellion began in January 1964, when Mulelist insurgents attacked government outposts, mission stations, and company installations. On January 22 and 23, four European missionaries were killed, and on February 5 the chief of staff of the ANC was ambushed and killed. Troops were immediately sent to the area, and by April a measure of stability had been restored to the area. The Kwilu rebellion did not finally end until December 1965, however.

The central figure behind the eastern rebellion was Gaston Soumialot, who, in January 1964, was sent to Burundi by the CNL, with the mission of organizing the rebellion.

With the full support of the Burundi authorities, and thanks to his own skill in exploiting local conflicts and working out tactical alliances with Tutsi exiles from Rwanda, Soumialot was able to recruit thousands of dedicated supporters in eastern Kivu, along the border with Burundi. On May 15, the town of Uvira fell to the rebels, and, shortly thereafter, so did Fizi." – (Herman Kinder and Werner Hilgemann, *The Anchor Atlas of World History, 2*: *From the French Revolution to the American Bicentennial*, New York: Anchor, 1978, p.268).

The Simba rebellion spread quickly throughout the east and towards the south. In the northern part of Katanga, the mineral-rich province in southeastern Congo, the town of Baudoinville – which was renamed Virungu, and now Moba – fell on 19 July 1964. Others followed.

Kindu, in Maniema, was taken on July 24th. And in early August the Soumialot forces, now calling themselves the National Liberation Army – *Armée Nationale de Libération* (ANL) – captured the Lumumbist stronghold of Stanleyville. It was a great victory for the nationalist forces.

Units of the Congolese national army were routed and fled, leaving a lot of weapons behind which Soumialot's forces added to their arsenal as they pushed forward into other parts of the country to capture more territory and consolidate their gains. The Simba fighters pushed on north and west of Stanleyville, eventually penetrating as far west as Lisala on the Congo River in the western part of the country hundreds of miles away from the east.

Prospects seemed bleak for the central government in Leopoldville.

By 5 September 1964, with the proclamation of a revolutionary government under the leadership of the National Liberation Council in the provisional or new capital of Stanleyville, almost half of the entire country was in rebel hands. And seven local capitals out of 21 had also been captured by September 5th.

It seemed the nationalist forces were headed for victory.

But the United States intervened, with a vengeance, to stop the advance of the nationalist forces.

However, it must be conceded that the nationalist forces themselves were partly responsible for undermining their victory. As the rebel movement spread across the country, discipline became a problem among many of its fighters and atrocities were committed by some of them, unleashing terror and terrorising villagers for no apparent reason and without provocation.

The people who were seen as liberators now became enemies of the people, especially those who were :westernized,: an euphemism for "privileged," "educated" or "civilized." These were usually the middle-class "guilty of" aping the consumption proclivities of the West.

But American intervention played a much bigger role in neutralizsing the nationalist forces in spite of the fact that the Simba rebels also played a role in undermining themselves because of the excesses of many of their fighters who could not be contained or disciplined.

The United States increased its support for the central government in Leopoldville and the CIA organised an air force for aerial bombings of the Simba nationalist forces and their targets to support the weak Congolese national army fighting the rebels. Now the Simba rebellion faced its biggest and toughest opponent.

Also on the side of the government and the CIA in the Congo were the white mercenaries, many of them from apartheid South Africa, Rhodesia, Belgium and France. And the bombing missions masterminded by the CIA against the nationalist forces of the Simba uprising had Cuban pilots flying the planes.

These were some of the same Cubans who had been involved in the abortive Bay of Pigs invasion against Cuba on 17 April 1961 during the Kennedy administration when President Kennedy tried to overthrow Castro by using Cuban exiles living in the United States and trained by the CIA for the Cuban invasion. After the disastrous Cuban invasion, they went on another mission, this time in Congo, again at the behest of the CIA.

The CIA also had high-speed patrol boats on Lake Tanganyika to interdict supply lines for the Lumumbist nationalist forces. A lot of supplies which passed through Tanganyika, later renamed Tanzania, were shipped across the lake and some of them were intercepted by the CIA and the mercenaries. Some of the weapons sent to the rebels through Tanzania came from Egypt, which was then known as the United Arab Republic, a strong supporter of Lumumba's former vice premier Antoine Gizenga who was the head of the revolutionary government in Stanleyville.

Yet, in spite of American intervention and clandestine efforts by the CIA to undermine the insurgency, the Simba rebellion gained momentum and spread further, although it had its own weaknesses from internal dynamics which threatened to wreck the rebel movement.

Indiscipline among a significant number of its fighters remained a problem and threatened to alienate even more people whom the insurgents were supposed to be fighting for – the Congolese people in general – against the puppet government in Leopoldville. However, the insurgency was able to forge ahead in spite of its own weaknesses. And as

Herman Kinder and Werner Hilgemann further state:

"No less astonishing than the swiftness of rebel victories was the inability of the insurgents to consolidate their gains and establish an alternative system of administration to one they had so easily destroyed.

Corruption, administrative inefficiency, and ethnic favoritism turned out to be liabilities for the rebel leaders as much as they had been for previous provincial administrators. Heavy reliance on specific ethnic communities (Tetela-Kusu in the east, Pende and Mbunda in Kwilu) for manning the military and administrative apparatuses of the rebellions was seen by many as a reversion to tribalism.

Further complicating ethnic tensions between the ANL leadership and the Simbas, serious conflicts erupted at the *provincette* level over who should get the lion's share of the property seized from the enemy. Finally, countless disputes disrupted the CNL leadership in exile, stemming from personality differences as well as disagreements over questions of tactics and organization.

The rapid decline of popular support for the eastern rebellion is in large part a reflection of the very inadequate leadership offered by the CNL and local cadres.

The military setbacks suffered by the ANL in the fall of 1964 were not just the result of poor leadership, however; even more important in turning the tide against the insurgents was the decisive contribution made by European mercenaries in helping the central government regain control over rebel-held areas."– (Ibid.).

In a desperate move to unite the country, President Joseph Kasavubu invited Moise Tshombe in July 1964 to return to Congo and appointed him prime minister, replacing Cyrille Adoula. And the American government agreed to help Tshombe recruit a force of mercenaries to fight the Simba rebellion which the national army had failed to defeat. The CIA also decided to expand its air strike unit, using more firepower and aerial bombings against the rebels.

The CIA started using more advanced aircraft and more firepower in aerial bombings in August 1964. They were to prove decisive in the outcome of the conflict.

Cuban exile pilots learned how to use the aircraft as soon as the planes arrived in Congo in the same month of August. The Simba rebels had no antiaircraft guns to shoot down the planes and no aircraft of their own for aerial combat and bombing missions. Compounding the problem was the indiscipline and incompetence of the Simba rebels, making them easier targets and less effective in combat against the mercenaries directed by the CIA.

The central government under Prime Minister Tshombe relied heavily on the mercenaries who had a lot of combat experience. There were hundreds of them in Congo. Tshombe also used his former fighters, the Kantangan *gendarmes*, who fought for the secession of Katanga Province and went to live in neighbouring Angola after they lost the war.

He called them back and, with their combat experience, they proved to be effective fighters against the Simba rebels. They were also integrated into the Congolese National Army (ANC – *L'Armée Nationale Congolaise*). The mercenaries led the national army into combat against the rebels and proved to be very effective in the conduct of military operations.

The mercenaries had several advantages. They were experienced fighters; they had technical superiority; and they were a disciplined force. And with the support of air strikes against the rebels and rebel strongholds, they made impressive advances against the Lumumbist nationalist forces.

But the fighting became more intense and brutal as the mercenaries started to recapture rebel strongholds. And both sides committed atrocities which could not be justified under any rules of military engagement. Caught in the crossfire, and often deliberately targeted, were innocent civilians, men, women and children in villages and towns across the country.

As the fighting continued, the white mercenaries proved to be more and more effective. They played a decisive role in recapturing Lisala from the Simba rebels on September 15th, Buende on October 24th, and Kindu on November 6th.

The Lumumbist nationalist forces were now on the defensive and the revolutionary government in Stanleyville decided to take some local whites hostage as a bargaining tool in negotiations with the central government in order to reach some kind of compromise acceptable to both sides. About 1,650 whites, mostly Belgians and some Americans including priests and nuns, were taken hostage.

The Americans and the Belgians deliberately distorted and misinterpreted what the Simba rebels said, and their intention of holding some whites hostage, and used it as an excuse to launch an invasion of Stanleyville which cost countless lives. The invasion was a joint American-Belgian parachute rescue operation code-named Dragon Rouge, or Red Dragon, and was launched on 24 November 1964 to coincide with the arrival of some units of the Congolese National Army and the mercenaries in an area near Stanleyville, the capital of the eastern province. It lasted until November 27th.

Stanleyville was captured by the Americans and the Belgians, with the help of the mercenaries, in one of the bloodiest battles in Congo in the sixties. It was a devastating blow to the Simba rebels, and their leaders, Christophe Gbenye who led the rural rebellion in eastern Congo, and Gaston Soumialot, went into exile in Cairo, Egypt.

The invasion of Stanleyville by the Americans and the Belgians was widely condemned in Congo and across

Africa as well as in other countries. It was also discussed at the UN. Thousands of innocent lives were lost because of this American-Belgian operation.

And Moise Tshombe alienated many people in his own country and other parts of Africa and elsewhere around the world because he was the prime minister of Congo when Stanleyville was attacked by the Americans and the Belgians with his approval. The Americans, the Belgians and the mercenaries were now in full control of Stanleyville, with troops from the Congolese National Army playing only a subordinate role to these foreign invaders.

After the loss of Stanleyville, the Simba rebellion was seriously weakened. The rebels were demoralised, indiscipline continued to be a problem, some of them left, and by the end of the year, the eastern rebellion was reduced to isolated pockets of resistance without strong leadership and enough weapons to mount an effective counter-offensive, although the fighters continued to be inspired by the ideals of Lumumba.

The CIA brought in more combat aircraft and other weapons in January 1965 for mop-up operations and to effectively neutralise the rebels. And by the end of the year, the Simba rebellion had been suppressed in most areas.

Fighting continued here and there for more than one year after that but the war was, for all practical purposes, over by then. In late 1966 and early 1967, the CIA withdrew its most effective combat aircraft that were used against the rebels in the Congo.

The 1964 insurgency in Congo, and its failure to achieve its goals, provided a textbook lesson for other revolutionaries in the country and elsewhere in Africa. One of the things many of them did not learn through the years, no more than many other people aspiring to national office did, was that articulation of ideas is not enough by itself.

Lofty ideals may inspire the people, but they do not represent concrete reality. They must be implemented to be meaningful. And that requires national involvement which is impossible if the people don't identify themselves as a collective national entity.

Also, ethnic affiliations compromise national objectives if the leaders themselves appeal to ethno-regional loyalties to secure power ostensibly to implement a national agenda. That has been one of the biggest tragedies in Africa for decades since independence.

Leaders like Pierre Mulele and Antoine Gizenga may have been true nationalists, as they indeed were. But their inability to expand beyond their regional strongholds and win considerable support from the people of other ethnic groups across the country was a major setback for the insurgency.

Mulele was a Mbunda, and Gizenga, a Pende. And both leaders, like their ethnic groups, were native to Kwilu Province. Attempts by both leaders to transcend their ethnic and regional identities were not very successful.

There were other problems they had to contend with. And as Leonce Ndikumana and Kisangani Emizet explain what happened during that period in their paper, "The Economics of Civil War: The Case of the Democratic Republic of Congo":

"The Kwilu rebellion: 22 January 1964 - 31 December 1965

(i) The political and ideological background

In the post-Lumumba period, the United Nations invested diplomatic efforts to press for national reconciliation and unification of the Congo. The United Nations organized a conference including parliamentarians and leaders of the provincial governments of Katanga, South Kasai, Haut Congo, and Kinshasa in a neutral venue

288

at Lovanium University.

From the conference, a new central government was formed led by Adoula, who had unanimous approval from parliament. Adoula formed a diverse government, including such key pro-Lumumbists as Gigenza and Gbenye.

To appease regionalist demands, the Adoula government submitted to parliament an amendment to the *Loi Fondamentale* aimed at restructuring the country into 21 autonomous provinces (up from the six provinces initially created by the *Loi Fondamentale).* The amendment was promulgated on 27 April 1962.

While the Adoula government tried to find a constitutional solution to the political crisis in Congo, the opposition organized itself with the aim of a revolutionary overthrow of the regime. Pierre Mulele led the Kwilu rebellion while the *Conseil National de Libération* (National Liberation Council, CNL) organized the eastern rebellion

One of the most dedicated Lumumba supporters, Mulele, was Secretary General of the radical wing of the *Parti Solidaire Africain* (PSA) of Gizenga in 1959-1960 and served as Minister of Education in the Lumumba government. He also served as representative of the Gizenga's Stanleyville provincial government in Egypt and in socialist countries. Having sojourned in Peking, Mulele was influenced by Maoist ideology.

At the end of the Stanleyville government in August 1961, Mulele refused national reconciliation and chose exile, during which he perfected his revolutionary ideology and prepared his strategies for organizing a peasant guerilla force.

Mulele accused the central government of having sold out to the interests of the West and advocated a second 'liberating independence,' which attracted enthusiastic support from rural mass

289

(ii) Support for the rebellion:
Ethnic base with no mineral resource base

Mulele was from the Mbunda ethnic group while Gizenga was an ethnic Mpende, both groups were from the Kwilu province and claimed to be marginalized by the central government. The ethnic orientation of the Mulelist rebellion facilitated recruitment of combatants but also prevented the rebellion from gaining ground beyond the Mbunda-Mpende territory.

Unlike the Katangan and Kasai rebellions, the Kwilu rebellion was not motivated by the control of provincial mineral resources. Thus, the rebellion could not count on external economic interests for support. The war effort was entirely supported by the local population.

There are no specific factors that triggered the Kwilu rebellion. Upon his return from exile in July 1963, Mulele mobilized and trained his combatants who were subjected to a rigid code of discipline. The Mulelist rebels posed stiff resistance to government troops despite the rudimentary nature of their military equipment.

The rebellion was eventually defeated in December 1965, leaving only pockets of isolated resistance in the rural area.

The eastern rebellion:
15 April 1964 - 1 July 1966

(i) The political context

The Adoula government failed in its mission of national unification and instead became a vehicle of recolonization of the Congo by Belgium via military occupation and control of the economy.

Antagonism between the parliament and the government - this time with the president and the prime minister on the same side - led President Kasavubu to suspend the parliament on 29 September 1963. The same day, opposition nationalist parties opened an extraordinary conference that ended on October 3 with the creation of the CNL whose objective was to overthrow the Adoula government and to achieve "total and effective decolonization of the Congo thus far dominated by a coalition of foreign powers" (Vanderlinden, et al. 1980: 124)..

(ii) The ideological factor

The leaders of the CNL fled to Brazzaville and formed a cartel of Lumumbist- nationalist parties, the most important ones being MNC-Lumumba led by Gbenye and PSA led by Gizenga (Vanderlinden, et al. 1980).

The CNL had a socialist orientation with both pro-Soviet and pro-Chinese leanings. This socialist orientation proved useful in mobilizing the masses against the central government, which was accused of selling out to capitalist interests, but it also prevented the CNL from obtaining foreign assistance.

(iii) Organization of the rebellion

In January 1964, the CNL sent Gaston Soumialot and Laurent Kabila to Burundi with the mission of preparing the rebellion in the east (Kabila in north Katanga and Soumialot in Kivu).

On 15 April 1964, the rebellion started in the Ruzizi plain south of Bukavu and a month later, Uvira was under the control of the simba (which means lions), the rebel forces of the *Armée Populaire de Libération* (Popular Liberation Army, APL) of the CNL.

The rebellion drew its forces from the large population of young, uneducated, and unemployed Congolese. The APL advanced quickly with little resistance from the government forces. The Simba were believed to possess magic powers acquired from taking a traditional potion that was purported to transform enemy bullets into water (Verhaegen, 1969).

In two months, the rebels conquered northern Katanga, Maniema, Sankuru and Orientale province. On 5 September 1964, the "people's government" of Stanleyville was installed in Haut Congo, headed by President Gbenye of the MNC-Lumumba who was also president of the CNL.

By the end of September, about half of the country was under control of the APL. The rich endowment in mineral resources of the eastern provinces was a major motivation and source of financing for the rebellion. In this respect, the eastern rebellion has numerous similarities with the secessionist wars of Katanga and southern Kasai. Furthermore, like the Katangan, southern Kasai, and Kwilu rebellions, the eastern rebellion was also supported by a large ethnic base dominated by the Bakusu and Batetela.

(iv) Tshombe returns and defeats the rebellion

The Adoula government continued to experience instability and its army was unable to contain the rebellion. The government turned to Tshombe (in exile in Spain) who still had some influence in the Katanga region and had the backing of Belgian officials and private actors. More important, he had contacts with both the CNL and the Adoula government. Tshombe was believed to be the man who could achieve national reconciliation and control the rebellion (Gibbs 1991).

He returned on 26 June 1964 and President Kasavubu gave him the mission of forming a transitional government. To the surprise and anger of many, Tshombe's government did not include representatives from key opposition groups, most notably the CNL.

Tshombe rallied his former Katangan gendarmes with

the assistance of Belgian mercenaries and advisers and with backing from the United States and Belgium.

The rebels unsuccessfully tried to use white hostages to stop the advance of Tshombe's forces. Stanleyville was captured on 24 November 1964, but as many as 200 Europeans and some 46,000 Congolese were killed.

The leaders of CNL retreated from the provincial capitals but continued to fight in rural areas. It was only in 1967 that the Orientale province and Maniema province were fully controlled by government forces.

The APL retained limited control over some rural areas in southern Kivu (Fizi and Baraka) under the command of Kabila. The rebellion was completely defeated by 1968." - – (Leonce Ndikumana and Kisangani Emizet, "The Economics of Civil War: The Case of the Democratic Republic of Congo," Peri Working Paper No.63, 1 July 2003).

In spite of Tshombe's success in fighting the Simba rebels in his capacity as prime minister of Congo during that period, he did not last long in power. He became involved in a power struggle against President Joseph Kasavubu and lost.

In October 1965, he was replaced by Evariste Kimba as prime minister and returned to Spain, where he lived before, after he failed in his secessionist effort to keep Katanga out of Congo.

Kasavubu remained president but not for long. On November 25th the same year, he was overthrown by Joseph Mobutu who became the new head of state.

In spite of all those changes during that period, the year 1964 stood out as the most decisive one in the history of nationalist resistance in the sixties when the Simba rebels were finally defeated by a combined force of American and Belgian paratroopers.

When they lost Stanleyville, the capital of their revolutionary government, they knew their days were numbered. And they never recovered from that loss.

Elsewhere in Africa, 1964 was also an important year. In the case of South Africa, it assumed even greater significance as an important milestone in the struggle against apartheid. It was the year of the Rivonia Trial.

The Rivonia Trial was a significant event, not only for South Africa but for the entire continent. It was a defining moment in the struggle against apartheid and it influenced the course of African history during the post-colonial era because of the involvement of other African countries in the liberation struggle throughout southern Africa, and not just in South Africa.

But South Africa posed special problems because it was the strongest nation and the bastion of white supremacy on the continent. And the Rivonia Trial provided an opportunity for the opponents of apartheid to expose the evils of the diabolical system of racial oppression. The trial also showed that the apartheid regime was determined to maintain its grip on the country, especially on the restive black majority, and was not ready to make any concessions to its opponents.

The most prominent of those opponents was Nelson Mandela, leader of the African National Congress (ANC) and commander of Umkhonto we Sizwe, the Spear of the Nation, which was the military wing of the ANC.

The Rivonia Trial took place between 1963 and 1964 involving 10 leaders of the African National Congress, including Mandela. It was a treason trial. The accused were tried for 221 acts of sabotage intended to start a violent revolution and overthrow the government.

On 11 July 1963, 16 leaders of the African National Congress were arrested at Liliesleaf Farm in Rivonia, a Johannesburg suburb. The farm was owned by Arthur Goldreich and was used as a private meeting place and hideout for leaders of the African National Congress.

Among those arrested were Walter Sisulu, Govan Mbeki, Raymond Mhlaba, Andrew Mlangeni; Elias

Motsoaledi, trade union and ANC member; Ahmed Kathrada; Dennis Goldberg, a Cape Town engineer and leader of the Congress of Democrats; Lionel "Rusty" Bernstein, architect and member of the South African Communist Party (SACP); Bob Hepple, Arthur Goldreich; Harold Wolpe, prominent attorney and activist; and James "Jimmy" Kantor, brother-in-law of Harold Wolpe.

Charged together with those who were arrested at Liliesleaf Farm were Nelson Mandela and Walter Mkwayi. Mandela was brought to the trial in Pretoria from Robben Island where he was already serving a five-year sentence since 1962 for sabotage and leaving the country illegally.

Most of those who were charged in the Rivonia Trial were black. Four of them – Goldberg, Bernstein, Hepple and Goldreich – were Jews. And one, Ahmed Kathrada, was Indian.

The prosecutors and the police considered Goldreich, the owner of Liliesleaf Farm, to be "the arch-conspirator" and were infuriated when he and Wolpe managed to escape from prison on 11 August 1963, after they bribed a prison guard.

The people who were arrested at the farm owned by Goldreich had been forced to go underground by the apartheid regime's repressive laws. The ANC had been operating underground since being outlawed in April 1960, one month after the Sharpeville Massacre. The police had collected hundreds of documents from the ANC hideout at Rivonia about Operation Mayibuye – Operation Comeback – which they used against the defendants.

Under the new General Law Amendment (Sabotage) Act of 1962 and the Suppression of Communism Act, the defendants faced the death penalty.

The defence lawyers did not even have enough time to prepare their case. They were unable to see their clients until two days before the indictment on October 9th. The defence team was led by Bram Fischer, a prominent

Afrikaner lawyer. He was assisted by George Bizos, Joel Joffe, Harold Hanson and Arthur Chaskalson who became a distinguished judge after the end of apartheid. In June 1994 President Mandela appointed Chaskalson the first president of South Africa's new Constitutional Court. On 22 November 2001, he became the Chief Justice of South Africa.

At the end of October 1964, Bob Hepple was struck off the list of the accused and left the dock after he agreed to testify for the prosecution. He later fled the country instead of testifying against his compatriots.

The star witness for the prosecution was Bruno Mtolo, a member of the ANC and its armed wing, Spear of the Nation – Umkhonto We Sizwe (MK) – in Durban, Natal. He betrayed his colleagues and was the most prominent witness among the 173 who testified against the accused. His testimony was also the most damaging, although much it was fabricated. But he was "believable" because he was a member of the inner circle.

He also testified during cross-examination by the defence that he turned against his colleagues because he was not paid by the ANC for his work as the leader of the MK (Umkhonto We Sizwe) in Natal.

The prosecution team was led by Dr. Percy Yutar, a Jew, who was the assistant attorney-general of the Transvaal, the northern province.

His conduct of the case was reminiscent of the Rosebergs' trial in New York in the United States in the early 1950s in which Julius Rosenberg and his wife Ethel were accused of spying for the Soviet Union and giving the Soviets secret information on the atomic bomb.

Both the prosecutor and the judge in this case were Jews who are said to have been too harsh on the Rosenbergs to prove to the American government that although they were Jews themselves like the accused, their patriotism could not be questioned; they were good American citizens and fiercely loyal to the United States.

The prosecutor was Assistant US Attorney Roy Cohn. And the judge was Irving Kaufman.

The Rosenbergs were convicted and sentenced to death in April 1951 and were executed in June 1953, although many observers believed that Ethel was innocent of espionage and played only a minor role, if any, in helping her husband provide Soviet agents with nuclear secrets.

Dr. Yutar also, as Jew, may partly have been motivated by his desire to prove to the Afrikaner-dominated government that he was a true patriot by seeking a harsh sentence for the defendants in the Rivonia Trial, among whom were some of his fellow Jews opposed to apartheid.

The charges against the accused were:

- Recruiting persons for training in the preparation and use of explosives and in guerilla warfare for the purpose of violent revolution and committing acts of sabotage.

- Conspiring to commit the aforementioned acts and to aid foreign military units when they invaded the Republic.

- Acting in these ways to further the objects of communism.

- Soliciting and receiving money for these purposes from sympathizers in Algeria, Ethiopia, Liberia, Nigeria, Tunisia, and elsewhere.

- Production requirements for munitions for a six -month period were sufficient, the prosecutor Percy Yutar said in his opening address, to blow up a city the size of Johannesburg.

It was the most celebrated, and most sensational, trial in the history of South Africa.

The trial began on 26 November 1963 and ended on 12 June 1964 when the defendants were sentenced to prison. Each of the 10 accused pleaded not guilty.

James "Jimmy" Kantor was discharged at the end of the prosecution, and Lionel "Rusty" Bernstein was acquitted. But Bernstein was rearrested, released on bail, and placed under house arrest. Later he fled the country.

The case had some dramatic aspects including daring

297

escapes. Arthur Goldreich escaped from prison disguised as a priest; Walter Mkwayi escaped during trial; and Harold Wolpe and James Kantor also escaped.

The trial was condemned by the UN Security Council but nothing was done to punish the apartheid regime, although the Security Council members talked about imposing sanctions on the South African government. It was more rhetoric than action. Race played a critical role in this.

The three Security Council members with veto power – the United States, France and Britain – besides the Soviet Union, were allies of apartheid South Africa. And their actions were motivated by racial considerations, not just geopolitical interests vis-a-vis the Soviet Union. As President Julius Nyerere, whose remarks were also appropriate with regard to the apartheid regime, stated in his article, "Rhodesia in the Context of Southern Africa" published in *Foreign Affairs* in April 1966:

"It is time for Britain and the United States of America to make clear whether they really believe in the principles they claim to espouse or whether their policies are governed by considerations of the privileges of their 'kith and kin'....

Despite the protestations of belief in human equality, the domination of a white minority over blacks is acceptable to the West."

As the treason trial continued, there was a distinct possibility that many of the accused, if not most or all of them, would get capital punishment.

In fact, Mandela was warned by his lawyers before the trial started not to bluntly tell the judge in his opening statement that he's ready for capital punishment; chances were he could get it since the judge would see that as a challenge to him. That is why, as he states in his autobiography *Long Walk to Freedom*, he qualified his remarks, "I am prepared to die," with "if needs be."

Although the prosecution would have preferred capital punishment, and had in fact originally requested the death penalty, worldwide protests against the trial and the ingenuity of the defence team helped to influence the outcome of the case. The death penalty was dropped and eight defendants, including Mandela, were sentenced to life imprisonment. One was acquitted.

Dennis Goldberg was sent to Pretoria Central Prison, at that time the only place where white political prisoners in South Africa were confined. He served 22 years. The rest were sent to Robben Island, the most harsh imprisonment facility in the South African penal system.

Probably the most dramatic moment during the trial was on 20 April 1964 when Nelson Mandela read his statement from the dock at the opening of the defence case in the Pretoria Supreme Court, "I Am Prepared to Die":

"I am the First Accused.

I hold a Bachelor's Degree in Arts and practised as an attorney in Johannesburg for a number of years in partnership with Oliver Tambo. I am a convicted prisoner serving five years for leaving the country without a permit and for inciting people to go on strike at the end of May 1961.

At the outset, I want to say that the suggestion made by the State in its opening that the struggle in South Africa is under the influence of foreigners or communists is wholly incorrect.

I have done whatever I did, both as an individual and as a leader of my people, because of my experience in South Africa and my own proudly felt African background, and not because of what any outsider might have said.

In my youth in the Transkei I listened to the elders of my tribe telling stories of the old days. Amongst the tales they related to me were those of wars fought by our ancestors in defence of the fatherland. The names of Dingane and Bambata, Hintsa and Makana, Squngthi and Dalasile, Moshoeshoe and Sekhukhuni, were praised as the glory of the entire African nation.

I hoped then that life might offer me the opportunity to serve my people and make my own humble contribution to their freedom struggle. This is what has motivated me in all that I have done in relation to the charges made against me in this case.

Having said this, I must deal immediately and at some length with the question of violence. Some of the things so far told to the Court are true and some are untrue. I do not, however, deny that I planned sabotage.

I did not plan it in a spirit of recklessness, nor because I have any love of violence. I planned it as a result of a calm and sober assessment of the political situation that had arisen after many years of tyranny, exploitation, and oppression of my people by the Whites.

I admit immediately that I was one of the persons who helped to form Umkhonto we Sizwe, and that I played a prominent role in its affairs until I was arrested in August 1962.

In the statement which I am about to make I shall correct certain false impressions which have been created by State witnesses. Amongst other things, I will demonstrate that certain of the acts referred to in the evidence were not and could not have been committed by Umkhonto.

I will also deal with the relationship between the African National Congress and Umkhonto, and with the part which I personally have played in the affairs of both organizations. I shall deal also with the part played by the Communist Party.

In order to explain these matters properly, I will have to explain what Umkhonto set out to achieve; what methods it prescribed for the achievement of these objects, and why these methods were chosen. I will also have to explain how I became involved in the activities of these organizations.

I deny that Umkhonto was responsible for a number of acts which clearly fell outside the policy of the organisation, and which have been charged in the indictment against us. I do not know what justification there was for these acts, but to demonstrate that they could not have been authorized by Umkhonto, I want to refer briefly to the roots and policy of the organization.

I have already mentioned that I was one of the persons who helped to form Umkhonto. I, and the others who started the organization, did so for two reasons.

Firstly, we believed that as a result of Government policy, violence by the African people had become inevitable, and that unless responsible leadership was given to canalize and control the feelings of our people, there would be outbreaks of terrorism which would produce an intensity of bitterness and hostility between the various races of this country which is not produced even by war.

Secondly, we felt that without violence there would be no way open to the African people to succeed in their struggle against the principle of white supremacy. All lawful modes of expressing opposition to this principle had been closed by legislation, and we were placed in a position in which we had either to accept a permanent state of inferiority, or to defy the Government. We chose to defy the law.

We first broke the law in a way which avoided any recourse to violence; when this form was legislated against, and then the Government resorted to a show of force to crush opposition to its policies, only then did we decide to answer violence with violence.

But the violence which we chose to adopt was not terrorism. We who formed Umkhonto were all members of the African National Congress, and had behind us the ANC tradition of non-violence and negotiation as a means

301

of solving political disputes.

We believe that South Africa belongs to all the people who live in it, and not to one group, be it black or white. We did not want an interracial war, and tried to avoid it to the last minute.

If the Court is in doubt about this, it will be seen that the whole history of our organization bears out what I have said, and what I will subsequently say, when I describe the tactics which Umkhonto decided to adopt. I want, therefore, to say something about the African National Congress.

The African National Congress was formed in 1912 to defend the rights of the African people which had been seriously curtailed by the South Africa Act, and which were then being threatened by the Native Land Act. For thirty-seven years - that is until 1949 - it adhered strictly to a constitutional struggle.

It put forward demands and resolutions; it sent delegations to the Government in the belief that African grievances could be settled through peaceful discussion and that Africans could advance gradually to full political rights. But White Governments remained unmoved, and the rights of Africans became less instead of becoming greater. In the words of my leader, Chief Lutuli, who became President of the ANC in 1952, and who was later awarded the Nobel Peace Prize:

'Who will deny that thirty years of my life have been spent knocking in vain, patiently, moderately, and modestly at a closed and barred door? What have been the fruits of moderation? The past thirty years have seen the greatest number of laws restricting our rights and progress, until today we have reached a stage where we have almost no rights at all.'

Even after 1949, the ANC remained determined to avoid violence. At this time, however, there was a change

302

from the strictly constitutional means of protest which had been employed in the past. The change was embodied in a decision which was taken to protest against apartheid legislation by peaceful, but unlawful, demonstrations against certain laws.

Pursuant to this policy the ANC launched the Defiance Campaign, in which I was placed in charge of volunteers. This campaign was based on the principles of passive resistance. More than 8,500 people defied apartheid laws and went to jail. Yet there was not a single instance of violence in the course of this campaign on the part of any defier.

I and nineteen colleagues were convicted for the role which we played in organizing the campaign, but our sentences were suspended mainly because the Judge found that discipline and non-violence had been stressed throughout.

This was the time when the volunteer section of the ANC was established, and when the word *Amadelakufa* was first used: this was the time when the volunteers were asked to take a pledge to uphold certain principles.

Evidence dealing with volunteers and their pledges has been introduced into this case, but completely out of context. The volunteers were not, and are not, the soldiers of a black army pledged to fight a civil war against the whites.

They were, and are. dedicated workers who are prepared to lead campaigns initiated by the ANC to distribute leaflets, to organize strikes, or do whatever the particular campaign required. They are called volunteers because they volunteer to face the penalties of imprisonment and whipping which are now prescribed by the legislature for such acts.

During the Defiance Campaign, the Public Safety Act and the Criminal Law Amendment Act were passed. These Statutes provided harsher penalties for offences committed by way of protests against laws. Despite this, the protests

303

continued and the ANC adhered to its policy of non-violence.

In 1956, 156 leading members of the Congress Alliance, including myself, were arrested on a charge of high treason and charges under the Suppression of Communism Act. The non-violent policy of the ANC was put in issue by the State, but when the Court gave judgement some five years later, it found that the ANC did not have a policy of violence.

We were acquitted on all counts, which included a count that the ANC sought to set up a communist state in place of the existing regime. The Government has always sought to label all its opponents as communists. This allegation has been repeated in the present case, but as I will show, the ANC is not, and never has been, a communist organization.

In 1960 there was the shooting at Sharpeville, which resulted in the proclamation of a state of emergency and the declaration of the ANC as an unlawful organization. My colleagues and I, after careful consideration, decided that we would not obey this decree. The African people were not part of the Government and did not make the laws by which they were governed.

We believed in the words of the Universal Declaration of Human Rights, that 'the will of the people shall be the basis of authority of the Government', and for us to accept the banning was equivalent to accepting the silencing of the Africans for all time.

The ANC refused to dissolve, but instead went underground. We believed it was our duty to preserve this organization which had been built up with almost fifty years of unremitting toil. I have no doubt that no self-respecting White political organization would disband itself if declared illegal by a government in which it had no say.

In 1960 the Government held a referendum which led to the establishment of the Republic. Africans, who constituted approximately 70 per cent of the population of South Africa, were not entitled to vote, and were not even consulted about the proposed constitutional change.

All of us were apprehensive of our future under the proposed White Republic, and a resolution was taken to hold an All-In African Conference to call for a National Convention, and to organize mass demonstrations on the eve of the unwanted Republic, if the Government failed to call the Convention. The conference was attended by Africans of various political persuasions.

I was the Secretary of the conference and undertook to be responsible for organizing the national stay-at-home which was subsequently called to coincide with the declaration of the Republic. As all strikes by Africans are illegal, the person organizing such a strike must avoid arrest. I was chosen to be this person, and consequently I had to leave my home and family and my practice and go into hiding to avoid arrest.

The stay-at-home, in accordance with ANC policy, was to be a peaceful demonstration. Careful instructions were given to organizers and members to avoid any recourse to violence. The Government's answer was to introduce new and harsher laws, to mobilize its armed forces, and to send Saracens, armed vehicles, and soldiers into the townships in a massive show of force designed to intimidate the people. This was an indication that the Government had decided to rule by force alone, and this decision was a milestone on the road to Umkhonto.

Some of this may appear irrelevant to this trial. In fact, I believe none of it is irrelevant because it will, I hope, enable the Court to appreciate the attitude eventually adopted by the various persons and bodies concerned in the National Liberation Movement. When I went to jail in 1962, the dominant idea was that loss of life should be avoided. I now know that this was still so in 1963.

I must return to June 1961. What were we, the leaders of our people, to do? Were we to give in to the show of force and the implied threat against future action, or were we to fight it and, if so, how?

We had no doubt that we had to continue the fight. Anything else would have been abject surrender. Our problem was not whether to fight, but was how to continue the fight. We of the ANC had always stood for a non-racial democracy, and we shrank from any action which might drive the races further apart than they already were. But the hard facts were that fifty years of non-violence had brought the African people nothing but more and more repressive legislation, and fewer and fewer rights.

It may not be easy for this Court to understand, but it is a fact that for a long time the people had been talking of violence - of the day when they would fight the White man and win back their country - and we, the leaders of the ANC, had nevertheless always prevailed upon them to avoid violence and to pursue peaceful methods.

When some of us discussed this in May and June of 1961, it could not be denied that our policy to achieve a nonracial State by non-violence had achieved nothing, and that our followers were beginning to lose confidence in this policy and were developing disturbing ideas of terrorism.

It must not be forgotten that by this time violence had, in fact, become a feature of the South African political scene. There had been violence in 1957 when the women of Zeerust were ordered to carry passes; there was violence in 1958 with the enforcement of cattle culling in Sekhukhuniland; there was violence in 1959 when the people of Cato Manor protested against pass raids; there was violence in 1960 when the Government attempted to impose Bantu Authorities in Pondoland. Thirty-nine Africans died in these disturbances. In 1961 there had been riots in Warmbaths, and all this time the Transkei had been a seething mass of unrest.

Each disturbance pointed clearly to the inevitable growth among Africans of the belief that violence was the only way out - it showed that a Government which uses force to maintain its rule teaches the oppressed to use force to oppose it.

Already small groups had arisen in the urban areas and were spontaneously making plans for violent forms of political struggle. There now arose a danger that these groups would adopt terrorism against Africans, as well as Whites, if not properly directed. Particularly disturbing was the type of violence engendered in places such as Zeerust, Sekhukhuniland, and Pondoland amongst Africans.

It was increasingly taking the form, not of struggle against the Government - though this is what prompted it - but of civil strife amongst themselves, conducted in such a way that it could not hope to achieve anything other than a loss of life and bitterness.

At the beginning of June 1961, after a long and anxious assessment of the South African situation, I, and some colleagues, came to the conclusion that as violence in this country was inevitable, it would be unrealistic and wrong for African leaders to continue preaching peace and non-violence at a time when the Government met our peaceful demands with force.

This conclusion was not easily arrived at. It was only when all else had failed, when all channels of peaceful protest had been barred to us, that the decision was made to embark on violent forms of political struggle, and to form Umkhonto we Sizwe. We did so not because we desired such a course, but solely because the Government had left us with no other choice. In the Manifesto of Umkhonto published on 16 December 1961, which is Exhibit AD, we said:

'The time comes in the life of any nation when there remain only two choices - submit or fight. That time has now come to South Africa. We shall not submit and we have no choice but to hit back by all means in our power in defence of our people, our future, and our freedom.'

This was our feeling in June of 1961 when we decided to press for a change in the policy of the National Liberation Movement. I can only say that I felt morally obliged to do what I did.

We who had taken this decision started to consult leaders of various organizations, including the ANC. I will not say whom we spoke to, or what they said, but I wish to deal with the role of the African National Congress in this phase of the struggle, and with the policy and objectives of Umkhonto we Sizwe.

As far as the ANC was concerned, it formed a clear view which can be summarized as follows:

1. It was a mass political organization with a political function to fulfil. Its members had joined on the express policy of non-violence.

2. Because of all this, it could not and would not undertake violence. This must be stressed. One cannot turn such a body into the small, closely knit organization required for sabotage. Nor would this be politically correct, because it would result in members ceasing to carry out this essential activity: political propaganda and organization. Nor was it permissible to change the whole nature of the organization.

3. On the other hand, in view of this situation I have described, the ANC was prepared to depart from its fifty-year-old policy of non-violence to this extent that it would no longer disapprove of properly controlled violence. Hence members who undertook such activity would not be subject to disciplinary action by the ANC.

I say 'properly controlled violence' because I made it clear that if I formed the organization I would at all times subject it to the political guidance of the ANC and would not undertake any different form of activity from that

308

contemplated without the consent of the ANC. And I shall now tell the Court how that form of violence came to be determined.

As a result of this decision, Umkhonto was formed in November 1961. When we took this decision, and subsequently formulated our plans, the ANC heritage of non-violence and racial harmony was very much with us. We felt that the country was drifting towards a civil war in which Blacks and Whites would fight each other. We viewed the situation with alarm.

Civil war could mean the destruction of what the ANC stood for; with civil war, racial peace would be more difficult than ever to achieve. We already have examples in South African history of the results of war. It has taken more than fifty years for the scars of the South African War to disappear. How much longer would it take to eradicate the scars of inter-racial civil war, which could not be fought without a great loss of life on both sides?

The avoidance of civil war had dominated our thinking for many years, but when we decided to adopt violence as part of our policy, we realized that we might one day have to face the prospect of such a war. This had to be taken into account in formulating our plans.

We required a plan which was flexible and which permitted us to act in accordance with the needs of the times; above all, the plan had to be one which recognized civil war as the last resort, and left the decision on this question to the future. We did not want to be committed to civil war, but we wanted to be ready if it became inevitable.

Four forms of violence were possible. There is sabotage, there is guerilla warfare, there is terrorism, and there is open revolution. We chose to adopt the first method and to exhaust it before taking any other decision.

In the light of our political background the choice was a logical one. Sabotage did not involve loss of life, and it offered the best hope for future race relations. Bitterness would be kept to a minimum and, if the policy bore fruit, democratic government could become a reality. This is what we felt at the time, and this is what we said in our Manifesto (Exhibit AD):

'We of Umkhonto we Sizwe have always sought to achieve liberation without bloodshed and civil clash. We hope, even at this late hour, that our first actions will awaken everyone to a realization of the disastrous situation to which the Nationalist policy is leading. We hope that we will bring the Government and its supporters to their senses before it is too late, so that both the Government and its policies can be changed before matters reach the desperate state of civil war.'

The initial plan was based on a careful analysis of the political and economic situation of our country. We believed that South Africa depended to a large extent on foreign capital and foreign trade. We felt that planned destruction of power plants, and interference with rail and telephone communications, would tend to scare away capital from the country, make it more difficult for goods from the industrial areas to reach the seaports on schedule, and would in the long run be a heavy drain on the economic life of the country, thus compelling the voters of the country to reconsider their position.

Attacks on the economic life lines of the country were to be linked with sabotage on Government buildings and other symbols of apartheid. These attacks would serve as a source of inspiration to our people. In addition, they would provide an outlet for those people who were urging the adoption of violent methods and would enable us to give concrete proof to our followers that we had adopted a stronger line and were fighting back against Government violence.

In addition, if mass action were successfully organized, and mass reprisals taken, we felt that sympathy for our cause would be roused in other countries, and that greater pressure would be brought to bear on the South African Government.

This then was the plan. Umkhonto was to perform sabotage, and strict instructions were given to its members right from the start, that on no account were they to injure or kill people in planning or carrying out operations. These instructions have been referred to in the evidence of 'Mr. X' and 'Mr. Z'.

The affairs of the Umkhonto were controlled and directed by a National High Command, which had powers of co-option and which could, and did, appoint Regional Commands. The High Command was the body which determined tactics and targets and was in charge of training and finance. Under the High Command there were Regional Commands which were responsible for the direction of the local sabotage groups.

Within the framework of the policy laid down by the National High Command, the Regional Commands had authority to select the targets to be attacked.

They had no authority to go beyond the prescribed framework and thus had no authority to embark upon acts which endangered life, or which did not fit into the overall plan of sabotage. For instance, Umkhonto members were forbidden ever to go armed into operation. Incidentally, the terms High Command and Regional Command were an importation from the Jewish national underground organization Irgun Zvai Leumi, which operated in Israel between 1944 and 1948.

Umkhonto had its first operation on 16 December 1961, when Government buildings in Johannesburg, Port Elizabeth and Durban were attacked. The selection of targets is proof of the policy to which I have referred. Had we intended to attack life we would have selected targets where people congregated and not empty buildings and power stations.

The sabotage which was committed before 16

311

December 1961 was the work of isolated groups and had no connection whatever with Umkhonto. In fact, some of these and a number of later acts were claimed by other organizations.

The Manifesto of Umkhonto was issued on the day that operations commenced. The response to our actions and Manifesto among the white population was characteristically violent. The Government threatened to take strong action, and called upon its supporters to stand firm and to ignore the demands of the Africans. The Whites failed to respond by suggesting change; they responded to our call by suggesting the *laager*.

In contrast, the response of the Africans was one of encouragement.

Suddenly there was hope again. Things were happening. People in the townships became eager for political news. A great deal of enthusiasm was generated by the initial successes, and people began to speculate on how soon freedom would be obtained.

But we in Umkhonto weighed up the white response with anxiety. The lines were being drawn. The whites and blacks were moving into separate camps, and the prospects of avoiding a civil war were made less. The white newspapers carried reports that sabotage would be punished by death. If this was so, how could we continue to keep Africans away from terrorism?

Already scores of Africans had died as a result of racial friction. In 1920 when the famous leader, Masabala, was held in Port Elizabeth jail, twenty-four of a group of Africans who had gathered to demand his release were killed by the police and white civilians.

In 1921, more than one hundred Africans died in the Bulhoek affair. In 1924 over two hundred Africans were killed when the Administrator of South-West Africa led a force against a group which had rebelled against the imposition of dog tax. On 1 May 1950, eighteen Africans died as a result of police shootings during the strike. On 21

March 1960, sixty-nine unarmed Africans died at Sharpeville.

How many more Sharpevilles would there be in the history of our country? And how many more Sharpevilles could the country stand without violence and terror becoming the order of the day? And what would happen to our people when that stage was reached? In the long run we felt certain we must succeed, but at what cost to ourselves and the rest of the country? And if this happened, how could black and white ever live together again in peace and harmony? These were the problems that faced us, and these were our decisions.

Experience convinced us that rebellion would offer the Government limitless opportunities for the indiscriminate slaughter of our people. But it was precisely because the soil of South Africa is already drenched with the blood of innocent Africans that we felt it our duty to make preparations as a long-term undertaking to use force in order to defend ourselves against force.

If war were inevitable, we wanted the fight to be conducted on terms most favourable to our people. The fight which held out prospects best for us and the least risk of life to both sides was guerilla warfare. We decided, therefore, in our preparations for the future, to make provision for the possibility of guerilla warfare.

All whites undergo compulsory military training, but no such training was given to Africans. It was in our view essential to build up a nucleus of trained men who would be able to provide the leadership which would be required if guerilla warfare started. We had to prepare for such a situation before it became too late to make proper preparations.

It was also necessary to build up a nucleus of men trained in civil administration and other professions, so that Africans would be equipped to participate in the government of this country as soon as they were allowed to do so.

At this stage it was decided that I should attend the Conference of the Pan-African Freedom Movement for Central, East, and Southern Africa, which was to be held early in 1962 in Addis Ababa, and, because of our need for preparation, it was also decided that, after the conference, I would undertake a tour of the African States with a view to obtaining facilities for the training of soldiers, and that I would also solicit scholarships for the higher education of matriculated Africans.

Training in both fields would be necessary, even if changes came about by peaceful means.

Administrators would be necessary who would be willing and able to administer a non-racial State and so would men be necessary to control the army and police force of such a State.

It was on this note that I left South Africa to proceed to Addis Ababa as a delegate of the ANC. My tour was a success. Wherever I went I met sympathy for our cause and promises of help. All Africa was united against the stand of White South Africa, and even in London I was received with great sympathy by political leaders, such as Mr. Gaitskell and Mr. Grimond.

In Africa I was promised support by such men as Julius Nyerere, now President of Tanganyika; Mr. Kawawa, then Prime Minister of Tanganyika; Emperor Haile Selassie of Ethiopia; General Abboud, President of the Sudan; Habib Bourguiba, President of Tunisia; Ben-Bella, now President of Algeria; Modibo Keita, President of Mali; Leopold Senghor, President of Senegal; Sekou Toure, President of Guinea; President Tubman of Liberia; and Milton Obote, Prime Minister of Uganda.

It was Ben-Bella who invited me to visit Oujda, the Headquarters of the Algerian Army of National Liberation, the visit which is described in my diary, one of the Exhibits.

I started to make a study of the art of war and revolution and, whilst abroad, underwent a course in military training. If there was to be guerilla warfare, I wanted to be able to stand and fight with my people and to share the hazards of war with them.

Notes of lectures which I received in Algeria are contained in Exhibit 16, produced in evidence. Summaries of books on guerilla warfare and military strategy have also been produced. I have already admitted that these documents are in my writing, and I acknowledge that I made these studies to equip myself for the role which I might have to play if the struggle drifted into guerilla warfare.

I approached this question as every African Nationalist should do. I was completely objective. The Court will see that I attempted to examine all types of authority on the subject - from the East and from the West, going back to the classic work of Clausewitz, and covering such a variety as Mao Tse Tung and Che Guevara on the one hand, and the writings on the Anglo-Boer War on the other. Of course, these notes are merely summaries of the books I read and do not contain my personal views.

I also made arrangements for our recruits to undergo military training. But here it was impossible to organize any scheme without the co-operation of the ANC offices in Africa. I consequently obtained the permission of the ANC in South Africa to do this. To this extent then there was a departure from the original decision of the ANC, but it applied outside South Africa only.

The first batch of recruits actually arrived in Tanganyika when I was passing through that country on my way back to South Africa.

I returned to South Africa and reported to my colleagues on the results of my trip. On my return I found that there had been little alteration in the political scene save that the threat of a death penalty for sabotage had now become a fact.

The attitude of my colleagues in Umkhonto was much the same as it had been before I left. They were feeling their way cautiously and felt that it would be a long time before the possibilities of sabotage were exhausted. In fact, the view was expressed by some that the training of recruits was premature.

This is recorded by me in the document which is Exhibit R.14. After a full discussion, however, it was decided to go ahead with the plans for military training because of the fact that it would take many years to build up a sufficient nucleus of trained soldiers to start a guerilla campaign, and whatever happened the training would be of value.

I wish to turn now to certain general allegations made in this case by the State. But before doing so, I wish to revert to certain occurrences said by witnesses to have happened in Port Elizabeth and East London.

I am referring to the bombing of private houses of pro-Government persons during September, October and November 1962. I do not know what justification there was for these acts, nor what provocation had been given. But if what I have said already is accepted, then it is clear that these acts had nothing to do with the carrying out of the policy of Umkhonto.

One of the chief allegations in the indictment is that the ANC was a party to a general conspiracy to commit sabotage. I have already explained why this is incorrect but how, externally, there was a departure from the original principle laid down by the ANC.

There has, of course, been overlapping of functions internally as well, because there is a difference between a resolution adopted in the atmosphere of a committee room and the concrete difficulties that arise in the field of practical activity. At a later stage the position was further affected by bannings and house arrests, and by persons leaving the country to take up political work abroad. This led to individuals having to do work in different capacities.

But though this may have blurred the distinction

316

between Umkhonto and the ANC, it by no means abolished that distinction. Great care was taken to keep the activities of the two organizations in South Africa distinct. The ANC remained a mass political body of Africans only carrying on the type of political work they had conducted prior to 1961. Umkhonto remained a small organization recruiting its members from different races and organizations and trying to achieve its own particular object.

The fact that members of Umkhonto were recruited from the ANC, and the fact that persons served both organizations, like Solomon Mbanjwa, did not, in our view, change the nature of the ANC or give it a policy of violence. This overlapping of officers, however, was more the exception than the rule.

This is why persons such as 'Mr. X' and 'Mr. Z', who were on the Regional Command of their respective areas, did not participate in any of the ANC committees or activities, and why people such as Mr. Bennett Mashiyana and Mr. Reginald Ndubi did not hear of sabotage at their ANC meetings.

Another of the allegations in the indictment is that Rivonia was the headquarters of Umkhonto. This is not true of the time when I was there. I was told, of course, and knew that certain of the activities of the Communist Party were carried on there. But this is no reason (as I shall presently explain) why I should not use the place.

I came there in the following manner:

1. As already indicated, early in April 1961 I went underground to organize the May general strike. My work entailed travelling throughout the country, living now in African townships, then in country villages and again in cities.

During the second half of the year I started visiting the Parktown home of Arthur Goldreich, where I used to meet my family privately. Although I had no direct political association with him, I had known Arthur Goldreich socially since 1958.

2. In October, Arthur Goldreich informed me that he was moving out of town and offered me a hiding place there. A few days thereafter, he arranged for Michael Harmel to take me to Rivonia. I naturally found Rivonia an ideal place for the man who lived the life of an outlaw. Up to that time I had been compelled to live indoors during the daytime and could only venture out under cover of darkness. But at Liliesleaf [farm, Rivonia,] I could live differently and work far more efficiently.

3. For obvious reasons, I had to disguise myself and I assumed the fictitious name of David. In December, Arthur Goldreich and his family moved in. I stayed there until I went abroad on 11 January 1962. As already indicated, I returned in July 1962 and was arrested in Natal on 5 August.

4. Up to the time of my arrest, Liliesleaf farm was the headquarters of neither the African National Congress nor Umkhonto. With the exception of myself, none of the officials or members of these bodies lived there, no meetings of the governing bodies were ever held there, and no activities connected with them were either organized or directed from there. On numerous occasions during my stay at Liliesleaf farm I met both the Executive Committee of the ANC, as well as the NHC, but such meetings were held elsewhere and not on the farm.

5. Whilst staying at Liliesleaf farm, I frequently visited Arthur Goldreich in the main house and he also paid me visits in my room. We had numerous political discussions covering a variety of subjects. We discussed ideological and practical questions, the Congress Alliance, Umkhonto and its activities generally, and his experiences as a soldier in the Palmach, the military wing of the Haganah. Haganah was the political authority of the Jewish National Movement in Palestine.

6. Because of what I had got to know of Goldreich, I

recommended on my return to South Africa that he should be recruited to Umkhonto. I do not know of my personal knowledge whether this was done.

Another of the allegations made by the State is that the aims and objects of the ANC and the Communist Party are the same. I wish to deal with this and with my own political position, because I must assume that the State may try to argue from certain Exhibits that I tried to introduce Marxism into the ANC.

The allegation as to the ANC is false. This is an old allegation which was disproved at the Treason Trial and which has again reared its head. But since the allegation has been made again, I shall deal with it as well as with the relationship between the ANC and the Communist Party and Umkhonto and that party.

The ideological creed of the ANC is, and always has been, the creed of African Nationalism. It is not the concept of African Nationalism expressed in the cry, 'Drive the White man into the sea'. The African Nationalism for which the ANC stands is the concept of freedom and fulfilment for the African people in their own land.

The most important political document ever adopted by the ANC is the 'Freedom Charter'. It is by no means a blueprint for a socialist state. It calls for redistribution, but not nationalization, of land; it provides for nationalization of mines, banks, and monopoly industry, because big monopolies are owned by one race only, and without such nationalization racial domination would be perpetuated despite the spread of political power.

It would be a hollow gesture to repeal the Gold Law prohibitions against Africans when all gold mines are owned by European companies. In this respect the ANC's policy corresponds with the old policy of the present Nationalist Party which, for many years, had as part of its programme the nationalization of the gold mines which, at

319

that time, were controlled by foreign capital.

Under the Freedom Charter, nationalization would take place in an economy based on private enterprise. The realization of the Freedom Charter would open up fresh fields for a prosperous African population of all classes, including the middle class.

The ANC has never at any period of its history advocated a revolutionary change in the economic structure of the country, nor has it, to the best of my recollection, ever condemned capitalist society.

As far as the Communist Party is concerned, and if I understand its policy correctly, it stands for the establishment of a State based on the principles of Marxism. Although it is prepared to work for the Freedom Charter, as a short term solution to the problems created by white supremacy, it regards the Freedom Charter as the beginning, and not the end, of its programme.

The ANC, unlike the Communist Party, admitted Africans only as members. Its chief goal was, and is, for the African people to win unity and full political rights. The Communist Party's main aim, on the other hand, was to remove the capitalists and to replace them with a working-class government. The Communist Party sought to emphasize class distinctions whilst the ANC seeks to harmonize them. This is a vital distinction.

It is true that there has often been close co-operation between the ANC and the Communist Party. But co-operation is merely proof of a common goal - in this case the removal of white supremacy - and is not proof of a complete community of interests.

The history of the world is full of similar examples. Perhaps the most striking illustration is to be found in the co-operation between Great Britain, the United States of America, and the Soviet Union in the fight against Hitler.

Nobody but Hitler would have dared to suggest that such co-operation turned Churchill or Roosevelt into communists or communist tools, or that Britain and

America were working to bring about a communist world.

Another instance of such co-operation is to be found precisely in Umkhonto.

Shortly after Umkhonto was constituted, I was informed by some of its members that the Communist Party would support Umkhonto, and this then occurred. At a later stage the support was made openly.

I believe that communists have always played an active role in the fight by colonial countries for their freedom, because the short-term objects of communism would always correspond with the long-term objects of freedom movements. Thus communists have played an important role in the freedom struggles fought in countries such as Malaya, Algeria, and Indonesia, yet none of these States today are communist countries.

Similarly in the underground resistance movements which sprung up in Europe during the last World War, communists played an important role. Even General Chiang Kai-Shek, today one of the bitterest enemies of communism, fought together with the communists against the ruling class in the struggle which led to his assumption of power in China in the 1930s.

This pattern of co-operation between communists and non-communists has been repeated in the National Liberation Movement of South Africa. Prior to the banning of the Communist Party, joint campaigns involving the Communist Party and the Congress movements were accepted practice.

African communists could, and did, become members of the ANC, and some served on the National, Provincial, and local committees. Amongst those who served on the National Executive are Albert Nzula, a former Secretary of the Communist Party, Moses Kotane, another former Secretary, and J. B. Marks, a former member of the Central Committee.

I joined the ANC in 1944, and in my younger days I held the view that the policy of admitting communists to the ANC, and the close co-operation which existed at times on specific issues between the ANC and the Communist Party, would lead to a watering down of the concept of African Nationalism. At that stage I was a member of the African National Congress Youth League, and was one of a group which moved for the expulsion of communists from the ANC.

This proposal was heavily defeated. Amongst those who voted against the proposal were some of the most conservative sections of African political opinion. They defended the policy on the ground that from its inception the ANC was formed and built up, not as a political party with one school of political thought, but as a Parliament of the African people, accommodating people of various political convictions, all united by the common goal of national liberation. I was eventually won over to this point of view and I have upheld it ever since.

It is perhaps difficult for white South Africans, with an ingrained prejudice against communism, to understand why experienced African politicians so readily accept communists as their friends. But to us the reason is obvious. Theoretical differences amongst those fighting against oppression is a luxury we cannot afford at this stage.

What is more, for many decades communists were the only political group in South Africa who were prepared to treat Africans as human beings and their equals; who were prepared to eat with us; talk with us, live with us, and work with us. They were the only political group which was prepared to work with the Africans for the attainment of political rights and a stake in society. Because of this, there are many Africans who, today, tend to equate freedom with communism.

They are supported in this belief by a legislature which brands all exponents of democratic government and African freedom as communists and bans many of them (who are not communists) under the Suppression of

Communism Act.

Although I have never been a member of the Communist Party, I myself have been named under that pernicious Act because of the role I played in the Defiance Campaign. I have also been banned and imprisoned under that Act.

It is not only in internal politics that we count communists as amongst those who support our cause. In the international field, communist countries have always come to our aid. In the United Nations and other Councils of the world the communist bloc has supported the Afro-Asian struggle against colonialism and often seems to be more sympathetic to our plight than some of the Western powers.

Although there is a universal condemnation of apartheid, the communist bloc speaks out against it with a louder voice than most of the white world. In these circumstances, it would take a brash young politician, such as I was in 1949, to proclaim that the Communists are our enemies.

I turn now to my own position. I have denied that I am a communist, and I think that in the circumstances I am obliged to state exactly what my political beliefs are.

I have always regarded myself, in the first place, as an African patriot. After all, I was born in Umtata, forty-six years ago. My guardian was my cousin, who was the acting paramount chief of Tembuland, and I am related both to the present paramount chief of Tembuland, Sabata Dalindyebo, and to Kaizer Matanzima, the Chief Minister of the Transkei.

Today I am attracted by the idea of a classless society, an attraction which springs in part from Marxist reading and, in part, from my admiration of the structure and organization of early African societies in this country.

The land, then the main means of production, belonged to the tribe. There were no rich or poor and there was no exploitation.

It is true, as I have already stated, that I have been influenced by Marxist thought. But this is also true of many of the leaders of the new independent States. Such widely different persons as Gandhi, Nehru, Nkrumah, and Nasser all acknowledge this fact. We all accept the need for some form of socialism to enable our people to catch up with the advanced countries of this world and to overcome their legacy of extreme poverty. But this does not mean we are Marxists.

Indeed, for my own part, I believe that it is open to debate whether the Communist Party has any specific role to play at this particular stage of our political struggle. The basic task at the present moment is the removal of race discrimination and the attainment of democratic rights on the basis of the Freedom Charter.

In so far as that Party furthers this task, I welcome its assistance. I realize that it is one of the means by which people of all races can be drawn into our struggle.

From my reading of Marxist literature and from conversations with Marxists, I have gained the impression that communists regard the parliamentary system of the West as undemocratic and reactionary. But, on the contrary, I am an admirer of such a system.

The Magna Carta, the Petition of Rights, and the Bill of Rights are documents which are held in veneration by democrats throughout the world.

I have great respect for British political institutions, and for the country's system of justice. I regard the British Parliament as the most democratic institution in the world, and the independence and impartiality of its judiciary never fail to arouse my admiration.

The American Congress, that country's doctrine of separation of powers, as well as the independence of its judiciary, arouses in me similar sentiments.

I have been influenced in my thinking by both West and East. All this has led me to feel that in my search for a political formula, I should be absolutely impartial and objective. I should tie myself to no particular system of society other than of socialism. I must leave myself free to borrow the best from the West and from the East....

There are certain Exhibits which suggest that we received financial support from abroad, and I wish to deal with this question.

Our political struggle has always been financed from internal sources - from funds raised by our own people and by our own supporters. Whenever we had a special campaign or an important political case - for example, the Treason Trial - we received financial assistance from sympathetic individuals and organizations in the Western countries. We had never felt it necessary to go beyond these sources.

But when in 1961 the Umkhonto was formed, and a new phase of struggle introduced, we realized that these events would make a heavy call on our slender resources, and that the scale of our activities would be hampered by the lack of funds.

One of my instructions, as I went abroad in January 1962, was to raise funds from the African states.

I must add that, whilst abroad, I had discussions with leaders of political movements in Africa and discovered that almost every single one of them, in areas which had still not attained independence, had received all forms of assistance from the socialist countries, as well as from the West, including that of financial support. I also discovered that some well-known African states, all of them non-communists, and even anti-communists, had received similar assistance.

On my return to the Republic, I made a strong recommendation to the ANC that we should not confine ourselves to Africa and the Western countries, but that we should also send a mission to the socialist countries to raise the funds which we so urgently needed.

I have been told that after I was convicted such a mission was sent, but I am not prepared to name any countries to which it went, nor am I at liberty to disclose the names of the organizations and countries which gave us support or promised to do so.

As I understand the State case, and in particular the evidence of 'Mr. X', the suggestion is that Umkhonto was the inspiration of the Communist Party which sought by playing upon imaginary grievances to enrol the African people into an army which ostensibly was to fight for African freedom, but in reality was fighting for a communist state. Nothing could be further from the truth.

In fact the suggestion is preposterous. Umkhonto was formed by Africans to further their struggle for freedom in their own land. Communists and others supported the movement, and we only wish that more sections of the community would join us.

Our fight is against real, and not imaginary, hardships or, to use the language of the State Prosecutor, 'so-called hardships'. Basically, we fight against two features which are the hallmarks of African life in South Africa and which are entrenched by legislation which we seek to have repealed. These features are poverty and lack of human dignity, and we do not need communists or so-called 'agitators' to teach us about these things.

South Africa is the richest country in Africa, and could be one of the richest countries in the world. But it is a land of extremes and remarkable contrasts. The whites enjoy what may well be the highest standard of living in the world, whilst Africans live in poverty and misery.

Forty per cent of the Africans live in hopelessly overcrowded and, in some cases, drought-stricken Reserves, where soil erosion and the overworking of the soil makes it impossible for them to live properly off the land.

Thirty per cent are labourers, labour tenants, and squatters on white farms and work and live under conditions similar to those of the serfs of the Middle Ages.

The other 30 per cent live in towns where they have

developed economic and social habits which bring them closer in many respects to white standards.

Yet most Africans, even in this group, are impoverished by low incomes and high cost of living.

The highest-paid and the most prosperous section of urban African life is in Johannesburg. Yet their actual position is desperate. The latest figures were given on 25 March 1964 by Mr. Carr, Manager of the Johannesburg Non-European Affairs Department.

The poverty datum line for the average African family in Johannesburg (according to Mr. Carr's department) is R42.84 per month.

He showed that the average monthly wage is R32.24 and that 46 per cent of all African families in Johannesburg do not earn enough to keep them going.

Poverty goes hand in hand with malnutrition and disease. The incidence of malnutrition and deficiency diseases is very high amongst Africans. Tuberculosis, pellagra, kwashiorkor, gastro-enteritis, and scurvy bring death and destruction of health. The incidence of infant mortality is one of the highest in the world.

According to the Medical Officer of Health for Pretoria, tuberculosis kills forty people a day (almost all Africans), and in 1961 there were 58,491 new cases reported. These diseases not only destroy the vital organs of the body, but they result in retarded mental conditions and lack of initiative, and reduce powers of concentration. The secondary results of such conditions affect the whole community and the standard of work performed by African labourers.

The complaint of Africans, however, is not only that they are poor and the whites are rich, but that the laws which are made by the whites are designed to preserve this situation. There are two ways to break out of poverty. The first is by formal education, and the second is by the worker acquiring a greater skill at his work and thus higher wages. As far as Africans are concerned, both these avenues of advancement are deliberately curtailed by legislation.

The present Government has always sought to hamper Africans in their search for education. One of their early acts, after coming into power, was to stop subsidies for African school feeding. Many African children who attended schools depended on this supplement to their diet. This was a cruel act.

There is compulsory education for all white children at virtually no cost to their parents, be they rich or poor. Similar facilities are not provided for the African children, though there are some who receive such assistance. African children, however, generally have to pay more for their schooling than whites.

According to figures quoted by the South African Institute of Race Relations in its 1963 journal, approximately 40 per cent of African children in the age group between seven to fourteen do not attend school. For those who do attend school, the standards are vastly different from those afforded to white children.

In 1960-61 the per capita Government spending on African students at State-aided schools was estimated at R12.46. In the same years, the per capita spending on white children in the Cape Province (which are the only figures available to me) was R144.57. Although there are no figures available to me, it can be stated, without doubt, that the white children on whom R144.57 per head was being spent all came from wealthier homes than African children on whom R12.46 per head was being spent.

The quality of education is also different. According to the Bantu Educational Journal, only 5,660 African children in the whole of South Africa passed their Junior Certificate in 1962, and in that year only 362 passed matric. This is presumably consistent with the policy of Bantu education about which the present Prime Minister said, during the debate on the Bantu Education Bill in 1953:

328

'When I have control of Native education I will reform it so that Natives will be taught from childhood to realize that equality with Europeans is not for them . . . People who believe in equality are not desirable teachers for Natives. When my Department controls Native education it will know for what class of higher education a Native is fitted, and whether he will have a chance in life to use his knowledge.'

The other main obstacle to the economic advancement of the African is the industrial colour-bar under which all the better jobs of industry are reserved for Whites only. Moreover, Africans who do obtain employment in the unskilled and semi-skilled occupations which are open to them are not allowed to form trade unions which have recognition under the Industrial Conciliation Act. This means that strikes of African workers are illegal, and that they are denied the right of collective bargaining which is permitted to the better-paid White workers.

The discrimination in the policy of successive South African Governments towards African workers is demonstrated by the so-called 'civilized labour policy' under which sheltered, unskilled Government jobs are found for those white workers who cannot make the grade in industry, at wages which far exceed the earnings of the average African employee in industry.

The Government often answers its critics by saying that Africans in South Africa are economically better off than the inhabitants of the other countries in Africa. I do not know whether this statement is true and doubt whether any comparison can be made without having regard to the cost-of-living index in such countries. But even if it is true, as far as the African people are concerned it is irrelevant.

Our complaint is not that we are poor by comparison with people in other countries, but that we are poor by comparison with the white people in our own country, and that we are prevented by legislation from altering this imbalance.

The lack of human dignity experienced by Africans is the direct result of the policy of white supremacy. White supremacy implies black inferiority. Legislation designed to preserve white supremacy entrenches this notion.

Menial tasks in South Africa are invariably performed by Africans. When anything has to be carried or cleaned the white man will look around for an African to do it for him, whether the African is employed by him or not. Because of this sort of attitude, whites tend to regard Africans as a separate breed.

They do not look upon them as people with families of their own; they do not realize that they have emotions - that they fall in love like white people do; that they want to be with their wives and children like white people want to be with theirs; that they want to earn enough money to support their families properly, to feed and clothe them and send them to school. And what 'house-boy' or 'garden-boy' or labourer can ever hope to do this?

Pass laws, which to the Africans are among the most hated bits of legislation in South Africa, render any African liable to police surveillance at any time. I doubt whether there is a single African male in South Africa who has not at some stage had a brush with the police over his pass. Hundreds and thousands of Africans are thrown into jail each year under pass laws. Even worse than this is the fact that pass laws keep husband and wife apart and lead to the breakdown of family life.

Poverty and the breakdown of family life have secondary effects. Children wander about the streets of the townships because they have no schools to go to, or no money to enable them to go to school, or no parents at home to see that they go to school, because both parents (if there be two) have to work to keep the family alive. This leads to a breakdown in moral standards, to an alarming rise in illegitimacy, and to growing violence which erupts not only politically, but everywhere.

Life in the townships is dangerous. There is not a day that goes by without somebody being stabbed or assaulted. And violence is carried out of the townships in the white living areas. People are afraid to walk alone in the streets after dark. Housebreakings and robberies are increasing, despite the fact that the death sentence can now be imposed for such offences. Death sentences cannot cure the festering sore.

Africans want to be paid a living wage. Africans want to perform work which they are capable of doing, and not work which the Government declares them to be capable o Africans want to be allowed to live where they obtain work, and not be endorsed out of an area because they were not born there. Africans want to be allowed to own land in places where they work, and not to be obliged to live in rented houses which they can never call their own.

Africans want to be part of the general population, and not confined to living in their own ghettoes. African men want to have their wives and children to live with them where they work, and not be forced into an unnatural existence in men's hostels. African women want to be with their menfolk and not be left permanently widowed in the Reserves. Africans want to be allowed out after eleven o'clock at night and not to be confined to their rooms like little children.

Africans want to be allowed to travel in their own country and to seek work where they want to and not where the Labour Bureau tells them to. Africans want a just share in the whole of South Africa; they want security and a stake in society.

Above all, we want equal political rights, because without them our disabilities will be permanent. I know this sounds revolutionary to the whites in this country, because the majority of voters will be Africans. This makes the white man fear democracy.

But this fear cannot be allowed to stand in the way of

the only solution which will guarantee racial harmony and freedom for all. It is not true that the enfranchisement of all will result in racial domination. Political division, based on colour, is entirely artificial and, when it disappears, so will the domination of one colour group by another. The ANC has spent half a century fighting against racialism. When it triumphs it will not change that policy.

This then is what the ANC is fighting. Their struggle is a truly national one. It is a struggle of the African people, inspired by their own suffering and their own experience. It is a struggle for the right to live.

During my lifetime I have dedicated myself to this struggle of the African people. I have fought against white domination, and I have fought against black domination. I have cherished the ideal of a democratic and free society in which all persons live together in harmony and with equal opportunities. It is an ideal which I hope to live for and to achieve. But if needs be, it is an ideal for which I am prepared to die."

On 11 June 1964, at the conclusion of the trial, Mandela and seven others – Walter Sisulu, Govan Mbeki, Raymond Mhlaba, Elias Motsoaledi, Andrew Mlangeni, Ahmed Kathrada and Denis Goldberg – were convicted of treason. But although Mandela was found guilty on four charges of sabotage and like the others was sentenced to life imprisonment, he and his colleagues did not give up the fight.

In fact, Mandela was even offered freedom in the 1960s if he was going to abandon the struggle and return to his home region, the Transkei, and live a quiet life.

But he turned down the offer and said he would be back in prison as soon as they let him out if the government was not going to allow blacks and other non-whites to enjoy the same rights enjoyed by whites.

It was not until almost 30 years later, on 11 February 1990, that Mandela and his compatriots were released from prison, undefeated, after the government finally agreed to start dismantling apartheid. It was a major concession by the government and a victory for the anti-apartheid movement.

In fact, the 1964 Rivonia Trial was a warning to the architects and adherents of apartheid that this abominable institution would one day come tumbling down under the sustained assault of its opponents as long as the anti-apartheid forces refused to compromise on fundamental issues of freedom and justice for all.

Freedom and justice cannot be compromised. They can only be upheld to be meaningful. You are free or you are not free. You have justice or you don't have justice.

While 1964 will be remembered as a year of major setbacks for the liberation struggle in South Africa, especially with the imprisonment of the leading figures in the anti-apartheid movement, it will also be remembered as a year of victory against colonialism on the continent. People in two African countries celebrated the end of colonial rule only about two months apart.

On 6 July 1964, Nyasaland won independence from Britain and became the new nation of Malawi. And on October 23rd, neighbouring Northern Rhodesia, another British colony, became independent and was renamed Zambia.

During colonial rule, Northern Rhodesia and Nyasaland together with Southern Rhodesia constituted what was known as the Federation of Rhodesia and Nyasaland.

Formed on 7 September 1953, it was also known as the Central African Federation. Salisbury, now Harare, which was the capital of Southern Rhodesia was also the capital of the federation.

The federation was dissolved ten years later on 31 December 1963 because of strong opposition to the union by African nationalists in all three countries when the wind of change was sweeping across the continent during the struggle for independence in the fifties and sixties.

After the federation was dissolved, independence was only months away for Northern Rhodesia and Nyasaland, except for Southern Rhodesia which did not become independent until almost 20 years later on 18 April 1980 as Zimbabwe.

After Malawi and Zambia became independent in 1964, there were many other African countries which had not yet won independence. But, like the rest of the countries on the continent which had won independence, the march towards freedom for them was inevitable. Nothing could stop them. It was the dawn of a new era for Africa marking the end of colonial rule.

1965

THE YEAR 1965 was one of the most important milestones in the history of post-colonial Africa. Most African countries had won independence by 1965, and almost all by 1968.

But there were other important events which took place on the continent in that year. And they helped change the course of history on the continent.

One of those events was the military coup which took place in Algeria. It was one of the first three military coups in Africa which set the trend on the continent in the following decades and was preceded by the military coup in Togo in January 1963.

The other military coup took place in Congo-Leopoldville in November 1965 as we learned earlier.

The 1960s went down in history as the decade in which African armies started to intrude in politics and overthrow civilian governments, instituting military rule. And they had a profound impact on the course of Africa history.

The military coup in Algeria was one of the most

dramatic on the continent because of the kind leader who was ousted from power.

On 19 June 1965, President Ahmed Ben-Bella, a hero of the independence movement, was overthrown by his defence minister Colonel Houari Boumedienne. He was imprisoned for 15 years. All political parties were banned except the National Liberation Front (FLN) famed for its revolutionary zeal during Algeria's struggle for independence.

Ben-Bella was one of the most prominent, and most influential, African and Third World leaders. He led the struggle for his country's independence and became one of the most eloquent spokesmen for the liberation of Africa.

He was also one of the first leaders on the continent to offer troops to help liberate the countries in southern Africa which were still under white minority rule and was ranked, together with Nkrumah, Nasser, Sekou Toure, Modibo Keita and Nyerere, as one of the most committed Pan-Africanist leaders. As Ben-Bella himself said in an interview in 1995, the six leaders constituted what was known as "the Group of Six" within the Organisation of African Unity (OAU) and regularly worked together secretly on African issues. And as Professor Ali Mazrui states in his book *Towards A Pax Africana*:

"When Algeria attained independence another militantly Pan-African power emerged from the Arab world. At times Ahmed Ben-Bella seemed prepared to go further in identifying with African causes than Nasser had done – for he seemed prepared to be militarily involved at a significant scale in the remaining liberation movements in Africa.

In his short dramatic speech at the Summit Conference at Addis Ababa in May 1963 (when the OAU was founded) Ben-Bella said:

'There has been talk of a Development Bank. Why have

we not talked of setting up a blood bank? A blood bank to help those who are fighting in Angola and all over Africa....Ten thousand Algerian volunteers have been waiting for a chance to go to the assistance of their brothers in arms....

A ransom had to be paid for Algeria's liberation....So let us all agree to die a little, or even completely, so that the peoples still under colonial domination may be free and African unity may not be a vain word.'

Yet on balance Egypt has done more for Pan-Africanism than Algeria has done – particularly since the Ben-Bella regime was overthrown in Algeria. Nevertheless, the Algerian leadership remains on the whole more Afro-centric than Nasser's regime has been....

In concrete terms Nasser's Pan-Africanism has consisted in granting scholarships to African students, in allowing Cairo to become the first major centre of refuge for nationalists from colonial Africa; in converting Cairo Radio into an instrument of anti-colonialism in Africa as well as in the Arab world; in active involvement in the conference diplomacy of African states; in establishing 'cultural links' with Muslims elsewhere in Africa; in undertaking the responsibility of looking after Lumumba's children on his death; and in active participation in the 'struggle against the forces of neo-colonialism in the Congo.'" – (Ali Mazrui, *Towards A Pax Africana*, op.cit., pp. 111, and 110).

Although the new Algerian ruler Colonel Boumedienne and his regime continued Ben-Bella's policy of being actively involved in black Africa, he did not have the same stature Ben-Bella had as a major Pan-Africanist leader in the same league with leaders such as Nkrumah and Nyerere who – together with a number of other black African leaders – regarded Arabs in Algeria, Egypt and elsewhere on the continent as fellow Africans, and not as "foreigners" or "non-Africans."

Ben-Bella not only led the liberation struggle for his country; he also became a legendary figure as a survivor during the liberation war which cost one million Algerian lives and lasted for about seven years.

The National Liberation Front – *Front de la Liberation Nationale*(FLN) – which fought for independence started fighting French forces on 1 November 1 1954. The French had an army of 500,000 troops but failed to suppress the revolt until the war ended with a cease-fire on 18 March 1962.

Algeria won independence from France on 3 July 1962, and Ben-Bella became president after a power struggle among the FLN leaders.

He gained control in August 1962. A new constitution was approved in 1963 and Ben-Bella was elected in October the same year as Algeria's first president. But he did not last long in power.

Fidel Castro blamed Abdelaziz Bouteflika, Algeria's minister of foreign affairs under Ben-Bella who retained the same post under Boumedienne, for Ben-Bella's ouster from power. He strongly criticized Bouteflika in 1965 for being the person who was mainly responsible for Ben-Bella's downfall more than anybody else and relations between Cuba and the new Algerian regime became strained as a result of that.

Relations between Cuba and Algeria did not start to improve until November 1968 when Bouteflika visited Cuba. but Castro remained bitter over the ouster of Ben-Bella with whom he had excellent relations when he was president of Algeria. According to *Africa Contemporary Record: Annual Survey and Documents 1968 – 1969*:

"A new era in relations with Cuba began with M. Bouteflika's visit to Havana in November. He had been attacked by President Castro in 1965 for being mainly responsible for M. Bouteflika's downfall. Relations improved as a result of the Middle east crisis in 1967, and a Cuban Ambassador was appointed to Algiers to replace the Charge d'Affaires. A visit to Algiers of a member of the political bureau of the Communist Party in July was a further step towards official reconciliation." — (Colin Legum and John Drsydale, eds., *Africa Contemporary Record: Annual Survey and Documents 1968 – 1969*, London: Africa Research Limited, 1969, pp. 69 – 70).

More than 30 years later, Bouteflika himself became president of Algeria after winning a controversial election in April 1999. The opposition candidates said it was rigged and refused to take part in the electoral contest.

The year 1965 had mixed results with regard to the independence struggle on the African continent. Only one country won independence in 1965. That was Gambia, the smallest country on the continent which won independence from Britain on February 18th.

Although many people celebrated Gambia's independence, Africa suffered a major setback when the white minority rulers of Southern Rhodesia unilaterally declared independence many months later in the same year, totally excluding the black African majority from the new dispensation. It was the ultimate defiance of the wishes of Africans not only in Rhodesia but all over the continent.

Southern Rhodesia declared independence on 11 November 1965 under the leadership of Ian Smith who was the country's prime minister and head of the Rhodesian Front, a party of white settlers which had won the general election in which only whites were eligible to vote. During that period, Rhodesia had a population of about 250,000 whites, mostly of British origin, and about 4 million black Africans.

The country was a British colony and African leaders asked Britain to intervene to end the rebellion by Ian Smith and his colleagues who constituted the white minority regime. African ministers of foreign affairs and other leaders attended a meeting of the Organisation of African Unity (OAU) on 2 December 1965 in Addis Ababa, Ethiopia, to discuss the Rhodesian crisis and passed a resolution asking all African states to break off diplomatic relations with Britain on December 15th if nothing was done by the British government to bring down the Smith regime before that date.

The deadline was almost exactly one month from the day Rhodesia unilaterally declared independence, what came to be known as UDI (Unilateral Declaration of Independence). African leaders formulated and invoked a principle known as NIBMAR - No Independence Before Majority Rule.

But the British government under Prime Minister Harold Wilson of the Labour Party refused to intervene. African countries responded by breaking diplomatic relations with Britain. The ultimatum which the OAU gave the British government essentially said: "Break Ian Smith or Africa will break with you."

The first country to sever ties was Tanzania under Nyerere, followed by Ghana under Nkrumah the next day, and by Egypt and the rest.

Malawi under Dr. Hastings Kamuzu Banda refused to follow suit and publicly defied the OAU resolution. As Nyerere stated in his speech to the Tanzania National Assembly – parliament – on 14 December 1965, entitled "The Honour of Africa" which is included in his book *Freedom and Socialism: A Selection from Writings and Speeches 1965 - 1967*:

"My purpose today is to explain the policies and attitudes of the Tanzanian Government one month after the illegal declaration of independence by the racist minority government in Southern Rhodesia.

340

Africa's Objectives

The policies of Tanzania, and of Africa, in relation to Southern Rhodesia, have always had one object, and one object only. That was, and is, to secure a rapid transition to independence on the basis of majority rule. On this subject every action we have taken, every speech we have made, has been intended to further that purpose. We have no other.

The declared policy of the British Government – successive British Governments – in relation to all her colonies has been the same. Our past disagreements with Britain have been on the basis of her performance in particular places at particular times – not really on the basis of ideas.

The basic friendship between our two countries, and between Africa and Britain, has been based on our belief that underlying any current disagreement was a present-day, similar purpose, of bringing all colonial territories - including those dominated by white minorities - to democratic independence.

The Charge Against Britain

Why then is Africa now quarrelling with Britain to the extent that Africa has said if certain things are not done by the 15th of December - tomorrow - we shall break diplomatic relations with that country? When the enemy is the Smith regime in Southern Rhodesia, why are we breaking relations with Britain when she says that she is an enemy of the Smith regime?

There is a very simple reason. In an ordered society, when a man is wronged by an illegal act he does not, and should not, take the law into his own hands. He applies to the law, and to those responsible for enforcing the law, for

341

redress. And he expects that action will be taken to relieve him of the wrongs which he is suffering because of an illegal action.

It is by such procedures that peace and justice are maintained within states. It is by similar procedures that international peace and justice can be maintained between states. Nations which are wronged by the action or inaction of another nation call upon the nation responsible to relieve them of their wrong; or they call upon the United Nations for assistance against the country responsible.

If an individual who is suffering from a continuing illegal act finds that the organs of law and order fail to act in his defence, what is he supposed to do? Even more, if those organs which are meant to protect him appear to be helping the criminal instead, what must his reaction be? He will say - and he will be entitled to say - 'This is enough; I will have nothing more to do with you unless and until you demonstrate to my satisfaction that you propose doing something effective against those who continue to wrong me.'

That is the meaning and implication of the resolution passed by the Organization of African Unity foreign ministers at Addis Ababa. Africa is saying to Britain, 'This is enough.'

Mr. Speaker, this is a very serious thing for one country to say to another. It is still more serious when 36 countries say it through an organization for unity which they have themselves established.

The people of Africa, and indeed the people of Britain themselves, are entitled to ask for an explanation. They need to understand the evidence which causes Africa to say to the British Government – 'This is enough.'

Before Africans can support their leaders on such a serious matter they must be sure that Britain is the country responsible in law for the wrong to Africa, and the country which must therefore undertake to remove that wrong.

They must be sure too, that any failure is a failure of intent and not merely an inefficiency of execution.

I believe these two charges against Britain must be made, and can be sustained, in relation to the events in Southern Rhodesia. I believe further that it is Africa's inescapable duty to make these charges, and to take action in accordance with the evidence.

Let me make the charges clear.

Africa maintains that Southern Rhodesia is at present a colony of the United Kingdom, and that ultimate responsibility for events there resides, in consequence, with the government of the United Kingdom in London.

That government may delegate its responsibility if it wishes, but it cannot escape it; if it entrusts its responsibility for the government of Southern Rhodesia to other people, then it is responsible for their actions. If the British Government disagrees with what is being done by those to whom it has entrusted power, then it must replace those people. If those people assume powers which have not been entrusted to them, then the British government must reassert its authority and get rid of those who have usurped its power.

The first charge is thus that Britain is the right place to go for redress.

The second charge is that Britain has not shown serious determination either to get rid of those in Southern Rhodesia who have usurped British power, or to replace them by representatives of the people. For it is not the independence of Rhodesia that Africa is complaining about; it is independence under a racialist minority government.

What is the evidence to support those charges?

Britain's Responsibility

Southern Rhodesia is a British colony; its constitution is subject to the will of the British Parliament. As an international entity Southern Rhodesia does not exist. Internationally, by both law and custom, there exists only Britain and its colony.

The colony of Southern Rhodesia has been self-governing since 1923; for 43 years increasing *de facto* power has been exerted by a government based in Salisbury. But the constitution under which that government operated reserved certain powers to the British government and parliament in London.

The fact that successive British governments did not use their powers to prevent acts which were contrary to the interests of the African people does not alter the existence of these 'Reserved Powers,' nor the ultimate responsibility of the British government for the actions of the Southern Rhodesian government.

In saying this there is no need to argue abstract cases in law. Britain herself accepts responsibility for Southern Rhodesia. More, she claims that responsibility. Britain claims that she, and she alone, can decide what is to be done about Southern Rhodesia.

The only time she has ever used the veto in the United Nations was when Ghana (under Nkrumah) proposed a resolution which would have blocked the transfer to the Southern Rhodesian government of the air force which had been built up by the defunct Federation of Rhodesia and Nyasaland.

In the Commonwealth Conferences of 1964 and 1965, the government of Britain maintained this stand, and it was conceded by the rest of the Commonwealth – including the African members. And only just over a week ago – on 6 December 1965 – Mr. Wilson, the prime minister of Britain, is reported to have said once again, 'Rhodesia is Britain's responsibility.'

There is thus no dispute between Britain and Africa about the British responsibility. What then of the manner in which that responsibility has been, and is being, exercised?

British Record

I do not propose to go back further than October 1964 in an examination of the British record. The record before that date is a shameful one; time after time the interests of the African majority were subjected to the selfish power hunger of the settler minority.

Even after 1947, when other colonies in Africa began to feel some hope of ultimate freedom, the settlers of Southern Rhodesia were able to extend their sway. In return for some concessions on the periphery of power, some verbal acceptance of the theory of 'partnership,' they were able to secure dominance in a federation of Rhodesia with the countries which are now Zambia and Malawi.

In 1961, with the tide running hard against them, and when they were concerned to try and save their federation, they still managed to secure a constitution for Southern Rhodesia which entrenched minority power while only appearing to make some concessions to the African population. And in 1963, at the break-up of the federation, they secured into their own hands the real instruments of power – the aeroplanes, the equipment, and the administration of the army and the air force.

For the settler government of Southern Rhodesia even this was not enough. In 1963, and even in 1964, they began to demand independence for themselves.

That was the position in October 1964. It was an extremely difficult position for anyone to deal with. The effects of mistakes, errors, or sins, do not disappear because one regrets them; they create their own difficulties and reduce the area of possible movement. It is legitimate to sympathize with the problem facing anyone assuming responsibility for Southern Rhodesia in October 1964.

Africa did sympathize. Tanzania did sympathize. We sympathized the more because we felt that a new element had entered into the situation, and that there was hope that the long series of betrayals would end and be replaced by some attempt to implement the principles of human justice.

A good start was made. On 27 October 1964, the prime minister of Britain said openly to Mr. Smith, the prime minister in a British colony, that a unilateral 'declaration of independence would be an open act of defiance and rebellion, and it would be treasonable to take steps to give effect to it.' These strong words meant that Africa was heartened despite the fact that the statement went on to speak only of the economic consequences of such a declaration.

In November, however, the Smith government called for a referendum in support of independence for Southern Rhodesia under the 1961 constitution. He received 58,000 votes in support. I ask that this House should take particular note of that number; it is less than the total registered voters in the Dar es salaam South constituency of Tanzania. And even that vote was only obtained after Mr. Smith had said that he was not asking for a vote in support of an illegal declaration of independence!

Threats of illegal action nonetheless continued to come from Salisbury and, apart from warnings about what would happen if they were carried out, nothing was done to those who made the threats. Indeed, by the end of the year there were indications from London that independence might be granted without majority rule.

Mr. Bottomley, the British Commonwealth secretary, was reported as saying, 'We must be satisfied that the basis on which independence is to be granted is acceptable to the people as a whole.' This ambiguous statement was clearly deliberate, and it succeeded in one of its designs. Africa thought that this was merely a tactical move, an endeavour to avoid provoking Smith before Britain was ready to deal with him.

There is no need for me to dwell on the long months of negotiation, threat, and counter-threat, between Britain nd

Smith in the first ten months of this year. It is sufficient to remember that Mr. Smith went to London once, and that Mr. Wilson went once to Salisbury, in addition to two other ministerial visits from the metropolitan capital to the colony.

To these negotiations Africa had no objection; on the contrary, it welcomed them as indicating that Mr. Wilson was genuine in his desire to avoid UDI (Unilateral Declaration of Independence) and was not going to complicate the issue by standing on his dignity.

But while Africa accepted Britain's willingness to negotiate it had cause to get increasingly worried about the content of the negotiations. There were two causes for this unease; one of them has already proved to be justified, and the other has increased in intensity.

Although UDI was declared to be an act of rebellion there was a studious avoidance by British ministers of the statement that the rebellion would be brought down by all necessary means, including the use of force. The Smith group were never faced with that prospect. On several occasions British ministers said, 'We shall not use force to impose a constitutional solution' to the Rhodesian situation. They never went further. Africa worried and waited.

Even more serious for Africa was the deliberate vagueness about the ultimate objective of the negotiations and the opposition to UDI.

Majority Rule

Africa does not oppose UDI because it wishes Southern Rhodesia to remain forever a colony of Britain. And it certainly does not find the maintenance - or the reassertion - of the 1961 constitution an acceptable goal. The goal of Africa is independence on the basis of majority rule for Southern Rhodesia.

Its opposition to UDI is because the hope of attaining

majority rule, peacefully and reasonably quickly, is compromised by the usurpation of power from a country which is, at least in general principle, committed to that goal for its colonies. Africa would have been equally opposed to a legal granting of independence to Southern Rhodesia if this were done before majority rule had been attained.

Yet Britain's 'five principles' which had to be met before independence would be granted by the British government did not specify the existence of majority rule. On the contrary, they clearly showed that if certain 'safeguards' were enshrined in a document, then majority rule would not be insisted upon. There was only one ambiguous statement in principle five which many genuine people - including African leaders - believed provided a safeguard.

Principle five stated that 'any basis proposed for independence must be acceptable to the people of Rhodesia as a whole.' Many of our friends said that the people of that colony could not possibly agree on an independence without majority rule, and that therefore, so long as this principle was maintained, Rhodesia would not become completely a second South Africa without hope of peaceful progress.

Tanzania was less sanguine; in the Commonwealth Conference I therefore demanded that the words *independence on the basis of majority rule* be included in the final communique.

They were not included; and in consequence Tanzania disassociated itself from the Southern Rhodesia section of the communique. Our friends thought us needlessly suspicious. But it was quite clear to us that the British government was willing to grant independence on the basis of minority rule.

Now it is one month after the minority government of Rhodesia has seized power. There is no longer, surely, any problem about 'not complicating the negotiations' or 'allowing Britain to go step by step in her discussions.' But have we yet had the assurance which Tanzania sought in June? The answer is no.

The 1961 constitution remains in being, with some few powers having been resumed by the Government in London. This resumption having been forced upon Britain by Smith! Let me quote Mr. Wilson, the prime minister of the United Kingdom, speaking in the House of Commons, London, on 23 November 1965 - 12 days after the rebellion. He said (as reported in the *Times*):

'While we have power to revoke or amend sections of the 1961 constitution we have said we have no present intention of revoking it as a whole, and I cannot at this stage foresee circumstances in which we would do so.'

Mr. Wilson went on to deal with the role of this constitution in what he calls 'the resettlement period.' He said:

'When the Governor is able to report that the people of Rhodesia are willing and able to work on constitutional paths, we are prepared to work together with their leaders to make a new start. For this purpose the 1961 constitution remains in being, though the House will realize the need for those amendments which are required to prevent its perversion and misuse such as we have seen in the last fortnight, and those amendments, too, which are needed to give effect to the five principles to which all parties in this House have subscribed.'

It is perfectly true, Mr. Speaker, that later in the same speech Mr. Wilson said:

'All along we have made it plain – we did all throughout the negotiations – that while guaranteed and unimpeded progress to majority rule is the policy of all of us, we do not believe it can be immediate...But all of us are committed to an early attempt by the Rhodesian people to pronounce on their own future. That was the reason for the suggested referendum and for the Royal Commission.'

The thing which I notice in the last statement, Mr. Speaker, is that this was not an assurance about majority rule; it was an assurance against majority rule. There is still no statement that independence will be given only on the basis of majority rule.

At the end of last week the British Broadcasting Corporation (BBC) news service reported that Mr. Wilson had suggested that after all, when British authority was re-established in Southern Rhodesia, there might be a period of direct rule by the governor with advisers from all races. As this would mean the end of the 1961 constitution I had a moment of hope; we would begin over again.

But the report went on to say that Mr. Wilson stressed that majority rule could not come for a very long time - and still there was no suggestion that independence would be held up until this majority rule had finally been attained.

I have spent a long time on this matter because it is important that one thing should be understood. In this matter of objective it is not the timing which is causing Africa to become angry; we could argue about time. Our anger and suspicion arise from the fact that Britain is not even now – 14 December 1965 – committed to the principle: 'independence only on the basis of majority rule.'

I must, however, now move to the question of whether Britain has shown serious determination to get rid of those in Southern Rhodesia who have usurped her power. Africa maintains that she has not.

At this point let me make one thing clear. Africa is not hungry for blood. We do not demand that British troops should die in Southern Rhodesia; we do not demand that

350

Smith's forces should die. If this matter can be settled peacefully no one will be more happy than Africa. But IT MUST BE SETTLED. Further, it must be settled QUICKLY.

Great principles are at stake. But that is not all. It is also true that the safety of Africa, and particularly of Zambia, is at stake. Africa will therefore co-operate with any EFFECTIVE and determined attempt to deal with Smith without bloodshed; we shall support any proposal which reduces the danger of fighting to the minimum.

But we cannot acquiesce in token action, or in inaction. Africa contends that this is what we have had from Britain since 11 November. She has done the very minimum, and left an African state - an African state friendly to Britain - to live under threat to its livelihood from the rebels.

What has Britain done since 11 November?

On that date Mr. Wilson used some strong words: he said, 'It is an illegal act, ineffective in law; an act of rebellion against the Crown and against the constitution as by law established.' But he then went on to instruct the civil servants of Southern Rhodesia to 'stay at their posts but not to assist in any illegal acts.' He was unable to explain how they could do that when they were serving an illegal government.

As regards the use of force Mr. Wilson repeated his stock phrase despite the changed circumstances. Britain would not use force to impose a constitutional settlement he said, but he went on to say that the British government 'would give full consideration to any appeal from the governor for help to restore law and order.'

Mr. Wilson refrained from explaining how the law could be more broken than it had been by the usurpation of power, that is to say, by treason. He refrained later from explaining how the governor was to transmit his appeal once the telephone had been taken from him as well as all the furniture of his office, his staff and his transport.

Instead Mr. Wilson obtained the approval of the British

parliament for economic action against the regime. Capital exports to Southern Rhodesia were stopped; exchange restrictions were imposed; Commonwealth preference was suspended, and a ban was imposed on the British import of Rhodesian tobacco and sugar. The British foreign secretary was sent to the United Nations to secure international support for these actions.

The United Nations was highly critical: it demanded further action. Finally, on 20 November Britain accepted a Security Council resolution which included this phrase: 'Calls upon all states...to do their utmost in order to break all economic relations with Southern Rhodesia, including an embargo on oil and petroleum products.'

In response to this resolution first the United States of America, and then the Federal Republic of Germany, have both turned back cargoes of sugar coming from Rhodesia to fulfil the 1965 quota of that country.

The reaction of the country which claims responsibility for Rhodesia has been rather different. On 23 November Mr. Wilson spoke to the House of Commons, saying, 'We are going to study all aspects of trade and oil...we are not going in for a trade embargo or oil embargo alone.' And in explanation of this he said that there are many difficulties and 'there is the position of Zambia to be considered'!

That Zambia had supported the resolution appeared irrelevant to the British prime minister, who clearly thought he knew the business of that independent African state better than President Kaunda. On 1 December Mr. Wilson again said, 'We are not contemplating an oil embargo immediately.'

What is Africa expected to think of this mockery of a UN resolution which was already – at Britain's insistence – less than a firm, binding declaration of determination to defeat Smith?

On 1 December, however, Mr. Wilson announced new and much sterner economic measures against Rhodesia. Ninety-five per cent of Rhodesia's exports to Britain were then blocked, and financial measures taken which could have had a fairly quick and fairly severe effect on the economy of that colony. But Mr. Smith of Rhodesia was yesterday reported to have said that these have come too late to affect Rhodesia's economy.

I do not believe that he is bluffing. He has had weeks in which to prepare for these measures. But the timing is not my only criticism. I have argued that economic sanctions against Rhodesia will not work as long as South Africa is allowed to trade freely with the rebel colony. And it is Britain which has blocked obligatory sanctions under Chapter 7 of the UN Charter.

Commitment to Zambia

This brings me to my basic criticism of the British approach. It is a half-hearted approach, but one which leaves Zambia to pay a heavy price.

If effective and obligatory economic measures are instituted, and if alone they can bring down the Smith regime reasonably quickly and allow a new start to be made on the road to independence on the basis of majority rule, then on that basis I should be willing to support them: ON ONE CONDITION. That condition is that Zambia is not left alone to take the consequences of this procedure.

No African state is more concerned than Zambia that the Smith regime shall be defeated. No African president is more concerned that this shall be done without bloodshed and without unleashing a racial or ideological war. We in Tanzania join him in both these ambitions.

But the power supplies of the Zambian copperbelt are in rebel hands; the power station of the Kariba Dam has been occupied by troops of the rebel regime. Is Dr. Kaunda expected to sit quiet while increasing economic pressure on the rebels makes them more and more desperate, until they finally use their power to interfere with his power supply? What happens to his own economy, and his own peace meantime?

In November, a week after UDI, Dr. Kaunda called for British troops to guard the Kariba Dam. A British representative was sent to Lusaka to discuss this request. Later the British Commonwealth secretary was sent to Lusaka. The reason? That Britain was only prepared to send troops on conditions – and the conditions amounted to the defence of Rhodesia against attack quite as much as the defence of Zambia against attack from the rebels.

Dr. Kaunda accepted a Royal Air Force contingent because it was essential that his own country have some answer to the Southern Rhodesian and South African planes on his border. But, in the face of tremendous pressure, he has refused to accept ground forces under the conditions which Britain is imposing.

But the fact remains that the British government has been more willing to use Zambia's difficulties as an excuse for inaction, than it has been to use them as a reason for action. For a long time before 11 November, discussions about 'contingency planning' proceeded between Zambia, Britain and her allies, and Tanzania. When I opened this Assembly in October I said that Tanzania 'will give sympathetic consideration to any request which is made to us for help in furthering the cause of freedom and equality.'

What was this for if not to protect Zambia from the effects of any actions against an illegal Southern Rhodesia regime? And why is it not being used?

Let me make one thing clear at this point. Whatever happens as regards our relations with Britain, our commitment to Zambia remains. We continue to be ready to allow the transit of any goods or personnel, from any place, needed by Zambia to protect her interests and pursue the fight against Smith at the same time.

No one can drive a wedge between Zambia and Tanzania; neither can anyone hide behind Zambia's needs when they are trying to evade their responsibilities.

Mr. Speaker, that is an outline of the charge against the British government. I could amplify it and speak much longer. I do not think it is necessary. I believe that I have shown that Africa has reason for its action, reasons for saying that the British government has not shown serious determination either to get rid of those in Southern Rhodesia who have usurped British power, or to replace them by representatives of the people.

I believe that I have further shown that in so far as Britain has taken action which will, in the longer term, cause difficulties for the Smith regime, she has failed to safeguard the interests of that independent African state which stands in hourly threat from the regime. She has failed to live up to the responsibilities she has claimed, and she has failed to protect – or allow others to protect – an independent state which is threatened because of her failure to immediately overthrow the rebel regime.

The Addis Ababa Resolution

For these reasons I say that African action directed at Britain is both necessary and appropriate. Africa is entitled to say to this responsible authority, 'Act now, or allow others to act, or take the consequences.'

This is what the Addis Ababa resolution said. If Britain did not act against Smith before 15 December African states would break diplomatic relations with Britain.

Let me now move to a consideration of that resolution, and the consequent responsibilities for Africa.

The wording of the resolution can be – and has been – criticized. It called for Smith to be brought down by the 15th December. We are told – maybe correctly – that in 13 days this is impossible. But African states are not the fools that some people take them to be. To take an extreme example, it would clearly be absurd for Africa to break diplomatic relations with Britain if by the 15th British troops were moving towards Rhodesia. Africa clearly would not do such a stupid thing.

But it is not necessary even for things to have gone as far as that. If Britain has by the 15th demonstrated that at last she means to fulfil her responsibilities, and that she is prepared to pay the price in protecting others if she chooses a slower method, then again it would be absurd for Africa to take action against Britain.

I have myself suggested two things which Britain could do to demonstrate her determination. I understand her preference for economic sanctions; I even share it. But I have said that if she wants this time she must in the meantime protect Zambia.

She must apply the full pressure of economic measures, and while these are taking effect she must safeguard Zambia's power supplies by occupying the Kariba Dam and power station. This, Tanzania - and I believe every other African state - would recognize as willingness to act against Smith.

I have further suggested that, as long as the Kariba situation is safeguarded, it does not matter if the action taken is British. Let her call for the help of the United Nations in dealing with Smith. Let her, for example, ask the United Nations to apply Chapter 7 of the Charter which deals with the mandatory use of force by all members – economic or military force. This would give Britain time to allow economic sanctions to work; it would also give Africa the assurance that military force is not ruled if it becomes necessary.

This is my interpretation of the Addis Ababa resolution. I believe it is Africa's interpretation. I have no reason to believe that any other African state is going to be more illiberal in interpreting that resolution. All we are really asking is that Britain should recognize our interest, and that she should demonstrate to us her determination to defeat the Smith rebellion, and to put Southern Rhodesia once more on the path to democratic independence.

Britain's reaction so far – we have one day to go – has

not been encouraging. We have been told that Britain is not going to be pushed around. In a newspaper interview it is reported that Britain's 'not standing idly by' if Zambia's power supplies are cut off by Smith still means 'acting without bloodshed.'

And worst of all, because it is an action not words, an oil tanker, hired by a firm in which the British government hold 51 per cent of the shares, has been told by the same British government that it may continue on its way taking two weeks' supply of oil to Rhodesia.

Can Africa fail to implement its resolution?

Africa's Responsibility to Africa

Do African states meet in solemn conclave to make a noise? Or do they mean what they say?

The purpose of that resolution was to show that Africa requires action against Smith; if that action is not taken do we then shrug our shoulders and slink away without showing that Africa at least knows the meaning of the words it uses?

Can we - the African states - honourably do nothing to implement our own resolution, or would failure to do so not mean that we are improving on Britain's example of using big words and doing nothing – in our case – absolutely nothing? Britain at least has imposed economic santioncs after her big words. If we fail to implement our resolution we shall have nothing – less than nothing.

If we ignore our own resolution, neither our suffering brethren in Rhodesia, in Mozambique, in Angola, in South Africa, in South West Africa, nor the broad masses of the people of Africa, or for that matter the non-African members of the United Nations Organization could ever trust Africa to honour a pledge solemnly undertaken by Africa's leaders. Smith will rejoice; Verwoerd will rejoice; Salazar will rejoice. Where can we hide ourselves for shame?

The Addis Ababa resolution did just one thing which the Accra meeting of heads of State (in October 1965) had not done. At Accra we resolved on a series of measures to be taken under certain circumstances. At Addis Ababa the foreign ministers of those same heads of state selected one of those measures and put a date to it. Which of us can say we are not committed to carrying it out?

There are in fact two states in Africa which can absolve themselves if they wish. One is Malawi; the other is a state outside East and Central Africa. Both of these registered reservations, either at Accra, or at Addis Ababa, or both. There is one other state which no sane person could ask to implement it. That is Zambia. Zambia is bearing enough suffering in Africa's cause; far from asking her to accept more, Africa must try to reduce Zambia's present problems by being firm with Britain and Smith.

I make no pretence that the implementation of this resolution will be easy. There are few states in Africa for whom it is, perhaps, a matter of form. But for many of us the economic cost may be high. We cannot tell exactly how high.

But how can we criticize Britain for not being willing to pay the price of freeing Southern Rhodesia and meantime helping Zambia, if we ourselves are not prepared to a price to show our own determination? It is easy to call on others for sacrifice. Those who call on Britain without being ready themselves are guilty of a degree of hypocrisy which is unequalled up to now in Africa.

It is said that there is no point in paying this price, because it will have no effect. It will not secure the result we want. Mr. Speaker, I do not think the British government would agree. No country wishes to be cut off from Africa - free Africa – at this point in our history. They know as well as we do that we are economically and militarily weak. They also know that united we have a strength at the United Nations and elsewhere. If we are prepared to use it, and to be united.

For the Honour of Africa

Well, then, it is said, not every African state will in fact implement the resolution, and so there is no point in anyone doing so. Because this is an African commitment, not a commitment for one state or two, or even ten.

Mr. Speaker, I do not understand that line of argument. The Organization of African Unity (OAU) has twice passed a resolution. Each independent African state is a member of that organization, a sovereign independent member which has voluntarily formed and joined an organization to promote and develop the unity of Africa. They remain sovereign states; Africa is not yet united. Therefore, 36 separate actions have to be taken to implement the resolution instead of only one action.

But how can any of us argue that because some other sovereign state may not carry out its obligations, then we will not do so? It is each of separately which has this obligation; each of us separately which is responsible. It is we ourselves who will have to go to another meeting of the OAU and explain a failure to fulfil a responsibility. For it is our responsibility, and it is not a conditional one.

The OAU resolution does not say that this resolution comes into effect once it has been ratified by such and such proportion of states in Africa. One can argue that perhaps it should have done; but it does not. Each separate African state committed itself – with the exceptions I have named – to take action. If we have any respect for international obligations how can we fail to observe our own resolution? If the OAU has any meaning to us, how can we ignore its resolutions?

Earlier I criticized Britain for accepting a United Nations resolution and then failing to implement it. I did not – Africa does not – accept her justification that there is no point in her acting on her own. How then can we use this justification ourselves in relation to another international body of which we have claimed to be loyal members?

Tanzania participated in the resolution at Accra and in the resolution at Addis Ababa. We are committed to this. We are responsible only for the actions of this nation. But for those we, and we alone, are responsible.

The government feels that Tanzania has no honourable alternative but to abide by that resolution if the conditions are not fulfilled. There is very little time left.

I do not intend, on behalf of this country, to take action in accordance with that resolution one minute before we have to do so. We are not proposing to break diplomatic relations with Britain because we wish to do so; we shall do it only if it becomes necessary for our own honour, for the honour of Africa, and as a means of showing our determination never to falter in the campaign against racialism on this continent.

The Resolution and the Commonwealth

I should perhaps add that breaking diplomatic relations with the British government does not at present mean that Tanzania will be leaving the Commonwealth. The Commonwealth is a multinational organization, and although it is still true that Britain, for historical reasons, has a very special place in the Commonwealth, it is no longer the British Commonwealth – it is a Commonwealth of free nations.

We recognize that because of Britain's special place in this organization, a diplomatic break by any other member with Britain will impose great strains on it. We hope it will be possible for the organization to withstand those strains and still remain true to its principles.

But loyalty to the Commonwealth, and support for its principles, are impossible without loyalty to the Organization of African Unity.

This is a very simple and inescapable fact, and it should be recognized by those African countries which are now asking us to consider the effect on the Commonwealth of a breach with Britain. Disloyalty to one international organization of which a country is a member implies a lack of trustworthiness in relation to all other international organizations. If we are disloyal to the OAU how can we be trusted to be loyal to the Commonwealth - or to the United Nations for that matter?

Can a country which has a record of committing itself in an international organization, and then ignoring its own commitment, be respected in other organizations? Will they respect themselves? And will the Commonwealth really be an organization of equals if some members ignore their international commitments while others abide by them?

The time for African states to consider the effect on the Commonwealth of a breach with Britain was before passing the Accra resolution – or at least before the Addis Ababa resolution. Not now. If the African members of the Commonwealth are loyal to the OAU then the Commonwealth has a chance to survive, because its members will respect each other. Otherwise it will be in danger of becoming a shibboleth, and self-respecting heads of Commonwealth countries will go to Commonwealth conferences only if they enjoy them as a form of relaxation.

I repeat, for the sake of the Commonwealth, as well as for the sake of the OAU, Africa must honour its commitment.

We Oppose Racialism

There is one further thing I wish to say, Mr. Speaker, and it is of equal importance with the rest. I ask that every member of this House accepts full responsibility for ensuring the understanding and the implementation of what I am now about to say.

If it becomes necessary for us to break diplomatic relations with Britain we shall be doing so in support of the principles on which our nation is based. Those principles include anti-colonialism and African unity, and commitment to international obligations. They also include non-racialism.

We are not opposing Smith because he is white; we are not proposing action against the British government because it is a white government. We are opposing Smith because he is a racialist. If there were to be even one person among us who used this time as an excuse to indulge in racialism directed against white people residing here, that would be a betrayal of our country and the cause we are fighting for. This government of Tanzania deals firmly with treachery.

In the last elections the people of this country demonstrated that they cared about people, not their race or religion. This is a further, and harder, test of that principle. I am confident that the people of Tanzania will again rise to the challenge.

Let me say a further word about British subjects – for by no means all the white people here are British subjects, or of British origin. We do have working in our public services, and in business, a number of people from Britain. Many of them, indeed I suspect most of them, are highly critical of their government on this matter. Most of them, I believe, will be willing to stay and continue to work with us in Tanzania even if diplomatic relations are broken off between the two governments.

I have already stated that we in Tanzania hope that they will stay. Our need for them will be even greater if the carrying out of our development plan becomes complicated by a diplomatic break. I realize that some of these expatriate officials may have financial problems if a break comes; we shall do our best to help where this occurs; and at the moment this matter is under very urgent consideration.

I realize, however, that even more important to the majority is the atmosphere in which they and their families live and work. I have already given the assurance of the Tanzania government that their personal safety will not be endangered by their staying on after the British high commission staff has gone.

I am now asking that, in addition, our people should try to make those who stay realize that we understand their personal unhappiness at this quarrel between the two governments with both of which they are involved, and that we appreciate their choosing to continue serving the people of Tanzania. And those, if any, who wish to go must be allowed to go in peace. This is a quarrel between governments, not between people.

Mr. Speaker, honourable members, I do not again expect to address this sitting of the National Assembly. If it becomes necessary I shall ask the Leader of the House to bring a message to you. But I ask you, as always, to conduct any discussions on this very serious matter with a full realization of the importance of your words. You are leaders of our nation; you have a right, indeed a duty, to ask the ministers for further details of the implications of this decision, this commitment of the government. You have a right to criticize the government for making this commitment.

I hope you will not – as a body – ask the government to renounce its commitment. Because it cannot do so and remain the government. But whatever the House, or the individual members, say, I beg that the words be chosen carefully to serve our objective.

Our objective is the furtherance, on this continent, of justice and peace between men, regardless of race, tribe, or religion.

Mr. Speaker, I ask for the support of this House, and thank you for your attention." – (Julius K. Nyerere, *Freedom and Socialism: A Selection from Writings and*

Speeches 1965 – 1967: Dar es Salaam, Tanzania: Oxford University Press, 1968, pp. 115 – 133).

Although Tanzania was the first country to sever diplomatic ties with Britain, it did not rule out restoring those ties until Rhodesia was free.

It was ready to resume diplomatic relations with its former colonial ruler if certain conditions were met. And it did so in July 1968. As President Nyerere said in his message to British Prime Minister Harold Wilson on the resumption of diplomatic ties:

"Tanzania's conviction that there would be no compromise on the British pledge of no independence in Rhodesia before majority rule has made possible this resumption of normal diplomatic relations." – (Julius Nyerere, quoted by Colin Legum and John Drysdale, *Africa Contemporary Record*, op.cit., p. 220).

And the official organ of Tanzania's ruling party (TANU), *The Nationalist*, had this to say after Tanzania resumed diplomatic relations with Britain:

"Tanzanians are honoured and satisfied that it has been their consistent and uncompromising stand which has influenced Britain to declare NIBMAR (No Independence Before Majority Rule)...The resumption of ties will enable Tanzania to press Britain more effectively to implement NIBMAR." (Ibid.).

The illegal declaration of independence by the white minority regime in Southern Rhodesia was one of the most important developments in the history of post-colonial Africa. And it influenced the course of events in a profound way, especially in southern Africa, as independent African countries rallied behind the nationalist forces in that colony in their quest for freedom.

The liberation struggle also had a direct impact on the frontline states – Tanzania, Zambia, Mozambique, Botswana and Angola – which suffered in different ways and in varying degrees when the guerrilla war was going on during that period. It was most intense in the 1970s.

But it was not until years later that Southern Rhodesia finally won independence as Zimbabwe under majority rule on 18 April 1980 after one of the bloodiest liberation wars in the history of Africa since the advent of colonial rule.

Appendix:

Army Mutiny in Tanganyika: An Eyewitness Report

THE army mutinies in the three East African countries of Kenya, Uganda and Tanganyika in January 1964 were some of the most significant events in the history of post-colonial Africa.

They demonstrated the power of the soldiers and the potential they had to influence the course of events in their countries against the wishes of civilian governments.

They were also among the first manifestations of military power in the political arena and a demonstration of the military as the most powerful institution in the newly independent African countries. And they helped change and shape the course of African history by encouraging soldiers in other African countries to overthrow governments in the following years.

The army mutiny in Tanganyika took place one week after the Zanzibar revolution and about three months before Tanganyika united with Zanzibar to form the United Republic of Tanzania.

One of the people who was in Tanganyika during that time was John D. Gerhart from Harvard University who was teaching in Dar es Salaam under a programme called Project Tanganyika. He sent the following report which was published in *The Harvard Crimson* daily newspaper on 10 March 1964:

Tanganyika Embarrassed By Need for British Assistance – Calls for Pan-African Force To Aid Future Crises

The city of Dar es Salaam woke early on the morning of Saturday, January 25.

At about 6.15 a.m. citizens all over the sprawling capital were shaken out of bed by what some thought at first was an early onset of the monsoon season.

But the evenly-spaced rumblings in the distance were not thunder; they were a diversionary barrage from the anti-aircraft guns of the British aircraft carrier Centaur.

By 7 a.m., when government workers began leaving for their 7:30 jobs, Tanganyika's five-day-old army mutiny was over and East Africa's oldest independent government was back in control.

The short, well-timed action which put down the revolt was carried out by the Royal Marine Commandos with an efficiency that will probably win it a glowing place in British military history.

While the barrage went on, helicopters lifted some 60 commandos to a ravine behind the Tanganyika Rifles' barracks about six miles north of the city. As the Tanganyikan soldiers spilled out of their barracks, they were quickly captured from behind by the British troops.

One mortar shell broke up the resistance; only three

Rifles members were killed; and though several hundred soldiers escaped in the bush, all but a handful were quickly recaptured.

The exercise was directed by the commanding officer of the Tanganyikan forces, a Britisher who had escaped the mutiny on Monday and had been hiding in European homes in Dar's fashionable Oyster Bay area during the week.

The Marines' performance was most remarkable because they accomplished it virtually unarmed.

According to an official in the British High Commission here, the British quartermaster in Aden had furnished the Marines with the wrong calibre of rifle ammunition, and the mistake was not discovered until shortly before the landing was to take place. The only effective weapons available were mortars and a few pistols.

When the troops landed they went immediately taken to the Tanganyikan armory to rearm themselves, which explains why so many of the Tanganyikan soldiers were initially able to escape. The quartermaster in Aden has since been returned to England for court-martial.

Though they had never been in danger during the revolt, Dar's British citizens were thrilled to have the "shocking do" over with, and "the boys" standing guard.

The New Africa Hotel did a landslide afternoon tea business. There was a band concert by the forces on the following afternoon. Smiling Scotsmen bought cases of beer and Fanta for the troops.

Our neighbors spoke to us for the second time in six months, the first time having been on Monday when the "do" began.

But in spite of the local European reaction, there were no neo-colonialist overtones. The British offered to withdraw immediately on the wishes of the Tanganyika government, and the President, Julius K. Nyerere dispelled further doubts in a speech given Saturday afternoon. "Any independent country is able to ask for the help of another independent country," he said. "Talk that the British have come back to rule Tanganyika again is rubbish."

Request Difficult

"But," continued the President, "asking for help in this way is not something to be proud of. I do not want any person to think that I was happy in making this request."

The decision was undoubtedly a painful one for Nyerere, who had worked so long to gain Tanganyika's independence from the British, but in the end, it was the only choice he could make and be sure of his government's survival.

What had begun on Monday as simply an army revolt for higher pay was beginning to take on much more threatening tones. The story of this deterioration in the situation is the real story of the army revolt. The mutiny began shortly after midnight on January 20 when the troops of the Tanganyika (formerly King's African) Rifles First Battalion seized the arms at Colito Barracks and arrested their European officers and NCOs.

Soldiers then proceeded to surround the State House and to take over the radio station, airport, telegraph office, and other key points throughout the city. Several ministers were arrested before dawn, but President Nyerere and Vice President Rashidi Kawawa escaped.

Though Nyerere reappeared the next day, rumors circulated wildly that he had gone to Arusha in the north of the country, gone to Nairobi, been captured, or was hiding in the embassy of "a friendly country."

In actuality, Nyerere remained in Dar es Salaam, but he let his Defense Minister Oscar Kambona come to terms with the soldiers. This was probably because he felt that his first duty to the nation was to survive unharmed, and also because he did not want to demean his office by dealing with the mutineers.

Throughout the mutiny, troop movements were confined almost entirely to the town proper and to the African business quarters of Magomeni and Kariakoo (named for the German Carrier Corps stationed there in 1918). The large European and African suburbs to the north and south of the town were not entered.

The first indication I had of the trouble was about 8 a.m. when, upon reaching the Tanganyikan school where I teach, I found classes dismissed and the headmistress, a close friend of Nyerere's, in tears.

Cars Halted

With two other teachers, I headed toward the downtown area. We passed milling crowds of Africans and Arabs in the streets, but saw no signs of other vehicles or of soldiers. However, we soon reached a bridge leading to the town's center and ran directly into a roadblock of soldiers who, pointing guns at our tires and faces, quickly persuaded us to return the way we had come. Though not proficient in Swahili, we found that our comprehension was almost perfect.

About noon on Monday the road blocks were removed and another teacher and I, with a Tanganyikan friend, took the opportunity to drive through Kariakoo to the Muhimbili hospital, where my friend had a surgical appointment. This time cars were in sight, but most of them contained soldiers with large guns who had commandeered taxis and private vehicles for cruising the streets.

Looters Shot

Entering the first rotary intersection in the bazaar district, however, we saw a frightening sight. Looting had broken out during the mid-morning and the soldiers, aided by normal police forces, were firing at and beating looters in the street.

On the opposite side of the intersection a hatless soldier was casually aiming his rifle, not at a looter, but at a family of Indians watching the scene from a fourth-story apartment nearby. The bullet smashed over their heads.

The soldier laughed, turned backdown the street and shouldered his weapon.

Proceeding down the main street about two blocks from the African market, we were soon stopped by a group of soldiers and forced to wait outside the car for about twenty minutes. Actually, this provided us with a relatively safe viewpoint from which to watch the soldiers in action.

They seemed content to let the more efficient police restore order; the streets cleared rapidly and occasional shots rang out, often fired into a trash can "for effect."

Civilians Killed

We soon continued to the hospital where casualties were being brought in. One of the first was a soldier with a bullet fired clean through the chest. His agonized expression seemed to frame an ironic question about the value of his comrades' revolt.

On Monday, four soldiers, six Arabs, and about a dozen African civilians were killed, all in "non-military" action.

On Monday afternoon the government agreed to give "urgent consideration" to the troops' demands for a pay increase and the removal of all expatriate officers.

The soldiers returned to their barracks and Kambona

announced he had "mediated a dispute between African and British soldiers in the Tanganyika Rifles" and that the troops were still "loyal to the government."

On Tuesday the capital returned to almost normal.

As the week continued, it became increasingly apparent that the government could not continue to operate with the army able to seize power at will merely by entering and occupying the city. Negotiations over pay increases were conducted with the mutiny's leaders, but by Friday they had become, as Nyerere later said, "analogous to the negotiations between a blackmailer and his victim."

One reliable source says that the mutineers were demanding the right to name three new ministers. Nevertheless, the government wanted, if at all possible, to avoid calling in outside (namely) British help.

Strike Plotted

In the meantime, a group of politicians and trade union leaders including an Area Commissioner who had been a long-time TANU stalwart, had begun conspiring with the ringleaders of the mutiny to bring about a real overthrow of the government. They planned to initiate a general strike on Saturday, followed by a coup on the following Monday in which, it was rumoured, Nyerere and his ministers would be removed.

Nyerere got word of this on Friday afternoon and Friday evening he asked for British aid. Fortunately for the government, the British were close at hand and the more serious threat was stopped before it could materialize.

On Saturday night police detained about 200 persons, including officials of five major unions and the General Secretary of the Tanganyika Federation of Labour (TFL). Most of the officials are only now being released. The government has announced plans to disband the TFL and its eleven affiliated unions and to institute in their place a single, giant trade union representing all the workers in the country.

Though the trade unions have opposed the government in the past, they have paraded through Dar es Salaam almost daily for a week to demonstrate their present loyalty.

External Impact

In fact, the revolt may have more important implications for Tanganyika's external than its internal affairs. The 98 per cent of the nation's people who live outside the capital had little or no knowledge of the mutiny at all, and though the army is being disbanded and security measures increased, there are no sweeping changes in store for anyone outside the unions.

Nyerere is calling for a constitutional one-party state which will only make Tanganyika in name what it is in fact. The most widely felt "internal" result of the revolt so far has been the banning of the Nairobi-based *Daily Nation* for publishing an "exaggerated account" of the disturbances.

Conference Called

Externally, Tanganyika's reputation for stability was undoubtedly damaged. Foreign investors may lose confidence in the country, although such a loss would not be justified and should not be severe. And the fact remains that Tanganyika is embarrassed, though not apologetic, about having British troops in the country.

It was for this reason that Nyerere called for the emergency meeting of the Foreign Ministers of the Organization of African Unity, which opened in Dar es Salaam on Feb. 12, and which makes a proper concluding chapter to an account of the revolt.

The conference, with Tanganyika's Oscar Kambona as chairman, held its opening session in the attentive view of the world press, the TANU political hierarchy, and the local diplomatic corps.

Although the ambassador of the Chinese People's Republic was tactfully seated some distance from his American counterpart, the reporters from the New China News Agency vied openly with those of the USIS for picture positions, while the representative of the Vatican press religiously took notes.

Though the Moroccans looked like French grocers and the Liberians like American businessmen, the assembly was an impressive one and Nyerere made an equally impressive opening address.

"The presence of troops from a country deeply involved in the world's cold war conflicts," he said, "has serious implications in the context of African nationalism and our common policies of non-alignment... The presence of British troops in Tanganyika is a fact which is too easily exploited by those who wish to...play upon natural fears of neo-colonialism in the hope of sowing seeds of suspicion between the different African states."

In a matter minutes, Nyerere neatly converted the revolt from an internal to a pan-African affair. He also pointed out that the African liberation movements, with headquarters in Dar es Salaam, might be damaged by the existence of just such a state of affairs in Tanganyika, and that this was also "the concern of the whole of Africa."

Nyerere then asked for an African armed force to help replace the British while Tanganyika trains its own forces. This proposal was accepted later in the week, though the practicalities of compiling an all-African force may be difficult.

Note:
When John D. Gerhart's article was published in _The Harvard Crimson_, Nigeria had already agreed to

send troops to Tanganyika to replace British soldiers until the country had a new army. – Godfrey Mwakikagile.

Morocco
Tunisia
Western Sahara
Algeria
Libya
Egypt
Mauritania
Mali
Niger
Chad
Eritrea
Djibouti
S
Guinea
B.Faso
Nigeria
Sudan
Ethiopia
IC
Gh
B
T
L
Sierra Leone
Cameroon
Cent Afr Rep
Somalia
Guinea Bissau
Equatorial Guinea
Gabon
Ug
Kenya
Gambia
Congo
Dem Rep of Congo
Rwanda
Burundi
Tanzania
Angola
Mozambique
Zambia
Madagascar
Namibia
Zimb
Bots
Malawi
Swaziland
South Africa
Lesotho

© 1800-Countries.com

377

www.ingramcontent.com/pod-product-compliance
Lightning Source LLC
Chambersburg PA
CBHW071220290326
41931CB00037B/1483